Doing Time
on the Outside

Doing Time on the
OUTSIDE

Incarceration and Family Life in Urban America

DONALD BRAMAN

University of Michigan Press
Ann Arbor

2007   2006   2005   2004   4   3   2   1

A CIP catalog record for this book is available from the British Library.

Library of Congress Cataloging-in-Publication Data

Braman, Donald, 1968–
    Doing time on the outside : incarceration and family life in urban
America / Donald Braman.
        p.   cm.
    Includes bibliographical references and index.
    ISBN 0-472-11381-X (cloth : alk. paper)
        1. Imprisonment–United States.   2. Imprisonment–Social aspects–
United States–Case studies.   3. Criminal justice,
Administration of–Social aspects–United States–Case studies.
I. Title.

HV9950.B7   2004
362.82'95'0973–dc22   2004003467

Contents

Introduction

There is only one sure basis of social reform and that is Truth—a careful, detailed knowledge of the essential facts of each social problem. Without this there is no logical starting place for reform and uplift.

—W. E. Burghardt Du Bois and
Augustus Granville Dill

W hen Davida was born, her father, David, was seventeen and serving his first adult sentence on a drug conviction.* A small-time drug dealer in Washington, D.C., he has been in and out of prison for his daughter's entire life. For all the anger and disappointment that come with having a father who is addicted to and sells drugs, Davida loves him and cherishes her first memory of his return home from prison. She was getting off the school bus and saw him waiting for her outside her grandmother's house. "I just looked, and I was, like, 'Daddy!' And I just ran." "At that time," she says, crossing her fingers, "we was like this, you know?" Thinking back on the time when she, her father, and her grandmother all lived together, she smiles, shaking her head: "I mean, it was just so much that me and my father did. I missed that when he got locked back up." Her father's subsequent arrest remains a similarly vivid memory:

> I remember the night the police came. They chased him in the house, and I was sitting there screaming, like, "Daddy! Daddy!" And he ran to the back door, but the back door was locked. The police came, and they pushed him down on the floor. He got up and pushed them off and ran through the front door, so I ran behind him, and I was just running

*A more detailed account of Davida's story and that of her family is given in chapter 6.

right behind him . . . running right behind him. I seen the police behind me, and my father ran in through the alley. And I came, and I seen the police coming, so I ran behind the gate, by where my father was at. They didn't see us. My father, they came and pulled my father from under the car and started beating him. And I was standing there looking at them beating my father with night sticks, and they dragged him through the alley and put him in the paddy wagon. So they took my father.

The effect on Davida was, by her own assessment, powerful: "I was *upset* by that," she says, emphasizing the point. "I started hanging out more, started drinking. I wasn't going to school. I was, like, 'Forget school.' In sixth grade I dropped out of school completely. I didn't want to go no more."

In the next four years, Davida would be sexually assaulted by her stepfather, do time in a juvenile facility for girls, sell her body to help support herself and her grandmother, and be confined in a psychiatric institution. She hid what she could from her father, knowing there was little he could do for her from prison, but his inability to protect her makes Davida both angry and sad. "I try not to fault him, but I am a child still, and he wasn't there for me when I did this. He wasn't there for me when this happened to me. He would tell me, 'I can't do this for you. I can't do that for you.'" "Still," she says, "I love him to death because that's my Dad."

At the age of sixteen, as she and her grandmother watch the landlord remove all their belongings from the apartment they shared, Davida looks on incredulously, shaking her head, surprised not so much by the eviction as by her entire life:

By me not being old enough to get a regular job that maintains a stable place for us to stay, and my grandmother's retired, she only gets one check a month, we don't have much money to do this, or, you know, food or whatever. She's not with Section 8 yet, public housing, food stamps, so it's, like, my father needs to be here. . . . I'm bending over backwards trying to keep everything intact while he's not here, and by me being my age it's hard, you know? I'm going through a hell of a life while he's not home.

Incarceration, something few families faced fifty years ago, is now an integral part of family life in urban America. About one out of every ten adult black men in the District of Columbia is in prison, and, at last count, over half of the black men between the ages of eighteen and thirty-five were under some type of correctional supervision.[1] If these conditions persist, over 75 percent of young black men in the District and nearly all those in the poorest neighborhoods can expect to be incarcerated at some time in their lives.[2] A few decades ago, these would have been staggering statistics in any city; but today, compared with other cities, the District is just average.[3] At a cost of over $40 billion a year, the United States now holds one out of every four of the world's prisoners.[4]

Nearly every longtime resident of the District whom I have spoken with has been able to name several friends or family members who had once been or were presently incarcerated, and many have themselves spent time in prison or jail. Our nation's capital city, a place of residence and work for many national policymakers who draft the federal criminal codes and sentencing guidelines that directly affect poor urban communities, epitomizes the high incarceration rates of American cities, a prime example of the recent dramatic expansion of the criminal justice system nationwide.

But while incarceration has become ever more common, the mainstream debate over our criminal law has had little to say about families or communities like Davida's. Focused intently on criminals, neither liberals nor conservatives pay much attention to the effects of criminal sanctions on nonoffenders. When liberals talk about reforming the criminal law, they generally talk about more expansive protection of suspect and offender rights throughout the criminal justice process.[5] They propose greater restrictions on police conduct, more restrictions on prosecutorial discretion, and significantly lighter sentences, particularly for drug offenses.[6] Conservatives, on the other hand, are less interested in the rights of those suspected or convicted of breaking the law and far more interested in sure and swift punishment.[7] They view offenders as a threat to the social order, and when they talk about reforming the criminal law they argue that the lengthy sentences meted out today are not enough.[8] Both forget that offenders not only offend against, but come from, communities.

Nor does either side really speak to the problems that people in Davida's world face. Liberal appeals to the rights of defendants and convicts ring hollow for the millions of families that live in communities with exceedingly high crime rates, communities historically devastated by both poverty and lax enforcement of the law. They take little solace in the thought that criminals would be less likely to be arrested and convicted if, under a more liberal regime, the rights of offenders were more vigorously protected.[9] But Davida and others living in impoverished neighborhoods are also deeply injured by mass incarceration. The disassembling of our society's most vulnerable families has wreaked material, emotional, and social havoc in the lives of millions, with consequences that will reverberate for generations.[10] The retributivist ideal is small consolation to those whose families and communities have become collateral damage in the war on crime.

This book parts ways with mainstream accounts on both sides. Unlike many liberal efforts, it does not argue that greater protection of the rights of criminal offenders will solve the problems that criminal sanctions exacerbate. Instead, this book suggests that our current regime of sanctions demands *far too little* accountability from offenders. Contrary to many conservative assessments, this book argues that the reforms of the last twenty-five years have done little to advance such accountability. Indeed, as currently practiced, incarceration not only provides offenders with an excuse for not contributing to the welfare of their families and communities, but it practically enforces their noncontribution. Indeed, if anything, the sentencing reforms of the 1980s and 1990s have enforced radical *irresponsibility* and *unaccountability,* and it is the families and communities of offenders that are bearing the burden.

The disconnect between the intent of our criminal law and the reality it partakes of is glaring. Despite a stable of elegant theories on issues of deterrence and desert,[11] and despite an intense debate over the effects of our increased reliance on incarceration on crime rates,[12] we don't really know all that much about how real people living in real families and communities respond to and cope with criminal sanctions.[13] And although legal academics and policymakers often justify criminal justice reforms by making reference to families and communities, real families and communities remain largely absent from their accounts.[14] Instead, those interested in the criminal law find mountains of statistics, moral philosophy, and conjecture. If we are to understand the full effects of our criminal law on what for the last thirty years has been described as "the urban crisis,"[15] we will need more detailed descriptions of what the law does than we have had to date. We need to ask how our criminal sanctions shape the lives not only of criminal offenders but of their children, partners, parents, and communities.

The central goal of this book is to describe the effects of incarceration on family and community life. In hundreds of interviews conducted in living rooms and kitchens, backyards, alleyways, and parks, and in jails, prisons, and halfway houses, the families described here–and those not described because of lack of space–showed me that most of what I had assumed about them was wrong and made the incoherence of my assumptions plain to me. While I employ many of the standard methods of inquiry, including statistical analyses, the central methodological lesson of this book is that any effective answer to the problems of those in impoverished neighborhoods will require an accurate and nuanced understanding of human motivation and that this understanding in turn requires intimate knowledge of the individuals whose families, lives, and deferred dreams have come to constitute that crisis.

An Anthropological Approach

I suspect most Americans sense that our criminal justice system is falling short of its promise of justice. But understanding how and why it is failing requires a shift in perspective from the traditional economic and philosophical models of deterrence and desert. Thus while the primary goal of the book is to describe the lives of families of prisoners, a secondary goal is to shake loose concepts and analytical frameworks that currently dominate discussions of criminal justice policy and to place more anthropologically grounded ones in their stead.[16]

The approach employed here is not new. Descriptions of kinship, exchange, and social norms have been refined over nearly a century of anthropological investigation and analysis.[17] What is new is the resonance they have gained as policymakers have become attuned to their importance. The study of exchange and reciprocity, for example, has reemerged in studies of "social capital,"[18] and a number of popular works, most notably Robert Putnam's *Bowling Alone*,[19] have helped to reassert the importance of family and community over and above the impersonal transactions that were long presumed to drive market capitalism. Similarly, the study of social norms, once an esoteric endeavor almost exclusively the domain of anthropologists,[20] has been taken up by economists and legal scholars, complicating and even displacing neoclassical economic theory in legal analyses.[21]

Although this should be heartening news, the lack of empirical detail in much of the recent work is troubling. For example, while the concepts that run through discussions of social capital—networks, reciprocity, and social norms—are useful, their application in popular discussions has been more along the lines of thought experiments or statistical inference than hands-on observation. Rather than describing how real people make use of and are used by social networks, academics have instead developed rather broad and generic analyses describing one or another measure of social capital, asserting that it is rising or falling or that it is, on the whole, either good or not so good.[22] What has been lost in these efforts is an understanding that social capital is a way of talking about real people's relationships with one another and that it is to these real people rather than abstract concepts that we should attend.

Popular depictions of social capital, for example, generally emphasize the positive aspects of social networks and the norms of reciprocity and resource sharing that inhere in them. By pooling both risk and resources, they note, individuals are better able to weather hardships than they could alone. In many instances, the accounts of the families in this book bear that out. But the accounts of families of prisoners also highlight the negative potential of sharing burdens and benefits. Because the material impact of incarceration reverberates through family and community ties, the rise of incarceration has not simply punished criminal offenders; it has disrupted and impoverished their families and communities as well. Thus, as incarceration rates have burgeoned over the last generation, so too have the costs to all of those in traditional networks of exchange and mutual aid. The result is that the relationships and norms described as social capital have increasingly become burdens rather than benefits to many inner-city families. This is no minor concern. These networks are the lifeblood of a healthy society, and their erosion is not just material but deeply social.

Popular studies of social capital that illustrate theoretical claims with statistical data alone have missed this point entirely.[23] It is not simply the case, for example, that social networks and reciprocity create social well-being; it is also the case that, where significant harm is spread through the relationships that individuals have with one another, individuals will withdraw from these relationships, effectively reducing their exposure to these costs, but also lowering the resources available to them in times of need. Rather than concluding, as many have, that social capital drives social wealth, health, and happiness, it is essential to understand that the norms and networks of social capital can be overburdened by systemic social costs. When policy transforms these relationships from benefits to burdens, the rational withdrawal of individuals can create a negative feedback loop, accelerating the spiral of entire communities into poverty, illness, and despair. The theoretical missteps made by academics in this area demonstrate the necessity of direct inquiry when asking how our most basic social relationships are developed, how they provide and tax common resources, and what they mean to the people who create and maintain them.

The latter concern–the matter of meaning–has been the subject of renewed interest in the law under the rubric of "social norms."[24] Like the literature on social capital, recent scholarship on social norms poses a direct challenge to economic models based on generic, wealth-maximizing individuals.[25] Rather than simply measuring efficiency or avarice, discussions about social norms have helped scholars of law and economics to investigate the richer kinds of meaning that humans create through their social interactions. Ironically, though, studies of social norms have been conducted largely in the methodological shadows of the economic models they challenge.[26] Like popular discussions of social capital, recent analyses of social norms have focused on generic reactions to the structure of legal and nonlegal norms rather than on the histories of actual relationships through which those norms become meaningful.[27]

This has led to a number of problematic claims. For example, recent scholarship on social norms suggests an expanded role for shame in criminal sanctions.[28] While shaming is an integral part of criminal sanctions, including incarceration, the accounts of families presented here show how the effects of stigmatization—like the economic costs of incarceration—are spread across families and communities. As a result, it is not only criminal offenders who bear the burdens of stigma but a host of nonoffenders as well—nonoffenders who are, by and large, the same population the law intends to protect. The broad impact of this stigma can make minefields of family members' relationships with relatives, neighbors, and co-workers. The social silence that this stigma creates extends from local settings such as church and work into the public arena, making it difficult for families to seek political remedies for the problems they encounter. The ethnographic account presented here should serve as a cautionary supplement to more theoretical scholarship on the effects of social norms and stigma.

These are more than academic issues. Policymakers need realistic assessments of how those in our nation's inner cities actually live their lives. The hard truth is that they are forced to struggle with the powerful pull of family, community, and the law under conditions that all too often set these social institutions against one another. The result has been a steady and silent corrosion of family and community in our inner cities and a public debate that fails to reflect how much families there still matter.

Overview of the Book

This book examines the criminal law through a series of family portraits, relating events and conversations in the District of Columbia over a four-year period. At its center are intimate accounts of family members whose relationships with each other, neighbors, co-workers, and other church and community members have been powerfully shaped by incarceration. Their accounts reveal the mixture of both relief and pain–though often more of the latter than the former–that incarceration can bring. Incarceration, as these families have found, is not limited to the time served in prison or jail. It includes what Jeremy Travis describes as "invisible punishments": the loss of voting rights, access to public housing, and job opportunities that prisoners face as the result of a criminal conviction.[29] But incarceration also reaches deep into the social life of families and communities, transforming fundamental social institutions of social exchange, kinship, and community–the habits and institutions that allow family and community members to rely on one another in times of need and to hold each other accountable.

The book is organized into four parts. Part I describes the structural shifts in population, political power, and economic opportunity that have influenced crime and criminal sanctions. Government housing and lending policies that led to concentrations of minority populations in impoverished inner-city neighborhoods, macroeconomic trends that shifted available jobs away from those same neighborhoods, welfare policies that discouraged marriage, and tax policies that disadvantaged poor families–all of these have had a prolonged and corrosive effect on the core social institutions of kinship and social exchange that normally sustain those living at the economic margin. These trends have helped to foster high rates of family dissolution, criminality, and, when combined with the sentencing reforms of the 1980s and 1990s, incarceration. As the remainder of the book describes, expanding the use of imprisonment as a response to social disorder has not only failed to address the core social problems of those living in impoverished inner-city neighborhoods, it has accelerated the very social disordering it was intended to remedy.

Part II describes the effect of incarceration on family structure and relationships. Incarceration forcibly restructures household composition and kin relations in many families. Some of the resulting effects are obvious, such as increasing rates of father absence and further skewing of already imbalanced gender ratios. But family accounts also suggest more subtle effects. Family members describe incarcerations as pitting material interests against the social norms of kinship, a conflict that contributes to a host of behaviors within families that are at once rational, socially destructive, and painful. They describe how incarceration encourages infidelity, distrust, abuse, and neglect–behavior consistent with many of the common stereotypes of poor, minority, inner-city families. What the stereotypes obscure, and what the accounts of the families bring into stark focus, are the ways in which criminal sanctions are intricately involved in the dissolution of the families the stereotypes describe.

Part III describes the material effects of incarceration on social life in greater detail. Because prisoners are effectively prevented from meeting their responsibilities to their families and because families provide help to prisoners, the costs of incarceration, though intended for offenders alone, ripple out through relationships between family members and have broad effects on communities where incarceration rates are high. The effects are most pronounced while offenders are incarcerated because most prisoners have few or none of the resources that would allow them to reciprocate the aid and care that family members provide them. But it is also true after offenders are released because a prison sentence–particularly without drug treatment or job training–dramatically lowers the employment options available to offenders. As a result, families of prisoners face significant burdens long after the release of their family member. The impact of mass imprisonment in the inner city helps to explain why significant racial disparities in income and wealth, and in human and social capital, have been so intractable during periods of economic expansion accompanied by soaring incarceration rates.

Part IV reports what is perhaps the most surprising finding of this study: Contrary to many popular accounts, the broad effects of stigma related to incarceration and criminality have not receded with the dramatic rise in incarceration rates–at least not for the families of prisoners. Strikingly, the accounts of families reveal that the burden of stigma persists and that it often falls more heavily on non-offending family members than on the offenders themselves. Whereas prisoners are held with other criminal offenders, family members live in communities where many of their friends and neighbors are victims of crime and where animosity toward criminal offenders often runs high. For this reason, many relatives hide the incarceration of a family member not only from friends, co-workers, and fellow congregants, but also other extended family members. The result, for many, is that relationships at the individual and community level are diminished and distorted to guard information about incarceration. At a broader political level, this social silence also obscures many of the effects of incarceration from public view.

It is my hope that the stories recounted here will help us to look at the law in a different way. The account developed here describes how the law interacts with the fundamental aspects of moral life: family and community, love and trust, gifts and exchange, status and shame–not only because they are important from an anthropological perspective but because they are essential to understanding the kind of justice that we should expect from our law, a justice that extends beyond the individual offender to the ties that bind our society together. Neither liberal nor conservative, these are concerns that give meaning to our lives every day. If we are going to hold criminal offenders accountable, and we should, we need not do so in a way that undermines the basic moral and material institutions that sustain those living at the margins. Those who most need the law to fulfill its promise need us to hold criminal offenders accountable to more than abstract ideas, they need us to hold offenders accountable to the victims, the communities, and the families they come from and return to. They need real justice, something that, at the present moment, is in short supply.

Part I What Went Wrong?

Two elderly women have come to blows. As they shove and wrestle, scuffling across the hard floor of the District government office building, they are yelling at each other. "That's my grandson you're talking about! Don't you talk about my grandson that way!" shouts one. "You love him so much, move to Ohio!" responds the other. The first woman is sent sprawling onto the floor, and the two are separated by others in a long line, all waiting to enter a public hearing about a proposed private prison slated for an abandoned industrial dump in a wooded area on the outskirts of Ward Eight, the poorest ward in our nation's capital city.* The Corrections Corporation of America (CCA), the company proposing to build the prison, already runs a private prison in Ohio that holds many District inmates.

The small meeting room quickly fills to standing room only, and people soon begin waving signs and shouting occasional comments at one another. On one side of the room is a small group of people, mostly women relatives of prisoners, there to support a local prison; on the other side is a much larger group of residents and local business owners opposed to the prison. At first the chants and shouts are direct:

Keep them home! We are family! Don't send them away!
No prison gates in Ward Eight! We don't need it, we don't want it!

Someone hands out T-shirts emblazoned with "KEEP THEM HOME," and most of the people in the family group put on the T-shirts, some a little hesitantly. The calls opposing the prison become heated. "Move the trash out of D.C.!" shouts one man, and it is clear that he is not talking about the District's garbage removal problem.

* Ward Eight is located in the southeastern corner of the District.

If your man had stayed home, he wouldn't be locked up now!
Thugs not wanted!

The small room is not made to hold this many people, and those packed into it begin to wipe their brows as the heat and humidity rise. A rumor circulates that the woman leading the prison family group is on the payroll of the company that wants to build the prison; another rumor goes around that the T-shirts were paid for and the families "bought and brought" with money and busses by the private corrections company. A new chant goes up:

Prison pimps go home!
Say no to prison ho's!

As the phrases are taken up as a chant, the families grow silent; people on both sides of the room begin to look very angry. A local council member announces that the meeting has been canceled for security reasons and will be rescheduled. Sweaty and worked up, a hundred or so people, most of them neighbors, begin to file into the street and go home.

Chapter 1 A Public Debate

T his strange public demonstration took place early in my fieldwork and provided a striking introduction to both local city politics and the increasingly complex politics of incarceration. It was followed by five public hearings,[1] the last two of which were open for comments from the general public. But even at the first hearing, the divergent perspectives within the community were quite clear.

The proposal that the CCA was presenting seemed, at least on the surface, to be an easy sell. Ward Eight is a community with the highest unemployment rate in the District, one where many families of prisoners lived. A large new correctional facility not only would provide hundreds of well-paying, recession-proof jobs to local residents but would keep prisoners closer to home, where family, counselors, and clergy could help with their rehabilitation. The proposed prison would be state-of-the-art, including a host of educational and job-training programs for inmates—in fact, the proposed programs were so extensive that some residents complained that they were "better than what we get out here,"[2] and CCA promptly added community scholarships and neighborhood job-training programs to the proposed package. To top it off, CCA noted, there were plenty of other communities around the country that would be happy to have the facility if the residents of Ward Eight refused it.

Marion Barry, the former mayor, who prided himself on having a broad constituency in Ward Eight, made all these points in his testimony on the first day of the hearings:

> Other states are trying to get the District to send their prisoners to their states so that jobs can be maintained in those states. In fact, in Youngstown, the Congressman there wants an addition of 2,500 beds built because of the economics of 450 jobs. And Ward Eight has the

highest unemployment rate of any in the city: some thirteen percent among adults, and some sixty percent among teenagers. We need these jobs in Ward Eight.[3]

Despite the chanting and cat calls from the first meeting, a few family members returned to testify for the proposal when public comment was finally allowed six months later. One mother spoke, generalizing from her concern about her own child to that of all the "wayward children" in prison:

> I am here today to pledge my strong support for the proposed correctional rehabilitation facility in Ward Eight. I was brought up to believe that we are responsible for every child, and that we are mothers and fathers to every one of them. We cannot toss our children aside when they are sick and in need of help. If we do not help them, then who will? Are we so insensitive as a society that we do not care about our children and their cries for help? Let us work together and make a productive people of our children and help those who need help the most. God said, "When you help the least of my people, you help me." Let me leave you with this final thought. What if it was your child? What type of help would you want to offer your child? I happen to know first hand. And I earnestly believe, that I would want to have available the assistance that this proposed correctional facility has to offer. What about you?[4]

Her comments touched not only on the feelings that many families of prisoners have about the lack of rehabilitation programs in most correctional settings but also on the responsibility of the community to take care of its own.

Over the course of the five hearings, however, it became clear that the opposition to the prison was overwhelming. The current mayor, Anthony Williams, the city council, and the local area neighborhood commissions all voiced strong opposition to the project,[5] as did the major and minor newspapers and nearly all the citizens' organizations in the District.* If the proposed prison would provide Ward Eight with

---

* The exception was the citizens' group organized with the express purpose of supporting the proposal.

valuable economic opportunity and an increased chance of rehabilitation for local residents involved in the criminal justice system, why were so many in Ward Eight opposed to it?

Opponents cited a variety of complaints, but a central theme that ran through the most poignant and persuasive arguments was that the prison was, for this community in particular, an indignity. As the Reverend Dennis Wiley argued at the final hearing, "Even the thought of placing such a complex in our community is but another indication of the low regard in which the citizens of this Ward are held."

> Building this facility in Ward Eight is not only unwise, it is wrong. In fact, Ward Eight ought to be the last place that anyone would think of building a prison. Why? Because the people of Ward Eight and especially the young people have for too long been stereotyped as residents of the most dysfunctional, pathological, and undesirable section of the city. Already this Ward has more than its share of programs, projects, institutions and facilities that no other Ward wants. Already the negative image that is constantly projected onto this Ward has taken its toll in broken dreams, lowered self-esteem, frustrated ambitions, misdirected lives, and untimely deaths. The burden, the shame, the indignity and the despair of trying to be somebody when everybody keeps telling you that you're nobody is often more than the human spirit can overcome. What I am saying is that the people of Ward Eight need hope. And at this critical juncture on the eve of the twenty-first century, any major facility that is built in that Ward ought to be a symbol of that hope. And I am sorry, no matter how you try to package it, no matter how you try to camouflage it, no matter how you try to fix it up and make it look attractive, a prison is not a symbol of hope.[6]

This concern was echoed in the testimony of David Pair, a member of a local youth advocacy organization, who suggested that those families of inmates who were supporting the proposed prison, far from advancing the welfare of their loved ones, were inadvertently supporting their demise and that of others in the community.[7]

> There are many people who support locating a prison in Southeast because it helps keep families closer. However, this statement seems to

say that people who reside in Ward Eight are the only perpetrators of crimes that occur in the District. . . . I can say that most of the young people, males anyway, will instill in their mind that yes, yes they've built a prison over here because of that. And all this, I feel as though it will be a bullet shot into minds of the young black males.[8]

Residents were not simply concerned with the potentially demoralizing effect of a prison on those who lived in Southeast D.C. As the Reverend Wiley's and Mr. Pair's arguments made clear, Ward Eight residents were also keenly aware of the perceptions of outsiders. This sensitivity to how the prison would color the perceptions of those who lived elsewhere was apparent when Damion Cain, a youth living in Southeast, argued that the construction of a prison in Ward Eight would "perpetuate [the] negative images that those outside of Southeast, D.C. have branded in their minds." The prison, he argued, would simply reinforce the preconceptions that people outside of Southeast had about the community:

> Because I usually go to Northeast and Northwest and [when someone asks] "Where are you from?" And I'm like, "Oh, Southeast, D.C." [They respond:] "Oh yeah, that's where the thugs at." "That's where the drugs at." "That's where everything at." You know, "It's hot around there." And stuff like that. That's what I hear. I hear it everywhere. . . . How do I feel about the prison? Well, I feel that it shouldn't be there. It's a negative image because Southeast, D.C. is already labeled as a prison, by the crime and all the drugs and the trades going on in Southeast. They are just looking at the surface of our community and not looking in the heart of the community to see what's good.[9]

The material implications of these negative perceptions were brought home by one longtime community activist, Robin Ijames. Voicing strong opposition, Ijames described how, after "the former Administration overlooked our distressed community for the designated Empowerment Zones and Enterprise Communities' benefits," residents of Ward Eight started their own "first-time home-buyers project" and a "first-time entrepreneurs project" but struggled to find investors "due to the fact that it's a redlined area."[10] By denying mortgages and insurance to poor and minority residents in "risky" neighborhoods, financial institutions that practice redlining severely restrict the ability of businesses and homeowners to invest in local properties, making the rehabilitation of inner-city neighborhoods difficult.[11] "I didn't even know what redlining was until I moved to Ward Eight,"* Ijames continued, "but, investors and lenders are very leery of Southwest and Southeast deals." Trying to "rise above the poverty and violence that has entrapped our community for many years" would be all the more difficult with a prison coloring the way outsiders looked at the community as well. Ward Eight didn't need a new prison, Ijames argued, because the distressed community was already "a prison without walls."[12]

This is true literally as well as figuratively. A majority of the men between the ages of eighteen and thirty-five in Ward Eight are under some type of correctional supervision, most on probation or parole.[13] Indeed, a large majority of the men in Ward Eight will spend time behind bars if current conditions persist.[14] The different meanings of the proposed prison to different people at the hearing give us some sense of how moral and practical concerns can be turned against one another as disadvantaged communities struggle with the terms of their own estrangement.

The struggle of two women in the corridor of the District's municipal building is symbolic of the struggle of the people in the District and across the nation as they grapple with poverty, crime, incarceration, and competing understandings of what has gone wrong and who is to blame.

---

* Redlining is the practice of refusing to serve particular geographical areas because of the race or income of the area's residents. Following integration, the U.S. Housing and Urban Development Department, along with lenders and banks, literally drew red lines on maps of minority neighborhoods and refused to insure loans there. For an introduction to redlining, see *From Redlining to Reinvestment: Community Responses to Urban Disinvestment* (Gregory D. Squires ed., 1992).

Chapter 2 "It's a Mess What's Happened"

Londa lives in the center of Washington, D.C., in a twenty-year-old housing project.* The project is one of the more modern in the District, spreading inhabitants out in a series of squat cement row houses. Her street is a small loop off of a main thoroughfare, and there is no traffic except for the cars of those living in or visiting the project. Kids and the occasional grown man ride bikes of varying quality up and down the street, some aimlessly riding, others watching for police. In the middle of the workday, the school day, the block is still populated by a scattering of people young and old. A run-down Dodge Neon is parked on the street with two halfway inflated balloons floating inside, one with a picture of a teddy bear, the other with "LOVE" written in large print. And, although it hides behind the doors of this project most of the time, there is a lot of love here.

Many of the residents are unemployed, but around five o'clock, when the working parents and their kids have come home, the street activity picks up. Parents, kids, and the occasional dog are in and out of the tiny cement tenements, playing and calling after each other. It is the typical puzzle of the inner-city project, with some folks working hard at being "decent" and others unable or unwilling.[1] Many of the younger kids alternately play at being "thugged out" and "respectable" to different people, caught between trying to impress their friends and please their mothers. It's the usual mix of loud and quiet, smart and foolish.

It's a mix that is better than most, in part because Londa's project is within walking distance of downtown. That means jobs are available

* A more detailed account of Londa's story and that of her family is given in chapter 5.

and more of the residents can find work than those living in other, more remote projects. And, rather than being a high-rise warehouse of dark and dangerous interiors, it is spread out, making the common spaces visible to all. The proximity to downtown and the visibility mean less violence than the more notorious projects of the District.[2] But it is also clear that a fair amount of the activity during the day here is, as it is around the corner and for several blocks, drug related.

In the last year, there were sixty-four arrests for drug possession and distribution within a two-block radius of Londa's residence.[3] Over 120 men living within the same two-block radius were admitted to the D.C. correctional system during that time, about one-quarter of them on drug possession or distribution charges. Many others, like Londa's husband, Derek, were incarcerated on other charges related to drug addiction.[4]

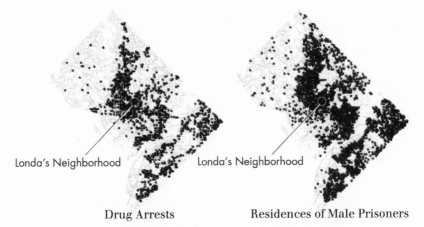

Londa's Neighborhood   Londa's Neighborhood

Drug Arrests   Residences of Male Prisoners
Fig. 1. Arrests and incarceration in the District

When we first meet, Londa has trouble opening the door because her leg is in a cast and her crutches get in the way. She's a solid woman, light skinned, with wide eyes and wrinkles just starting to form in the center of her forehead. When she's in pain they become deep furrows. Once inside her house, surrounded by the debris of family life–toys, a few empty kid-sized boxes of juice, dishes on the table from a lunch just finished, bottles and baby blankets strewn over the couch–she is apologetic for the mess. "But," she tells me, "I've got three kids, a broken leg, and a husband who's locked up." She has been fighting her husband's crack addiction and struggling to keep her family together for fifteen years. Gesturing out the window, she tells me, "I don't want to end up like everyone else. I guess I'm halfway there. But my kids need a father. I look around here and none of these kids have fathers. It's a mess what's happened."

What, exactly, has happened? Not just to Londa's family, but to the millions of families and thousands of communities like hers across America?

Chapter 3 The Creation of the Ghetto

In 1870, as freedmen were participating in their first local elections in the nation's capital, Frederick Douglass, like many blacks in the District, was celebrating newfound suffrage: "The ideas of progress, of self-dependence, and self-government," he wrote, "have taken root and are flourishing among our people. Each feels that he is a part of, and has an interest in, the welfare of the city, the District, and the nation."[1] Freed slaves were flocking to the city, which offered voting rights to blacks far earlier than most states. The Civil War had been won, and many thought that full citizenship was at hand. More so perhaps than even at the height of the civil rights movement of the 1950s and 1960s, blacks in the District during this period had a sense of possibility and prospective inclusion.

Unsurprisingly, as blacks flocked into the District, they moved, for the most part, into what were already largely black neighborhoods. Migrant groups typically follow the powerful pull of kinship, and black migrants were no exception. But if blacks migrated to predominantly black neighborhoods by choice, they were kept there by social and political forces that emerged quickly in the aftermath of the Civil War. By 1874, representative local government had been undone in the District, and all officials were appointed by the federal government.[2] The Supreme Court not only upheld segregation in *Plessy v. Ferguson*[3] but overturned the Civil Rights Act of 1875.[4]

The end of democratic rule in the District, the intransigence of the Supreme Court, and the social practices of whites in the District created a web of restrictions that effectively barred blacks from predominantly white neighborhoods. Once in the District, those who attempted to leave the confines of the black neighborhoods were blocked by zoning and exclusionary laws that were considered constitutional until 1917 and then by racially restrictive covenants until 1948.[5] Frustratingly, even after the abolition of formal segregation and the striking of private racial covenants, landlords, white landowners, banks, and real estate agents simply refused to rent, lend, sell, or show properties to blacks looking to leave black neighborhoods.[6]

At midcentury, the neighborhoods of Southwest, Foggy Bottom, and what would eventually be called Shaw had become crowded with black families, small towns within a city.[7] While still a minority in the District—blacks represented about one-third of the population in 1950—the black population had been growing more quickly than the white population. Over thirty thousand blacks in the District lived in "the Alleys," as the teeming and poorly constructed neighborhoods south and west of the Capitol were known.[8]

Many had parents and grandparents who were ex-slaves and had brought with them the extended networks of kin that have been described in numerous accounts of plantation life. As James Borchert has noted:

> While its forms varied considerably, the alley family facilitated indi-
> viduals' survival in difficult conditions. . . . These extended-augmented
> family networks represented adjustments to a new environment, dis-
> playing continuity with the slave and post-Civil War rural experience
> as well as with the larger ghetto experience of more recent years.[9]

Those who grew up in the Alleys recall the 1940s and 1950s with mixed emotions. Despite the impoverished conditions, most remember life there as rich with social support. As one woman who grew up in the Alleys described her childhood: "You almost had to be close to survive. Nobody had anything. We didn't lock doors, nobody locked a door. There wasn't anything to steal." "It was hard to go hungry, because everyone would feed you, take anybody's child and feed them."[10] Another woman, thinking back to her childhood, also remembered hardship mixed with a good deal of friendship: "In that awful place where I lived there was so much love and affection—not just in my house but in all of Southwest. We had a real community."[11] Despite poverty and decrepit housing conditions, inhabitants of the Alleys had what many of today's urban neighborhoods lack: a feeling of belonging and a sense that those around them cared.

The 1950s brought urban "renewal" and "redevelopment," during which these alley communities of Southwest were physically demolished, effecting the mass eviction of thousands of black families from the heart of the capital. As one woman, still angry over the destruction of her childhood neighborhood, told me: "When they torn it down, they destroyed it. It was never the same. [They told us,] 'It's going to escalate in value and this and that, and you can come back.' But once they got the people out, they never got back."* Most could not afford to move to better neighborhoods, instead relocating into more remote, but just as impoverished, areas of the District.

The 1950s were also the decade during which white Americans, drawn by billions of dollars in federal housing incentives, began to flee the city for the suburbs. While the rise of the American suburbs was financed with subsidized mortgages and tax write-offs paid for by all, they were granted almost exclusively to white families. The Federal Housing Authority (FHA), as a matter of policy, rejected mortgage funds for "high risk" neighborhoods, integrated communities, and female-headed households.[12] From 1934 to 1962, the FHA guaranteed and underwrote over $120 billion of home equity for over 35 million white families.

A massive capital subsidy for middle-class and upper-middle-class

---

* For this woman the difference wasn't so much the quality of the housing as the loss of community:

It was neighbor-neighbor. You didn't even have to lock your doors and if your mother—my grandmother raised me—when my grandmother went to work the neighbor watched me. . . . [Now] they're smothering you. You know, like downtown Washington—it's no shopping area. As a child I remember going up 7th Street. It was all kind of five-and-dimes and you know. And we don't have that in the District. Everything is malls. And once they smother you in you have to go. Southwest is horrible. It's a horrible place. And then they built one little project there in the middle. And they built all around it. And they had the nerve to say they should not of put those people there! Well they were there first. They were there first!

suburban white families that excluded black families, poor families, urban families, and single-parent families, these preferences were largely hidden from public view. To gain some sense of the power this preferential benefit has had over the last half century, consider that these properties have since appreciated to over $7 trillion in value today and are now worth "more than all the outstanding mortgage debt, all the credit card debt, all the savings account assets, all the money in IRAs and 401k retirement plans, all the annual profits for U.S. manufacturers, and our entire merchandise trade deficit combined."[13] As Dolores Hayden has noted, the "dream houses" that became the American standard of middle-class arrival for many families also helped to foster the racial balkanization of postwar urban and suburban communities, drawing two-parent families, particularly white families, out of the District.[14]

These incentives produced a large-scale shift in the geographic distribution of populations and wealth in the District and across America. As white families began a mass exodus from the District to suburban Virginia and, to a lesser extent, Maryland, black in-migration accelerated. Between 1950 and 1970, more than half of the white population of the District departed while, during the same period, the black population nearly doubled.

To help new suburban workers access the city, plans for highways were developed in the 1950s and implemented in the 1960s. The massive highway construction physically displaced thousands of black families, deepening the anger many felt over the leveling of the Alleys and forcing many to relocate farther from the city center.[15] The highways also physically separated many low-income and black neighborhoods from the jobs in the city center. (Often those living in these neighborhoods were the same families relocated from the Alleys and highway neighborhoods.) And, finally, the highways enabled those in the burgeoning white suburbs to access the growing number of government and service jobs available in the District, tilting the racial costs and benefits in ways that were readily apparent to those living in the District's black neighborhoods. Thus, as the number of jobs in the District grew, the job base for District residents actually shrank.

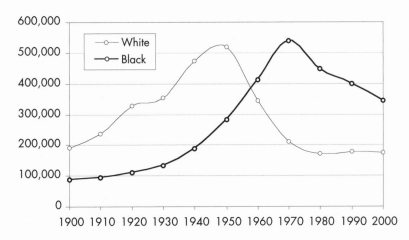

Fig. 2. Shifting population in the District, 1900–2000. *Source:* U.S. Census data.

While most of America was still basking in the afterglow of the pros-perous 1950s and early 1960s, the ghettos of the District, like ghettos across the nation, were becoming socially isolated, economically impoverished, and politically desperate. Public protests over the new highways and the lack of mass transit for local residents were regular features of Washington's political life in the late 1960s. As debate over the new highways reached its peak in 1968, Martin Luther King Jr. was killed, and rioting shook the city. Over seven thousand people were arrested, more than twelve hundred buildings burned, and property damage exceeded $24 million.[16] As in Watts in 1965 and Detroit in 1967, most of the damage occurred in the neighborhoods already hit hard by poorly considered policies.[17]

This was, of course, also a time of progress. The Second Reconstruc-tion–embodied in the freedom marches in Birmingham, Selma, Wash-ington, and across the South; in the passage of the Civil Rights Act and the Voting Rights Act; in the enforcement of those laws by the Civil Rights Division of the Attorney General's Office; and in court decisions leading up to and following in the spirit of *Brown v. Board*[18]–spoke to the American promise of equality, and the "withering injustice" of racial subordination despite that promise.[19] It was a broad movement with a deep conception of what can be described as "social justice"–a justice that extended beyond individual concerns to the problems of group conflict and inequality.[20]

But as the barriers to mobility fell away, and as middle- and upper-class blacks moved out, the District's ghettos–like many other inner-city neighborhoods–became communities highly concentrated not just racially but economically as well. It was during this time that what would become the most notorious symbols of inner-city life–massive housing projects that concentrated whole towns of poor families into massive, lawless structures–emerged.[21] When many of those who could leave did, they took a great deal of the social and human capital of the community with them. This, as William Julius Wilson has noted, was accompanied by a deep structural and geographic transformation of the American economy that moved jobs out of the inner city during the same period.[22] From 1960 on, the jobs left the inner cities for Southeast Asia or, particularly in the service sector, the suburbs.[23]

In the District and across the nation, the simultaneous movement of the middle class and entry-level jobs out of the inner city was devastating for the families left behind.[24] During the 1960s, 1970s, and 1980s the federal government added further injury, with successive cutbacks in programs benefiting parents–particularly married parents–with dependent children. There was a steady real-dollar decline in the federal per-dependent tax exemption, an exemption that would be worth well over six thousand dollars per child today, adjusting for inflation.[25] This decline accompanied dramatic reductions in "tax-splitting" benefits for married couples, significantly reducing the after-tax income available to families.[26] Added to this was the steady increase of the payroll tax–the most regressive regular tax on the income of working families. Sylvia Ann Hewlett and Cornel West recently described the effects this way: "1963 to 1985 was a period when tax policy turned fiercely against families with children."[27]

At the same time that housing, transportation, tax, and other policies*

* The generation that grew up on federal funding for family nutrition in the 1950s, 1960s, and 1970s also started shifting costs back onto poor families when they became adults, cutting back on the school lunch programs by $1.5 billion in the 1980s. *See*

turned against families living in the inner cities, there was significant growth in direct aid to poor single parents. One of the undeniable and largely unanticipated effects of welfare policies (particularly Aid to Dependent Children and Aid to Families with Dependent Children) was that poor women with children who chose to marry were punished with benefit reductions.[28] As the average income for the bottom quarter of wage-earning men in the District and across the nation steadily declined over the last thirty years, the cumulative economic pressures to avoid marriage grew.[29]

In retrospect, it seems utterly predictable that black families would be pulled apart in the social caldron of America's urban ghettos. Indeed, given all the factors working against low-income urban families, it is surprising how many remained intact. From segregation to housing policy to urban renewal and highway developments to regressive tax reforms to cutbacks in child-welfare programs to declining federal support for poor intact families and increased support for single-parent families, the pet policies of the Left and the Right combined to create an environment undeniably toxic to families, particularly poor families, living in the city.

Truly Needy; Let Them Eat Ketchup, ECONOMIST, Sept. 26, 1981, at 21. Because low-income families could afford these changes the least, and because these families were concentrated in inner cities, the reversal of family-friendly policies of the 1950s was an especially difficult blow to those struggling to get by there.

Chapter 4   Incarceration as a Response to Public Disorder

$\mathbf{A}$s families living in America's inner cities began to buckle under the weight of the shifts in policy and the economy, those outside its neighborhoods appeared blithely unaware. What many saw instead were minorities moving in, property values going down, businesses pulling out, and, perhaps most symbolically, crime on the rise.

In his 1968 campaign Richard Nixon described the District as the "crime capital of the United States," and it seemed to many that the District was another of America's fallen urban centers.[1] But as those who have documented the extreme disparities of opportunity in urban America have noted, cities with growing black populations such as Washington, Detroit, and Los Angeles did not so much fall as they were pushed by poorly conceived public policy.[2]

Examining the dramatic increase in reports of criminal victimization in FBI surveys (see fig. 3), it is important to keep several points in mind. First, aside from the years leading up to and following the riots in 1968, the crime rate in the District has roughly tracked that of the nation as a whole; however, because crime rates are generally higher in larger cities and areas with denser populations, the District has a crime rate lower than that of larger metropolitan areas like New York City but higher than that of most states (with which, in the Nixonian tradition, it is often erroneously compared).

Second, it is important to note that the FBI statistics almost certainly *underestimate* the overall increase in the crime rate. This is so in part because crimes defined as "victimless," generally drug possession and distribution, are not counted in FBI reports, and drug crimes have increased dramatically during the last forty years. This rise was due

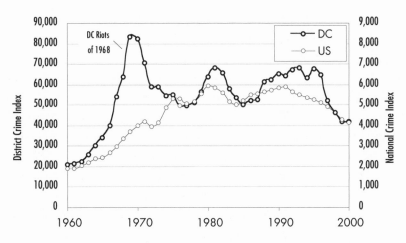

Fig. 3. Crime in the District and the nation, 1960–2000. *Source:* Crime Index, FBI Uniform Crime Reports, 1960–2000. Note that the index only counts victimization rates.

both to the increased criminalization of drug distribution, possession, and use as well as to the expanded distribution of heroin, powder and crack cocaine, PCP, and other drugs.[3]

In addition to the geographic and economic issues already described, the rise in crime was also driven by demographic trends. During the 1960s and early 1970s, in what many experts describe as one of the greatest influences on crime rates over the last century, the boys of the Baby Boom generation entered what are typically the most criminally active years of any generation, those between the ages of seventeen and thirty-five.[4] While, in retrospect, it may seem unsurprising that crime would also increase along with this demographic shift, liberal and conservative policymakers alike were caught off guard by the dramatic rise in crime rates in urban areas across the nation and in its capital city.[5]

There was also a shift in correctional outlook during this time. A major review of both community and correctional programs suggested that there was little evidence that, on balance, such programs were successful in rehabilitating offenders.[6] Although the study was thoroughly rebutted by subsequent studies,[7] the suggestion that "nothing works" resonated with many legislators, judges, and correctional administrators—and the implications for sentencing were obvious: If alternatives to incarceration were not ineffective, they shouldn't be used.

In the face of public concern about increasing crime rates and drug use, and faced with studies suggesting that community corrections weren't working, politicians responded by passing a series of laws criminalizing drug sale and possession, increasing the criminal penalties for other crimes, building up police and other law enforcement agencies, and restricting judicial discretion in sentencing.[8] Falling away during incarceration's rise were, on the one hand, "punitive" penalties such as hard labor, caning, and shame sanctions[9] and, on the other, "rehabilitative" penalties such as programs that provide drug treatment, education, and job training.

In the District, as in jurisdictions across the nation, the movement toward longer and more rigidly determined sentences was supported by a series of federal programs offering billions of dollars in federal aid during the last two decades:

- In 1984 the Comprehensive Crime Act and Sentencing Reform Act established mandatory minimum sentences for some federal drug offenders, abolished parole for all federal offenders, and required federal judges to use new sentencing guidelines.[10]

- In 1986 the Anti-Drug Abuse Act established mandatory minimums for all federal drug offenders, transferred sentencing power from federal judges to prosecutors, and provided $1.7 billion to states for new prison construction.[11]

- In 1988, the Omnibus Anti-Drug Abuse Act established mandatory minimums of five years for possession of five grams of crack cocaine and twenty years for continuing criminal enterprises and broadly expanded conspiracy.[12]

- In 1994 the Violent Crime Control and Law Enforcement Act established mandatory sentencing and lengthened minimum sentences for drug offenses.[13]

- In 1996 the Violent Offender Incarceration/Truth in Sentencing Act (VOI/TIS), which amended the 1994 Violent Crime Act, encouraged states to adopt sentencing guidelines with over $9 billion in incentives.[14]

33 Incarceration as a Response to Public Disorder

Just ahead of many other jurisdictions, the District began to implement mandatory minimum sentencing in the early 1980s for violent offenders, drug offenders, and, more recently, repeat offenders;[15] most recently, in response to VOI/TIS funding opportunities, the District has also adopted both determinate and "truth in sentencing" measures.[16]

Each of these reforms significantly increased the minimum criminal penalties that offenders faced, so that judges in the District's Superior Court had little discretion in sentencing those committing relatively minor drug offenses. As one attorney recounted, "a first time distribution was twenty months to five years, third time distribution was a mandatory seven to twenty-one year sentence–people were just getting slammed for selling small amounts of crack on the street corner and doing huge amounts of time, so the [prison] population just went through the roof." Incarceration rates from those years, as shown in figure 4, bear this out.

Incarceration rates also highlight the racial disparities found in prison populations. As shown in figure 5, black males between the ages of eighteen and thirty-five are incarcerated at a rate over seven times that of white males in the District. This is borne out nationally as well.

As a result, incarceration today no longer affects only a small portion of families in low-income neighborhoods in the District; rather, incarceration has expanded to touch a sizeable majority of such families. In fact, if conditions remain as they are today, over three-quarters of the boys growing up black in the District can expect to be incarcerated at some point in their lives.[17]

As a number of critics have noted, these rates are higher than any we've known in any nation at any time. They are higher than the rates at the height of apartheid in South Africa, higher than the rates at the height of the Gulag in Stalinist Russia. But these comparisons are somewhat misleading. Those in prison here are not in prison for political dissidence. They are in prison for violating criminal laws that most offenders and their community members, by and large, accept. This makes the American experience of incarceration radically different and all the more striking.

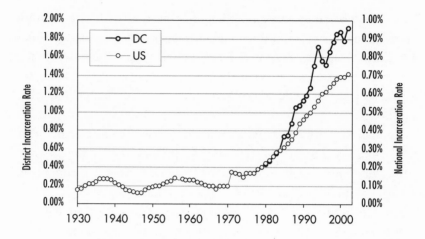

Fig. 4. Incarceration rates in the District and the nation, 1930–2000. *Note:* Data for the District begin in 1980.

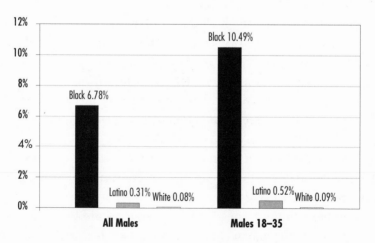

Fig. 5. District incarceration rates for blacks, Latinos, and whites

35   Incarceration as a Response to Public Disorder

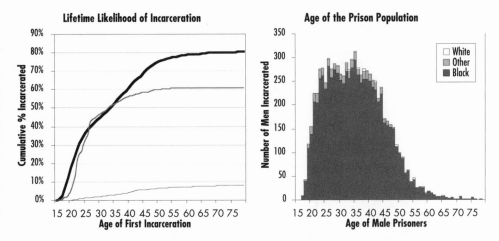

Fig. 6. Incarceration across the life cycle. *Note:* The chart on the left shows the percentage of inmates entering the D.C. correctional system for the first time in 1999. There are a number of caveats that must be attached to this chart. First, it almost certainly overestimates the age of first incarceration because many of these men have been incarcerated as juveniles or in other states (this is only their first time in the D.C. system). Second, it is valid only insofar as a person lives to be the age indicated. Thus, the lifetime likelihood of the average male is lower than that of the male who lives to be eighty. The chart on the right shows the age distribution of the D.C. inmate population in 1999.

But while incarceration is endemic in many inner-city communities, those making decisions about sentencing know very little–indeed next to nothing–about what it means to grow up in a neighborhood where most of the men will spend time behind bars. Does it influence the way that women and men approach their relationships with one another? What does it mean to children who come home from school to find that their fathers have been arrested–or whose parent is arrested in front of them? How does it affect their material lives? How do children feel the next day in school? How do their mothers feel the next day at work? Should a child tell her classmates that her father is in jail? Should a mother tell her co-workers or her supervisor? Should family members talk about it in church?

The accounts that follow show that families of prisoners wrestle with these and other questions every day.

Part II Kinship

[R]eciprocity [is] the most immediate form of integrating the opposition
between the self and others.

—Claude Lévi-Strauss, *The Elementary Structures of Kinship*

Kinship and marriage are about the basic facts of life.

— Robin Fox, *Kinship and Marriage*

Brenda and her sister, Janet, moved back into their childhood home
after their father passed away. It was a large, sprawling house, far too
large for their mother alone, with plenty of space for them and their
children. Their mother had encouraged the move, saying that she
needed their help, but in truth she knew that she was helping them at
least as much as they were helping her. The fathers of both Brenda's
and Janet's children were long gone, and all three women knew they
could live far better under the same roof than they could on their own.
Living together they could count on someone always being around to
look after a child, to give a ride, or to help out with one of the various
mundane crises that strike when children are present.

Their brother, Derek, his wife, Londa, and their kids would stop by
every day, and the house was, as Brenda described it, "overflowing
with family." They didn't have a lot of money, but, sticking together,
they managed to get by. "We'd just pull together, just take care of each
other." But Derek had a long history of addiction, and, even while he
was clean, the family worried about how long he could hold out without serious treatment. When Derek finally agreed to sign up for a slot in
a residential treatment program, they all pitched in to help pay for it.

And then their mother died, and Derek, devastated, was back on crack and in the streets.

Derek was at the old family home when the police came for him. He ran out the back door but didn't get far. Brenda yelled at him not to run and then at the police not to hurt him. He was unarmed, never held a gun, but they didn't know. Brenda's children watched quietly as, guns drawn, the police pushed him to the pavement. It was their uncle's fifth arrest on a drug-related offense. Brenda sat on the steps outside her front door with her daughter and cried. For her, Derek was still a brother, a family man with a wife, a daughter, and two sons. His wife, Londa, was her best friend. She thought of how Derek would work twelve-hour days, trying to hide from the streets, trying to make up for all the times he messed up. She thought of how much their family had sacrificed over the years, trying to get Derek out of prison, off drugs, and back with his family. The lawyers, the visits to prison, the collect phone calls–everyone made sacrifices, scraped and borrowed to try to make things work out. All the time, effort, money, and tears that they could muster, and their family was still falling apart.

One important lesson from nearly a century of anthropological studies of family and kinship is that, while family life in various locales around the world does not always look the same, the norms related to kinship rank among the most powerful in any culture. This is because they not only structure life in ways that are essential to material well-being, but they also lend emotional and moral meaning to people's lives. Materially and symbolically, families model the reciprocal relationships that are found throughout a society, often providing both the essential form and substance of political and jural institutions.[1] They provide, in essence, models for the sacrifice and commitment individuals must make in pursuit of any good that extends beyond themselves.

Materially, family members often help one another by spreading both costs and resources in predictable and reciprocal patterns, so that families are able to enhance their own well-being far more effectively than if individual family members simply acted out of their own narrow self-interest.[2] Socially, families also serve as symbolic resources, through which not only love and heartfelt advice are distributed but norms and modes of interaction are modeled as well. In particular, family life allows parents to express what Erik Erikson termed "generative" concern–a care that extends beyond the self to the next generation, most typically through one's children.[3]

A second lesson from the wealth of anthropological research into kinship is that, while many forms of family organization are adaptive to the material conditions that families encounter, because these conditions are varied and changing, the powerful pull to participate in family life can conflict with material necessity. When the cultural and material conditions of daily life are misaligned, as they are for many people in neighborhoods where incarceration rates are high, people are often required to transgress the norms of kin relations that inhere in the broader culture, and the costs–both emotional and material–can be immense.[4] Over time, the norms of familial relationships themselves can change and come into conflict with one another as people strive to meet some expectations only to fall short of others.

The primary goal of the next three chapters is to give greater definition to the effect that incarceration is having on the structure of families that experience it firsthand. Because incarceration is so common and because its effects are so pervasive, these chapters will also describe some of the aggregate effects that incarceration has on local norms that influence family formation and structure. Because criminal sanctions directly and indirectly affect the ability of family members to engage in these types of reciprocally supportive and socially generative relationships, they have a powerful influence not only on the material well-being of inner-city families but also on the structure and norms of family life itself.

Chapter 5 On the Ropes: Londa & Derek

Brenda's sister-in-law, Londa, is a mother of three. She broke her ankle a few weeks before we met and, worried about the impression the disarray in her apartment will give, she is quick to apologize about the mess. But, with her ankle broken and her husband, Derek, gone, she has trouble keeping the place as clean as she would like.

> What really messed me up [is that] because Derek's gone he's not helping, he can't contribute anything financially, and I broke my ankle, so I'm, like, "What am I gonna do?" I don't like asking nobody for anything. Even when I had my cast on and everything, I just started hopping to the store, I started cooking myself, and doing whatever. The only thing I hate, 'cause I had the crutches, I couldn't really carry anything, so that was really hard. . . . Oh, I can't stand to ask anybody to help me do anything, so I really hate asking my mother now, but I can't walk, I can't get around. So it's just really, really hard right now.

Londa and her three children—Pammy, who just turned eleven, Casper, who is two, and DJ, who is one—live in a small row house that is part of a housing project in central D.C. The neighborhood was devastated first by the 1968 riots, then by the heroin epidemic in the 1970s, declining public investment during the 1980s, and crack cocaine during the 1990s. Despite the efforts of numerous city and neighborhood organizations, the block she lives on is known today, as it has been for years, as a place where crack and heroin can be found on any street corner and at any hour.[1] Although the apartment is convenient to public transportation, Londa despises the drugs that permeate the area and has been waiting

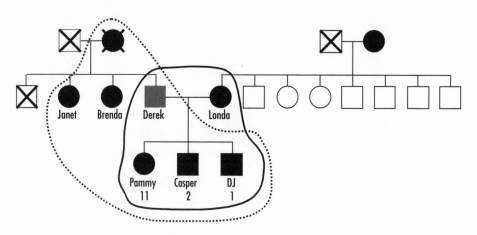

Fig. 7. Londa and Derek's family. *Note:* The heavy black line indicates
the members of Londa's household, though Derek's mother and sisters
often care for Londa's children when times are hard.

for a transfer to another Section 8 apartment in a better neighborhood
for four years now.

Over the three years that I have known her, Londa has struggled with
her commitment to her husband, Derek. She sees their current relationship as the culmination of fifteen years of struggle with Derek's
drug addiction and incarceration, a struggle that has left Londa feeling
utterly drained and Derek with years ahead of him in prison, both of
them unsure of what kind of father he'll be able to be to his children.
Their story is useful because, like the stories of so many families experiencing incarceration, it is neither one of flagrant injustice nor one of
triumph against the odds. Instead, their story shows a family facing
addiction, the criminal justice system's response to it, and the mixture
of hardship and relief that incarceration brings to many families of
drug offenders.

A Family Takes Shape

Londa and Derek grew up near one another. Londa was from a large family, with four girls and five boys; Derek's family was smaller, with two girls and two boys, but he had a large extended family in the area with whom he was close. Londa, who was shy as a teenager, was won over by Derek, her brother's bright and outgoing friend. He was spontaneous and generous, "a little over the top," but she liked that: "We use to just act silly and everybody would look at us like we crazy." Looking back on how they started, she remembers getting to know him during their long walks around the neighborhood, talking and joking. Soon they were in a full-fledged romance, and by the time they were out of high school, they were together nearly all the time.

Derek was a hard worker, making good money performing manual labor–laying carpet, working construction–any job that he could get to help them along. In many ways, Derek and Londa had a lot going for them. Despite Derek's wild streak and partying on the weekends, he kept himself in check and made it through his teens without any serious problems. Unlike many young men in the neighborhood where he grew up, Derek knew that he could earn a living if he worked at it, and he knew Londa was a good partner and would make a fine mother. Londa knew that Derek, though a little wild, cared about her and would be able to help support their children.

Londa had also developed positive relationships with Derek's mother and his two sisters, Janet and Brenda. "His family, his sisters, they're like close family to me. You know, I wouldn't call them my sisters-in-law, I would say they're my sisters." They spent a lot of time together, living the kind of family life that many people hope to be part of. They would cook for each other, watch each other's kids, help out with money in a pinch. Londa related one example:

When [Brenda's] daughter got ready to graduate she was upset–she was hurt. I know she was because you know, she had always said, "When my daughter gets ready to graduate, I'm gonna have a car waiting for her with a bow." You want to have so many things, and I understand that. I want all those things too. At the time she was out of a job. You know [her boss], he didn't care. I took my car. Waxed it, washed it, did everything. And I let her use my car for her graduation. I mean there was just a lot of things we did for each other.

Derek's sisters agree that he was a great family man early on, describing how he used to take care of his sisters' kids before he had any of his own. As Derek's sister Brenda told me:

We was like a big family. He used to take the family and they'd go to the park. Derek liked to play with kids. He's better than me, I don't have the patience for it. He'd take the kids. They'll just go and hang out. I mean, it's a thrill to him. I'm like, uh-uh, not me. [But] Derek is a kid person. I mean, he just, he must have got it from our mother, our mother was like that too.

To Londa, at the time, their prospects seemed exceptionally good. As she told me, "When he first came around [I thought] it's going to be me and that person forever, you know? And I guess I've always thought that about me and Derek."

Looking back on the same time, Derek now sees that his perspective on family life was neither equal to Londa's nor what he now thinks it should have been:

Thirteen years ago, before I had my daughter, [I said,] "I want a child." I wanted a child, but I wasn't prepared for the child. I didn't save up anything. I didn't prepare a home, a stable home or anything. I didn't prepare that me and Londa go ahead and be marrying, and she have her job, and I have a nice job. I didn't prepare for none of that; I was just living life on life's terms. I was living, listening to . . . I grew up with my uncle and them, around them all the time, and I thought the way that they was living was a way of life. That you go out here and work, and you got your wife at home, then you got a girlfriend over here. Then you can go stand over there on the corner, you know, how guys hang on the little block together? Go over there, and that's where they drink at and all that. Then I figure that you can come on the block riding on your car all cool, got your girl over there. You know, I thought this was a way of life, and also going down the parks and all. I really thought this was a way of life. Now that I look at it, I was following the wrong crowd–even my own peoples now–the wrong crowd. And I see this now.

At the time, though, it seemed to Derek, Londa, and their families that they would make a good couple. Both Derek and Londa wanted a child, and it wasn't long before Londa was pregnant. He was twenty-two, and she was twenty-one.

Family, Addiction, and Incarceration

Around the same time that Londa became pregnant, Derek's drug use became noticeable. By the time their daughter was born in 1987, Londa could see changes in Derek as he started covering for his growing addiction. Anyone with an addict in the family will know the litany of problems that Londa encountered: lying, erratic behavior, late night disappearances, pleading for money, and eventually stealing. Pretty soon the stealing was so bad that Londa would stay awake all night:

> As far as the drug addict, you can't really sleep around them because you're scared that when you wake up something is going to be missing. So you generally stay awake to try to keep them there or to make sure that things that you value or that you took your time out to get or spent your money on are still there when you get up in the morning.

Derek remembers this time, shaking his head. He had started selling drugs to support his habit: "I was out there at that time basically using–selling in order to use. . . . I was running and staying up all the time. I'd come in the house any time because of the addiction getting worse and worse."

Today, Derek makes no excuses for his behavior or his addiction. He acknowledges that his father was never around and that many of his family members–especially his male relatives–were hard drinkers and occasional drug users. But, on balance, he believes that his family was a positive influence. Given his family's stance, Derek told me, his continued drug use was a result of his being "hard-headed."*

> I was basically making my own decisions instead of listening to what they was trying to tell me. They always told me, "Derek, don't be going out there. Don't be doing this. Don't be. . . . I want you to stop using drugs." And they always stood a battle for me with the drugs, but I chose to do what I wanted to do.

When Londa realized how serious things had become, she tried to hold Derek accountable as a parent, something she felt like she deserved and their daughter needed. Londa was feeling more responsible now that they had a daughter, and she thought that Derek should as well:

> I felt like if I was going to grow up because I had to "be a mother" [then] he had to do it too. And I felt like that was only fair. He didn't have to be there all the time, but he just needed to grow up. And at the time he never got any help because he never felt like he had a problem. . . . I guess everybody [in his family] was upset because I wouldn't let him see our daughter. . . . But I felt like if I'm going to be sober and clean to see her, he has to be too.

When Derek did not go straight, she told him he couldn't come home and wouldn't be allowed to see their daughter until he did. "You get yourself together [and you can see her, but] I don't think she should get less from you and more from me. . . . The best you can do is to come over here like that? No. I'm sorry, she deserves more than that." And she cut him off. Shortly after that, Derek was arrested for possession and sentenced to eighteen months.

---

* While this phrase is sometimes used to describe a person who is intelligent and clear-headed, many prisoners and their families use it to indicate the reverse–someone who is hardened *against* good advice–and use it to explain illegal or self-destructive activities.

Cycling through the System

Although Derek did not enter drug treatment while he was incarcerated, he managed to stay off of drugs and felt like he had recovered from his addiction.* Londa was surprised to see that Derek once again seemed like the person she'd fallen in love with. At the height of his addiction, she had thought that his personality had permanently changed and that they would no longer be able to relate to each other in a meaningful way. But to her surprise, "the old Derek was back," and he was promising to reform his ways, writing long letters of regret, talking about his religious reform in prison, and suggesting that they get married on his release.†

* While it is not impossible to get drugs while incarcerated, it is both more difficult and riskier. For these reasons, many drug offenders either get clean or significantly reduce their drug habit in prison. It is worth noting, however, that one participant in this study died of a heroin overdose while in prison. Housed in Lorton's Central Facility, he had been, after extensive discussion of his habit in court, sentenced to drug treatment while incarcerated, inpatient treatment after release, and three years' probation for robbery. He was awaiting transfer (to be sent out in the next "load" of prisoners) to a federal facility where treatment was available when he died. Just before his death, he told me he knew he needed to get help soon:

> Right now, I'm just goin' through problems. I just wish they'd go ahead and send me on a load somewhere I can go somewhere. . . . They act like they don't want to send me on no load. I don't know. I'm just . . . I'm just here. I have never received any type of treatment. . . . This is gonna be my first time, so hopefully I'll get something out of it. I need it. I need it. I really do need it.

He was survived by his sister, his son, and his son's mother.

† Prison correspondence is, perhaps, the last great stronghold of the handwritten letter. Many of the men and women with whom I spoke described letter writing as crucial to their relationships while dealing with incarceration. This is, in part, because the collect phone calls are so expensive but also because it allows men to say things they wouldn't normally say aloud. Letters are also semipermanent objects that family members collect and read over several times, whereas phone calls, while allowing a more immediate kind of communication, are ephemeral.

Letter writing is part of a broader pattern of relationships that men and women enter into, however, and the moral and emotional quality of letters is colored by those patterns. Although prison is a remarkably public and social environment for men, one of the privileges afforded by incarceration is the relative privacy from female partners that men have in their correspondence and associations. The restrictions placed on when and how women can contact and visit with inmates allow incarcerated men to pursue relationships with several women at the same time, often with none of the women being the wiser. As one woman described it:

> The letters that they write you. . . . All of them got their jail line, their first line, it's like they teach them that line in a class or something: "How are you doing

Derek's family also pressured Londa to give Derek another chance. Concerned about Derek's morale, they were worried that his isolation from Londa and his daughter could push him back into his drug use. Eventually, Londa submitted to their pleas. "His mom and everybody has always felt like I could make a difference [in Derek's recovery]. And I guess they had me at the point where I was believing that I could too." Won over, Londa accepted Derek's proposal of marriage when he was released. Looking back, she says she feels like she married two people:

> I think when I got married I was thinking, too, that I really, really wanted this person that I knew. Not necessarily he had to be the same as that person or act the same way. I didn't want that person where the demons had taken over. You know? I just wanted my Derek back.

Once Londa had seen that Derek could be responsible when clean, she wanted to help him beat his addiction, but she had little idea how hard it would be.

Trying to gain control over an addiction can be all-consuming for family members as well as for the addicts. Londa felt that in order to understand how Derek could change so much, and to help him get off drugs so that they could stay together, she needed to become an "addiction expert":

> I had to learn about drugs. I had to learn. I had to study all of that and try to figure out "Why did he do this? Why does he do that? What makes him do this? What would he do if I did this?" So I learned about

---

emotionally and physically?" All of this shit. But the letters that they write you and the cards that they send, I mean, if you don't know no better. . . . Me, in my younger days, I didn't know no better. I was, like, "Oh, this man is sure enough in love with me." And the same thing he doing to me, he doing to the next woman! And I mean, they got it. The letters and the cards, they just make you feel like you everything. But all the time, you ain't everything. The next woman ain't everything. It's all of y'all.

This kind of behavior, however, runs the risk of discovery and loss. Many people I interviewed for this study described the emotional scenes that ensued when an inmate failed to manage who visited when and more than one of the women he was pursuing showed up for the same visitation slot.

it. I studied tapes, and read books, and went to the meetings, and I studied everything. I was maybe twenty-two, but I was old enough where I
could be sick and tired of it myself. I could be sick and tired of being
sick and tired![2]

During the following years of Derek's cycling through active drug
abuse and recovery, Londa would work with him every time he
returned to their home, accompany him to his Narcotics Anonymous
meetings, and keep on him about avoiding his old friends. Derek did
kick the habit each time he was incarcerated, but his recovery never
lasted longer than a year after being released from prison. He would
attend his meetings for a while, work hard, pay the bills, and then one
day he would stop off to see some "friends" on the way home, and it was
all over—another binge and another set of broken promises.

Family Aspirations

Addiction alone can strain and sour familial relationships, but incarceration adds an additional wrinkle to the problem that families struggling with addiction face. While incarceration can—and in many cases
does—save addicts from losing their families or their lives, it can also
extend the impact of addiction on families. Each incarceration allows
the offender another chance to reestablish family relationships that had
been curtailed out of frustration or anger. But because most drug
offenders do not receive treatment, the likelihood of relapse is high; and
because many offenders are released to their relatives, the influence on
family life can be drawn out and devastating. Incarceration without
treatment is, in many ways, a double penalty for families of prisoners:
the material and emotional costs of incarceration supplemented by the
equally devastating and—in the absence of treatment—highly likely
relapse of their family member. Given that most of the offenders added
to the prison rolls over the last twenty-five years have been incarcerated on drug-related charges, the human costs to the parents, partners,
and children of addicted criminal offenders are something that, while

receiving little attention in the press or policy debates, is of tremendous consequence.

Londa coped with the cycle of incarceration, release, and relapse by learning to identify clues in Derek's behavior and to protect herself whenever she saw signs of drug use. As soon as she found him back-sliding, she took away his keys, hid valuables, and kept an eye on him whenever she allowed him in the house. After Derek spent one of her paychecks, she also developed strategies for handling money. Whenever either of them got paid, she would guess at the amount of the next month's bills and send in her payments in advance.

> At first, you know, he helped me pay [the bills] and do everything. And then, you know, all of a sudden, he starts to do [drugs], and everything would just fall [apart]. I would try to keep money from him when he had it so that I could [pay my bills]. Whenever he would give me money, I would start paying everything, you know, putting more on it [than we owed]. I would do that. So it would kind of ease it a little bit by the time he starts back on drugs.

This way Londa got rid of all their money immediately and made sure the heat, electricity, and phone stayed on.

"Decent" and "Normal" Families

The pull of "normal" family life is powerfully attractive. What surprised me in my interviews was the degree to which that dream, against all odds, remained intact among families of prisoners. The assumption common in many policy circles is that few men or women in the ghetto have much interest in marriage or in what Elijah Anderson describes as "decent" living.[3] Liberals assume that single women like Londa might not want to be dependent on a relationship with a man and that benefits will enhance the options available to poor women. Conservatives assume that single women like Londa suffer from a value deficit that prevents them from placing proper value on family life. Neither recognize what numerous studies tell us: that those who live in poor and minority communities are firmly committed to marriage and family life but have low expectations of attaining what they hope for.[4] Nor does either camp seem to understand just how hard it is to keep a family together in the inner city. Londa acknowledges that few (indeed none) of the families she knows live in this arrangement, and her dedication to her marriage raised significant difficulties for her:

> I always thought that, "Okay, we want to raise our kids together." There's not too many [families], there's not any that I can think of at this time that's not a single parent family. I never wanted that for my kids. I wanted them to have something that I didn't have. So you try to give them this and you try to give them that. But to me it is more important to have both your parents there. And I've always thought, you know, "Okay, that will happen." I always thought that would happen.

If Londa doesn't fit the stereotype of the ghetto mother, she also doesn't fit the stereotype of the often invoked selfish rational actor. In trying to decide whether or not to stand by Derek, Londa wasn't simply evaluating him as a potential partner in an economic sense; her hope that Derek would eventually recover from his addiction was also based on their extensive history, their three children together, and the fact that both of them valued the institution of marriage itself. Divorce was not something Londa took lightly, and her adherence to that norm was something that she knew was costing her dearly.

The Last Time

The last time Derek was out of prison, Londa, his sisters, and his mother were close to cutting him off from the family altogether. His sister Brenda, recalling this time, looks down and frowns; things were worse than she had ever seen before: "He just didn't care no more. And he said he didn't care, and he wanted to die." Londa recalled that time and her daughter's reaction:

> It just really got worse. My daughter, she couldn't stand to be around him. She couldn't. She didn't want to be in the same room. And she loved her aunts, her grandmother, everybody over there. But she just

didn't want him, you know. She was just having fun as long as he wasn't in her face. I know one particular time she was just hitting on him and kept saying, "Leave my mommy alone!" She was just scream-ing and she was hitting. All of that swinging. And she kept saying, "Leave my Mommy alone! Leave my Mommy alone! Leave my Mommy alone! I don't want my Mommy to cry no more." I . . . it just, it shocked me. It really shocked me.

Even his mother, Derek's most tireless advocate, had had enough. As Londa recounted: "I could see that his mother was really, really upset." Derek's sister Janet remembered what she thought was the tipping point, a night when Derek brought a "friend" back to the house and started smoking crack in the basement with her. "My mother, she came downstairs with a knife, and me and my sister had to hold her back and hold him back."

But just when things seemed to get so bad that Derek's family gave up hope, he finally turned a corner and decided to check into a residential treatment program. As Brenda recalled, for "the first time ever after all the years, he was just able face it. He got three kids, a wife, and he wanted to raise the kids and everything, and he seen what he was doing to us. He was tearing us apart." Derek acknowledged that the threat of destroying or losing his family, particularly his mother, was what finally turned him around. "They could just cut me off, and they won't have nothing else to do with me. It was almost to that point." For the first time, he stopped using drugs on his own and made arrangements to enter an inpatient drug treatment program.

The day before Derek was supposed to start his program, however, his mother died. Londa cries thinking back on it. Derek had just left to pick up some food that his mother had prepared for her, Derek, and the kids. Londa called to let his mother know that Derek was on his way.

We were talking on the phone. She was telling me that he had called a drug treatment center himself and that he was going that next day, how he finally went through with everything. She was saying, "I'm so glad," you know. And she was saying how glad she was that he was finally his old self. And it was just . . . she was so happy about that. And she passed out while I was on the phone. . . . She just collapsed.

Derek's sisters called an ambulance, and the family followed it to the hospital. Janet, the younger of the sisters, remembered it this way:

We went back into the hospital and they put us in this special room, and that's when the nurse came in there and said that my mother had died. And then I'd say about 30 or 40 minute later, Derek had came on the truck, and he ran in there like to bust the door in and everything. He ran in there and he asked the nurse and the doctor, and he said, "Where is my mother? Where is my mother?" And so we took Derek back there; they let us go in back there where she was after they done cleaned her up and everything. And so we went back there, and Derek, he went back there, and that's when he fell out, when he seen his mother laying up there bloated up like that, and [that was] the first time I'd ever seen Derek like that. . . . I mean, it's nothing like losing your mother.

Derek's sisters and Londa were doubly devastated. Not only had they lost their mother, but they also knew that, despite his promises the week before, their mother's death would send Derek back to the crack pipe. As Brenda put it, "Usually we'd be the ones trying to get him to a program. But this time, Derek did it because he seen that we would have. We had just had it with him. And then my mother, she died that weekend. I knew right there, forget that, it won't go nowhere." Derek abandoned treatment and went on a month-long binge that lasted through the funeral and alienated most of his family. Londa recounted a litany of outrages:

He used drugs. He drank alcohol. He . . . I don't even know. Come to find out he was having money wired to him from somebody—everybody—and he was spending it on drugs. I mean, I had the kids down there. It was really bad. He cursed me out. We went to stay in a hotel that my mother paid for. Now, at the hotel he stole my father's car that night. He borrowed money from the hotel manager. He said, "My wife and kids are stuck. They don't have gas and I don't have no money on me. Can I borrow some money so I can get them some gas?" I didn't know any of this until I was sitting in the room and the guy says, "Well he told me that um he was waiting on you to get back with the money." And I'm looking at him like, what are you talking about? He borrowed money from his aunt [and] his uncle. They're married, but one was outside, one was on the inside, so he took from both of them. I mean it was just . . . I have never seen nothing unfold like it. It was so frustrating. It was so upsetting. I mean, I have never had so many hurtful things in one time just come at me like that.

Londa knew Derek was not headed toward recovery, so again she cut him off. It was not long before Derek was back in prison, not only for violating parole but with new larceny counts in both the District and Maryland.

Cycling through the System

Several families in this study described the cycle that drug offenders who don't receive treatment go through: the addicted family member would be incarcerated on some minor charge (usually possession or larceny), given a year or so in prison without drug treatment, and then released on parole. As was the case with Derek and Londa, the parole board would contact the family to make sure that the offender had a place to live and a supportive environment. Families, knowing full well that their loved one received little or no drug treatment and that he was thus likely to relapse, are put in a bind. If the family does not agree to take him in, they know that he will spend more time in prison or jail without treatment. If they do agree, they do so knowing that he is likely to relapse and reoffend. Unsurprisingly, most families—urged on by the pleadings of the incarcerated family member and ever hopeful that they will be able help him through recovery—agree to have him released to their care. Thus the cycle of good intentions and promises, followed by relapse, deeper addiction, and then reincarceration, goes on.

The cycle usually ends in one of two undesirable ways. The one that families fear most is death, and many drug offenders do die—victims of a drug overdose, an illness secondary to their addiction, or violence. Over the three years of this study, three of the fifty offenders who participated died drug-related deaths. But most survive, and often their cycle of abuse and incarceration without treatment ends another way: they commit a more serious offense or wear out the patience of a judge, garnering a lengthy sentence; eventually, if they do not die in prison, they are released late in life. While it is too early to say for sure, this appears to be what is likely to happen in Derek's case. After receiving several sentences for which he served less than two years apiece, Derek found himself in front of an unsympathetic judge who simply saw no reason to believe that this time would be any different from previous times. He had had his second, third, and fourth chances, the judge told him, and now it was time to take him off the streets for a long time. What might have garnered a suspended sentence or parole for a first-time offender got him eight to twelve years.

There are also, of course, far more desirable but also far less common ways of breaking the cycle. Fortunate offenders will be sentenced to mandatory inpatient drug treatment, followed by transitional treatment in a halfway house and then outpatient services. As a number of national studies have now demonstrated, this approach is highly effective when the quality of the treatment is high and the duration is reasonably long. Despite the widely held belief that treatment must be voluntary to be successful, this same research has demonstrated that mandatory treatment is at least as successful as voluntary treatment.[5]

One would think that mandatory drug treatment would thus be a popular sentencing option among judges and offenders alike. The chances of being sentenced to treatment, however, are slim. While some judges are perspicacious enough to sentence drug offenders to treatment, historically many have not been. And even those judges who support treatment have to confront the practical reality that treatment–both in the correctional setting and in the community–is frustratingly scarce. As Faye Taxman, a University of Maryland professor who studies the District, observes:

> [P]robably half of the sentences for probation have drug treatment required, but probably only ten percent get any type of services, and I

use the word "services" lightly. The system has been structured to provide the minimum. We provide something less than the minimum and say we are providing services.[6]

Over 40 percent of the District's offenders test positive for illegal drugs, and over 70 percent report current or recent drug use.[7] But while it is estimated that sixty-five thousand District residents need drug treatment, well over 80 percent cannot be placed because of lack of treatment facilities.[8]

The lack of available drug treatment also creates unintended incentives for inmates to avoid admitting to a drug problem and to submitting to drug treatment as part of their sentencing. Because inmates can wait months or even years to gain entry into a drug treatment program that is a requirement of their release, many inmates try to avoid sentencing that includes treatment even if they believe that treatment would help them. A surprising number of the inmates incarcerated on drug-related offenses in this study told me that they would rather be sentenced to "straight time" with no drug treatment and a definite release date than have their release be dependent on completing a drug program.[9] As one inmate told me, "Then, at least, you know. This other way, you maybe get out, you maybe don't. And then even if you do get out, you have to deal with all the nonsense with your parole officer."

Although Derek was in and out of correctional institutions for over a decade on drug-related offenses, he was never sentenced to or completed a correctional drug treatment program. For the years that Derek cycled in and out of prison without serious drug treatment, Derek's family members were trying to get him into a program, but with little success. Derek resisted seeking treatment at trial both because he thought he could kick his addiction on his own and because he knew that it could add significant time to his sentence. Once he was released, he also had bills to pay. As he told me, "I just thought I could kick it on my own. I was hard-headed that way." His sister Brenda would try to talk him into going to a residential program but had no success:

Derek is a workaholic when he's not on drugs. And he told me why he does it: to keep his mind off drugs. He wants to stay busy, because that's what he needs when he's first out. And like he told me, he also, he's scared of society. . . . He says, "It's scary out here," because he don't want to go back to jail. That's why, like I told him, I said, "Well, you need to get in a program, a real program that you can be there for awhile and take care of this sickness." He said, "Yeah, I know." But the point is getting there, getting in a program.

Small People and Big People

Derek will likely spend at least another eight years in Maryland and D.C. facilities, and it could easily be as much as twenty. While he is not happy to be separated from his family, he acknowledges that there are some benefits to his being incarcerated in Maryland, where there are drug treatment and job training programs available.

> I look at [my incarceration] as taking a burden off of them and look at it as giving me back my life. . . . Because if it had not been for this incarceration, either one of two things could have happened. First of all, I could have lost them completely first. It already got to the point where I was not living with my wife and kids before I came in here. And it was almost to the point that my sister and them was ready to let go. And also, now, I could have been sleeping in the grave and be dead. But through this incarceration . . . it's been a blessing to me. I'm not saying that I want to be here, but it was good that I came here. . . . because I never in my life want to do that again—to take my family what I took them through. And I made promises to my sister and them when my mom passed that I never held to. I promised to be there and help them, but now that I look at it, it seem like I made a promise to destroy them, because that's what I was doing.

It is hard not to agree with Derek that his current incarceration is, on the whole, better for his family than when he was out and using drugs. But Derek's sister Brenda views his predicament with less equanimity than he does, and her lament is one I heard from many family members of drug offenders. The cycle of release, relapse, and reincarceration is one that she thinks could and should have been avoided:

It's hard when people don't have the income or know how to find people that you can talk to, to know how to get them into [a drug treatment program], because a lot of people don't want to listen to smaller people like us. And you just kneel down, and you pray, and you just ask God to lead you in the right way, and just watch over us. Well, it's hard. And you're trying to survive for yourself. And my kids, my family, take care of my income and everything with my household, and it's difficult. Then he has a wife and his kids who are on the other side of town, and they're suffering, too, you know. [Wealthy people] got people, big people, helping them, pulling them out of situations. And when people, little people, get like that, that's a different story. For them, they get thrown away in jail and locked up, while people that's on in high places, they'll take them somewhere privately to a program, and then they get clean. Then they're around positive people and live in positive areas. But they don't do the same thing for people that's small people—they just throw them away in jail instead of them trying to say, "Well, I can make a deal here. If you spend such and such time in jail, and then you go from jail to a program out somewhere, until you feel like you got it mentally together, until you prove to me that I can trust you to go from step one to step two to step three." You know? That's what I believe. That's what I see. I mean, why they don't see that? I mean, they deal with us every day. I don't know why they don't see that. It's simple. Especially if they really want to.

Clearly, the efforts of police, judges, correctional officers, wardens, state administrators, congressmen, and citizens—all of whom have produced our correctional system—are not conspiracies against poor families and communities. Yet one can see why, from the perspective of many families dealing with the criminal justice system, it seems more like part of a calculated design to destroy and injure than a collective social attempt to help or protect.

Both Derek's and Brenda's perceptions seem right. For many drug offenders, arrest and conviction *do* offer them a chance at sobriety and a chance to reestablish the family relationships that they damaged while they were free. But, as is evident from all the times that Derek went through the system, incarceration without treatment gives drug offenders yet another chance to pull their families back into the cycle of addiction. As more offenders are incarcerated on drug-related charges, the disparities in the criminal justice system become ever more tightly bound up with the disparities in drug treatment. In both cases, people get the best their money can buy, and for those without money, for "small people," that is often nothing at all.

Straining Family Ties

Despite Derek's gratitude for being alive, his family life is a mess. While he is finally in a drug treatment program, for many in his family, it is too little too late. The first time I met Londa she was worried about how the rest of the family was thinking about Derek.

> He has an aunt now that, she's at the point where she doesn't talk to him, she don't want to see him, you know. She was like, "He needs to stay where he is," and, you know, not thinking about a turnover or anything like that. She's just really, really bitter about it. And I didn't know this until I spoke with her awhile back. And I didn't know she felt like that. But she was really, really headstrong about him. "He needs to stay where he is and he better never come see me again." It's hard. Like he tells me a lot, he tries to make amends with people, and he can't. . . . And it's because most people don't understand addicts. They just know that they are addicts and they don't want to have nothing to do with them.

While she had long been a supporter of Derek, Londa's mother was very upset by Derek's behavior at his mother's funeral and would berate Londa any time she talked about Derek. "I couldn't just say, 'Well I still love him' anymore [to her]. She'd be like, 'You . . . Are you crazy?'" So Londa stopped talking about Derek to her extended family, except for Derek's sisters.

One of the hardest issues for family members to talk about is the way that children are affected by their parent's incarceration. The most obvious difficulty is simply figuring out how to help the child deal with the absence of the parent. For Derek's daughter, Pammy, that he was occasionally a good father made the times that he wasn't all the harder. Londa described their relationship as a close one that slowly deteriorated. But Londa doesn't think that her daughter has ever forgotten what it was like when Derek was sober. "She really misses that, because when she was little they were really, really close."

Beyond simply missing her father, though, Pammy has had to navigate the social world of a young girl while managing the information about her father in her encounters with friends and teachers. This, for Londa, was the hardest part and led to several arguments with Derek about how to describe his situation to their daughter. Londa wanted to keep Derek's incarceration a secret while Pammy was young and to let her know as she got older. Derek, on the other hand, initially wanted to tell Pammy, but as Pammy grew more frustrated with him he began pleading with Londa not to tell her. Londa believes that Derek's incarceration has led her daughter, already a quiet girl, to become increasingly private and withdrawn.*

> It bothers her because, you know, everybody is dealing with their fathers and school and their mothers. They come see them in shows and stuff. . . . You could see the hurt. I mean it's not more or less she's gonna come out say it. But she's real quiet like me. She's gonna keep everything in 'til she can decide, "Okay, who do I want to talk to?" You know. Other than that she really is very, she is very private. But I could see it. She has girlfriends and stuff, but they don't know.
>
> He told me that he was sending her a watch or something, and I didn't tell her. And when it came in the mail, I said, "You got a package

---

* The reaction of children to incarceration is deserving of a great deal more study. One of the common responses that I found was that children generally guarded information about their incarcerated parent carefully, even when they knew that other people had full knowledge of the situation. As one aunt raising her nephew's son told me:

> He and I don't talk about it very much, but it does have an effect on him. It makes him kind of–when it comes to talking about his father–withdrawn. He has this "I don't want to talk about it" attitude. When his father calls he always talks to him on the phone, but anybody else, if you ask him, "Well, what did he say?" he won't tell you anything. It's like it's between him and his father. But otherwise he doesn't talk about his father.

in the mail." But I wasn't really thinking about it. . . . She said, "Oh it's from my father." I said, "Um-hmm." And she opened it up. She said, "Oh look what he got me!" She was really, really happy about it. Then her friends came along, and they were saying, "What's that?" "This is my new watch." And [her friend] said, "Oh that's cute. Where'd you get that?" She said, "My father gave it to me." [Her friend] said, "Your father gave it to you? When?" And she said, "Yeah. What you think, I don't have no father?" No father. You know?

And then her schoolwork, it showed in her schoolwork. And my daughter is a brain, you know, A's ever since she made kindergarten. She's never gotten a C. Never. Fifth grade everything just went [downhill]. He went to jail and everything just . . . she just really went down this . . . I kept talking to her. "What's going on? What's wrong." "Nothing." You know. She will not say it. Sometimes I sit and talk to her, and I try to pull it out of her. She'll say, "Yeah." Sometimes. You know. And I know that in the fifth grade year and I receive her report card and they said she had to repeat a grade, I cried, I . . . I hurt. It bothers me now. It still bothers me. You just think, you know, there is nothing that you can do. What can you do?[10]

Londa is both exhausted from years of trying to work it out with Derek and furious with him for backsliding at his mother's funeral. She still cares for Derek but is long past putting his desires before her own, let alone the needs of their children.

I think now I'm wiser. I know a lot, a lot more than, you know, than more average thirty-three-year-olds as far as dealing with drugs and kids, and I know where to draw the line. I know how to say, "So long," [instead of] "Okay, I'll give you one more chance." I know how to say, "No, that's it. You had your chance."

After the funeral of her mother-in-law, Londa began considering filing for divorce, but still reluctantly.

We have spent eighteen years together and I'm thinking, "Okay, I can't mess up now!" . . . The only kids he has are mine, you know. I think about all of that, and I think about, you know, why did I get married?

You know, was I so blinded, and the fact that I wanted to get married that I didn't look past that he-man stuff and doing drugs? Or [that] it hadn't been that long since he had stopped doing them. I mean . . . all the other times that he went back, and why did I think this was so different, you know? And I think about all of that, and sometimes I get mad at myself, because I look back, and I see all these things.

I mean, at first when we was dating, I could just walk away. But now, you know, I put a ring on my finger, and I'm married, and so it's more difficult now because I'm married to him. And I have more kids. I already had one, but I have more kids now. It would be a lot less pressure on me to stay, by me not being married to him.

Derek's Dilemma

The last time I interviewed Derek in person, he knew he was losing Londa. He was struggling to figure out how to cut his time down or to be relocated near D.C. so that he could avoid losing touch with his family altogether. Derek's sentencing judge told him he would consider reducing Derek's sentence if he completed a drug treatment program. But, as Derek notes, there are other considerations as well:

My problem now is this. I got to choose between the treatment route, the education route, and the job route. Now on the treatment route, I'll get nothing. Doing school, maybe just enough to cover cosmetics, but that's it. I go the job route, and I can send home some money and, see, that helps out Londa and keeps the family intact. The point is, though, that they ain't coming to see me here and ain't taking my calls 'cause they can't afford the collect. But if I take the job, I don't get the drug treatment. So I'm trying to focus on the family, but I'm also kinda trying to get out of here. But it's also to, I want to get back with them, even though I know I have to get the treatment first. But I just don't know. I know Londa's drifting away now.

And now I have two boys. One of them knows me but the other one was born while I was in here, and when I got out I only picked him up one time when he was a baby. And he's named after me, you know, but he don't know me from Adam. His mother may show him some pictures and things and say, "This is your father," or whatever. Maybe, I don't know. But I think my oldest son, he do know me a little bit. He's four years old now, so he may not know me as well, or maybe my face or something, you know, remember it. Well, now since I'm in here, I try to be a father to them, sending them money, you know, to be able to help the mother out. . . . I try to do that, you know. So if I keep up the job, I can send back money, keep Londa a little more happy, keep the kids knowing me. But then I just go in circles. The judge said I have to do the treatment here before I go for parole. . . . I mean, I look at it, and it would have been so easy to be a father out there. Maybe not easy, but it's like it's impossible here. You know Londa's talking about divorce.

I have often been surprised by the number of people who, while seeing their immediate world in terms of home, family, and community, shift their framework of understanding to one of radical individualism when discussing criminal justice. By conceptually stripping offenders of all their social relations, we are able to affix blame and mete out punishment. The isolated offender is a useful fiction in that regard, but a fiction that has come to so thoroughly dominate our analysis of what our criminal law should and can do that we are blind to its limitations.

Sitting in the office of a conservative congressman on Capitol Hill, I recounted an abbreviated version of Londa and Derek's story to a congressional aide. I was surprised by her response: "Why did she stay with that loser for so long? What these women need is to get out of these bad relationships." At the time, the aide's response seemed to contradict traditionally conservative "family values": here was a low-income African-American woman living in one of the most drug-ridden neighborhoods in our capital city making significant sacrifices to keep her family intact against all odds—and a white, politically conservative member of the middle class wondering why she bothered. That the congressman whom the aide worked for had publicly decried the casual attitude toward divorce encouraged by our culture had led me to think that the aide would be a sympathetic advocate for this family.

Having since spoken with many policymakers (both liberal and conservative), however, I would be far less surprised today than I was then. It is not that the aide did not value family; rather, it is that Derek's status as an offender prevented the aide from seeing that Derek is part of a family and that his family feels it would be *immoral* to abandon him. "For better, for worse, in sickness and in health" are the traditional vows of marriage, and many of the wives of prisoners whom I spoke with recited them to me when I asked why they chose to stay with their husbands. The stereotype of the offender is that of an individual isolated from all social relations. The aide's suggestion stemmed from a misunderstanding of the strength and meaning of family for the rest of Derek's relatives. Had it been her own brother or husband addicted to drugs and in prison, I suspect that she would have reacted differently.

Chapter 6 Falling Apart: Thelma & David

Thelma is sixty-two. While she never married, she had five children by a man who, though she doesn't like to talk about it, had a wife and another family with whom he spent most of his time and on whom he spent nearly all of his money. Although the two families never spoke to one another, their long-term affair was in many ways an open secret, as in the early years they attended the same church where Thelma's father was minister. While her children describe their youth as hard-scrabble living, often without enough food or clothing to go around, Thelma remembers the family church more than anything else.

> All my kids were baptized and belonged to the church, all of them. And my son, David, he was a usher in the church, a junior usher. All his sisters had a group, they sang. I sang with a group for thirty-six years, though I'm stopping now. And his father had a group, the Gospel Singers, a gospel group. And they went to Sunday school and church every Sunday. The bus picked them up at the roadside school, and when they came back, I was ready to go to church. All my children belong to the church. My father was the preacher, and my mother was the organist at the church at the age of six until she died.

While most of her children moved away, her youngest two, her daughter Rachel and her son David, stayed in the District and helped to care for her as she got older.

David is a young-looking man in his mid-thirties. His father abandoned his mother soon after he was born, so David remembers seeing his father only briefly, he says, "maybe eight times in my whole life." He used to drive up to his father's house and park in the convenience

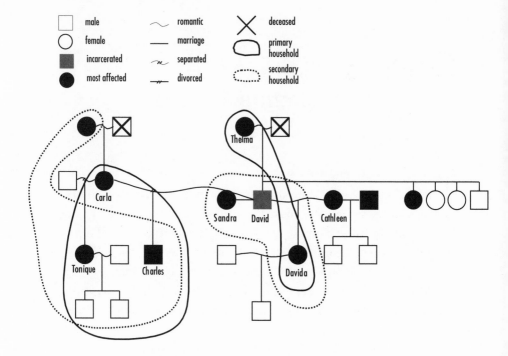

Fig. 8. Thelma and David's family

store across the street, watching his father's legitimate family, wondering what life was like for his father's other sons and daughters. David says that he wants to be there for his own children, to provide for them, so they can grow up knowing they have what he didn't, a father who cared.

Because I think that had my father been there to at least try to do more, that a lot of that stress that Mother had to bear, the responsibility, it would've been less of a burden. She could've did a lot of other things with her life. And so that's why it's just like, since that I've been gone, things are real hard for her. See, in my father's absence, my mother had to do everything. But at some point I got tired of asking my mother to do this and do that. Because as you see her do so much for you for so long, and her taking everything that she get, trying to pay rent. She worked six days a week. Traveling from D.C. to Springfield, Virginia, everyday, getting so to the point now, she don't have—she working six days a week, but she don't have nothing for herself. She taking her drawers, raggedy drawers, putting them back on the sewing machine, stitching them up just to put them back on just so we will have something to wear.

But then it came a point in, like junior high . . . I said, "Damn. I got to help my mother." I mean things got so bad for my mother, she started defecating on herself. Bowels breaking, she putting too much pressure on herself. At some point I say, man, "Fuck this, man." I started getting with these little dealers—at the time they was older than me, but they was still young—hanging out, where I wasn't doing it at first. Once I started hanging out and somebody showed me $20,000 in cash. "Where you get it from?" He said, "Shit, I got this in a matter of minutes." That's all it took.

David's claim that he got involved in drug dealing to help out his mother is a theme that ran through the stories of many petty drug dealers I spoke to.* As one told me:

Look, man, every dude in here had the same dream: "Make a little money and get my momma out of the projects." Some dudes need drugs, some do basically, you know, they want the clothes and all that, but you don't realize how much it mean to a lot of these guys to buy something for his momma.

---

* Even the few who stressed the financial rewards for themselves admitted to spreading their money around the family.

When I was selling drugs I would always take care of my family. I would make sure that they had money. Bills get paid. "Well, I'm going to the grocery store. Would you like anything?" "No. Here, here's two hundred more dollars to put some food in the house." Stuff like that. It was a lot of times that they would not accept the money But me just keep forcing it and forcing it. Forcing it and forcing and forcing and forcing it. And the large family we have, the money could be used. Even though people knew that the money was drug money, but still, it helped out. So when I got locked up, my family they support me to the fullest. When I need money order, they'll send me. When I need clothes package, they'll send me. But a lot of times they don't send it right away when I ask for it, because there are a lot of things that they have to take care of out in society that . . . I really have to understand that they are out there, and they have to take care of their bills and their living quarters.

David's mother, Thelma, agrees that David did help her out regularly when he was not incarcerated, although she claims ignorance about his drug dealing.*

While David may help justify his entrance into drug dealing this way, as he later told me, there were other factors involved as well. He started using heroin in high school, and dealing helped him to support his growing habit. At first, it seemed like just part of the lifestyle, and for many years, even though he had a regular and growing habit, he denied that he had any drug problem at all. From junior high on, though, David was in and out of juvenile facilities and, later, prison, using and selling heroin and a few other drugs up until three years ago, when he turned thirty.

While he says he's tired of the fast life now, at the age of seventeen, having just graduated from high school, he felt like he had turned his life around. By selling drugs, David was able not only to help out his mother but to dress sharply and buy a nice car with the money he earned. Although he was in and out of juvenile detention, there was no question in his mind that he was doing what he was supposed to be doing: "I thought everything was cool, for real, but I didn't know what was coming my way. I thought I was slick." That was just before his first adult conviction, which, as he put it, "turned my head a little bit, for sure."

David & Cathleen

Right after he started serving time for that conviction, David found out that one of his girlfriends, Cathleen, was pregnant. They'd met at a local club, and David knew she was out late every night of the week. As much as he liked the fast life himself, David worried that Cathleen wouldn't be able to care for their baby and convinced his mother to take in the baby while he was in prison. As David's mother, Thelma, tells it, Cathleen agreed to the arrangement and took their daughter, Davida, from the hospital straight to her house. The arrangement became permanent as the relationship between Cathleen and Thelma deteriorated.

* As I discuss in the next chapter, most family members do not claim ignorance.

Because Cathleen rarely visited or offered to help support her daughter, Thelma accused her of abandoning her child.

> Her mother never wanted her. Her mother brought her home from the hospital and dropped her in my lap. "Here's your granddaughter." Last month, I think it was, she told Davida that my son wasn't her real father. After sixteen years. You know it hurt him. My son is the only father she's ever known. And as far as she's concerned, he's still her father. I haven't gotten five cents from her since I had that baby. That baby has been with me for sixteen years. She hasn't given me five cents. And she ask her mother something, the boys got to have something. She still doesn't give it to Davida.

Cathleen, already a reluctant mother, simply stopped visiting altogether: "Why would I want to put up with all that abuse? I had my own problems at the time. If they want to keep telling me how bad a mother I am, well they can just do without me." Another reason for her absence, one that Thelma does not know about, is that about a year after Davida was born, Cathleen found out that an older man she was seeing was HIV positive. She tested positive and, in her depression, withdrew from many relationships. According to David, Cathleen later justified her absence by saying she was afraid of infecting Davida. "It was a time back then, people didn't know much about the virus. So, I do believe her in that."

David & Carla

Carla had already had a child at the age of fifteen, a daughter named Tonique. But after convincing her not to have an abortion, the father moved across the country, leaving Carla to raise their daughter alone. Carla moved in with her ailing grandmother and grandfather to help care for them. "My grandmother's wish on her dying bed, you know. She was, like, 'Just finish school and get you a job and take care of your baby.' Tonique was my only child at that time, so that's what I did." David's family lived right around the corner from her grandparents, and she and David had been flirting while he was seeing Cathleen.

When she heard that Cathleen and David had broken up, Carla convinced David's mother to bring her down to the jail to visit.

> Then I took care of my baby and David, because every Friday when I got paid I went to the store and then the post office to send him whatever he needed. And I mean, that's how it was for, like, ten years, but the first five years [during his first adult sentence] . . . then another [during his second]. At first, I was underage, so his mother would take me down there to see him. Then after I was going long enough until I turned of age to go by myself, and I started going by myself.
>
> Then he came home for a home visit one day, and I got pregnant with Charles. I stopped going down the jail, 'cause I was having morning sickness, and he got mad. Things changed right there when I stopped going down the jail to see him. But my child and my health was more important to me then, you know, but I still stuck by him, you know. I still took care of me, my two children, and him.
>
> You know, I worked from . . . Okay, I got both of my jobs the same day, at the National Zoo and Sears, August 1, 1985, I started both jobs. I was at the zoo from 8:00 to 4:00, and I was at Sears from 5:00 to 9:00. Then Sears wanted me full-time, so I did that for a year at the zoo and Sears, then I went to Sears from 8:00 to 4:45, and then I went to Wendy's from 5:05 until two o'clock in the morning.

During his incarceration, David's mother and Carla's mother helped to raise both Charles and Tonique, sharing childcare responsibilities while Carla worked. Both families treat David as the father of both children, though everyone is aware that he is not Tonique's biological father.

Although Carla sometimes denies it, by the accounts of other family members, they were engaged just before David was arrested again. But Carla eventually broke off the engagement with David, in part, she says, because he wouldn't give up using drugs. "Yeah, he was on drugs, and he wouldn't admit it, you know. That's what I don't like, because the ones in denial are the ones that's on it real bad—where you deny that you on drugs." But the drugs were not all that it amounted to. She was also upset by how little he helped her when he was released from his first five-year term. Not only did he not pay her enough attention, but all the promises he made about turning his life around and making a legitimate go of it amounted to nothing:

> I worked two jobs. I wasn't nothing but seventeen years old, but my grandfather still gave me a allowance, plus paid my thousand-dollar phone bills that David ran up, plus he used to send David money down the jail that I didn't even know he was sending David. My grandfather liked David. My grandfather passed away before David got out. David was hurt behind it, but at the same token, all the stuff that he told my grandfather, them promises he made my grandfather he still reneged on them too. You know, that's why I say he will never have no good luck, and I still believe that. He's never gonna have no good luck.

Eventually, she just grew tired of spending so much time and money on a relationship that gave her so little in return.

> I'd go way down there. I was down there every day. He was down Central Facility. They used to have where you could come seven days a week, and I went there seven days for him. That was a lot. Think about all the money I spent doing them buses–$1.25 going down, a $1.25 coming back–or the days I caught the van for $2.50 and stuff, all of that. The hot dogs that I ate and all that stuff going down there. Man, when I think about all the money I spent going down there every day. And I made sure I got money orders to send him money to put on his account, you know. I done so much for that boy, and the little bit I took from him on the street don't even compare.

When David was getting ready to come out the second time, Carla rekindled her relationship with him, but by that time he was already seeing another woman he knew from high school, Sandra. When David was released, he married Sandra, much to Carla's chagrin. Still, he would visit Carla and the children and help pay for diapers and occasionally groceries. Yet, Carla feels that he neglected the children when he was out:

But as the years went on, I was still working, so it really didn't matter to me, you know. The only thing that got me, because Charles had to have these bars put in his shoes from Boyce & Lewis. Children's Hospital would give me the prescription, and I would take the shoes to Boyce & Lewis, and I never put cheap shoes on Charles's feet anyway. I was on materialistic stuff, too, but I worked to get my kids the things that they wanted. I didn't sell drugs. I worked for everything that I wanted. If that meant for me to work two jobs, you know that's what I did. But it hurt me more when David got out, and David knew that I had to have these prescriptions in Charles's shoes, and them bars cost a hundred dollars for each pair of shoes, you know, and he couldn't help me with it. Yeah, that did start to hurt. You know, that was a hurting feeling right there, you know. But as time went on, I was like, "Forget it, you know. I'll buy this for my child. I'll do this for my child." And I was just to the point where I don't need him.

David argues that he tried to help Carla as much as he could but that he didn't have money right after he got out. "My thing is always to help out my family, so I'm always running by with something, or I drop it off for my mom to give her, when they was living next door." In fact, David feels that part of the reason he went back to dealing was because there was such intense pressure from his family to provide.

It seem like every time I come home, I'm gone to get this, that, or the other thing for someone. Everyone need me for money. But it's not them really. I say, "I want y'all to understand it's nothing that y'all done. These are my faults." I say, "I'm out there trying to do the wrong thing for the right reason. And the best thing that I can do—where I can rectify is to come over there and do the right thing for the right reason."

So David would give his mother money to help out Carla. Carla doesn't deny that Thelma helped to support the kids, she just doubts that David had much to do with it. Still, she says that she cares for David and that she hopes he is okay.

I mean, I still love him to this day, you know, I still love him. And my children know that. I just wish he'd get hisself together, and, you know, that's what I tell my children. "Your father just need to get hisself together." When I criticize him, I criticize him to hisself, you know, when it's me and him. I don't criticize him to them.

David believes that Carla isn't so much upset about money as she is about his marrying Sandra after she stuck with him for so many years. "The whole thing with her is that we're not together like she want us to be."

I told her, "Regardless if I've got a wife, I don't like to treat our relationship any different from when we came to be parents. When we came to be parents, we shall always be that. And more so it's important that we maintain a good relationship for the benefit of the kids. And whether you and I are together or not, we still have to get married to teach our kids marriage is a positive thing. Teach them the right way."

Carla's mother, Dora, although she dislikes David intensely, corroborated his account. "Carla's still angry at him for leaving her and marrying that other woman. That's the second man run off on her, so she don't like that. She still won't talk to his wife. I think she takes some of that out on the kids and everyone. She can get very nasty about it."

After his second five-year sentence, David did one more short sentence and then got into rehab. By all accounts, this last time out, David had finally turned himself around. Although he didn't have much money, he was drug free, visiting his parole officer regularly, and had a job as an insurance salesman, making about twenty thousand dollars a year. He joked about finally being able to put his hustling skills to use, and it may well be true that he has some transferable skills. Still, after being out a year and a half, he was again incarcerated on a possession charge.

David & Sandra

David's latest charge was the only one he contested. He claims that he was leaned on by a police officer who wanted information about a gun dealer in the area.[1]

They kept on about "This is a gun recovery unit. Or whatever. All we want–all we want is guns. Do you know where we can get guns from or do you know who owns this shops? Or who. Do I know these certain people?" And I say, "No. I don't know nobody." So from that point, they took my driving license from me. They ran my name through the joint. Find out I was on parole. "Shit. You on parole." "Yeah." "Okay, I tell you what. You help us, we can help you. We can call your parole officer." I said, "Man, I can't help you do nothing." "Okay, that's the way you want it."

David was assigned an excellent lawyer from the public defender's office. His lawyer laid out all of the evidence, describing his case as a fairly easy one.

Basically, number one, Officer Ramdan has a record of lying. Number two, you have the fact that his account of what occurred in the street directly contradicts his partner's account: Officer Ramdan says he saw David put something into his pants, his partner saw nothing; Officer Ramdan says he didn't search David until he got him back to the station, his partner says that he strip-searched him on the street–and we have witnesses. Number three, I have pictures and measurements from the area where the officer was located and time of day where he says he saw David put something in his pants, and it's a physical impossibility for him to have seen anything. Number four, Officer Ramdan's account of what occurred in the station directly contradicts the account of his supervisor. Ramdan contends that he strip-searched David in the presence of another officer and found a vial of heroin. His supervisor testifies that Officer Ramdan removed David to a room with no one else present and returned with the vial. Considering all these factors, David's description of the events seems more plausible.

The judge dismissed the case, but because David was on parole and because any arrest is a violation of parole, he also had to pass a hearing before a parole examiner, where the standard of proof is the preponderance of the evidence, a much lower standard than that of reasonable doubt that prevails at trial. At the hearing, the examiner found the

Putting numbers to the perceived disparity, we can see that perceptions reflect a real gender imbalance in the District–particularly in areas where incarceration rates are the highest. For about one-half of the women in the District–those living in areas with relatively low incarceration rates–the gender ratio is about ninety-four men per hundred women. The other half of the women in the District–those living in areas with relatively high incarceration rates–live in areas where the gender ratio is under eighty men per hundred women. And within this population, as the incarceration rate increases, so too does the imbalance. One-quarter of all women in the District live in areas where the incarceration rate exceeds 6 percent and where there are approximately seventy-five men per every hundred women. And for the 10 percent of District women who live in areas where the male incarceration rate is the highest–about 12 percent of adult men in these areas are incarcerated–there are fewer than sixty-two men per every hundred women.[4]

The fact that men and women both perceive a significant shortage of eligible men shapes the way they approach relationships in troubling ways. David, for example, found the perception of the "male shortage" widespread and influential:

> Oh, yeah, everybody is aware of it. . . . And the fact that [men] know the ratio, and they feel that the ratio allows them to take advantage of just that statistic. "Well, this woman I don't want to deal with, really, because there are six to seven women to every man."

As with David, the perceptions of many women and men in these neighborhoods exaggerated the actual gender ratios: "It's easily three women to every guy." "As they say, there are a lot of women–it's five women to a man, or something like that." "It's like it's all women and no men out here." This perceived imbalance in the ratio of available women to men affects how women approach relationships as well.[5] David described his own perception of the way that women look at men:

> A lot of the women, they just willing accept the lower things if they can get it from you, because they know that there's a hell of a ratio. And it

seem like everybody is aware of it. All the men is locked up, so they're willing to put up, or to make sacrifices for you, if they can get certain things in return, and they do it.

Women were painfully aware of the ways in which the "endangered" status of the eligible black man in the District affected women's behavior. As one prisoner's ex-wife lamented, women often had to lower their standards to find a man to date or marry, something that she found common and disturbing:

Women will settle for whatever it is that their man—even though you know that man probably has about two or three women—just to be wanted, or just to be held, or just to go out and have a date makes her feel good, so she's willing to accept . . . I think now women accept a lot of things. The fact that he might have another woman or the fact that they can't clearly get as much time as they want to. The person doesn't spend as much time as you would [like] him to spend. The little bit of time that you get you cherish.

The increase in the gender imbalance is only part of the larger picture. Incarceration also furthers the dissolution of premarital and marital relationships by making it harder for men to find legal employment upon release.[6] In this respect, the men in prison and in the community, while accepting some of the blame, also argue that women don't want to be in long-term relationships with them because of their diminished financial standing. As one young man, recently released from prison, told me:

You know, it's like women looking for, you know . . . Like this dude here might not have everything, but he a good man. He ain't no good-looking guy. He got a little job, he ain't got no car though. And they don't want him. See, they're asking for too much in a man. That's what that is.

This attitude reflects the impact of incarceration on the second part of what many social scientists argue is a deepening "eligibility gap" between men and women in inner-city communities. Not only are there fewer men than women, but there are even fewer with an income sufficient to attract a spouse. Women and men in this scenario, as William Julius Wilson has famously argued, can't find and can't afford marital partners.[7]

Incarceration works against marriage in more subtle ways as well. For example, by making marriage more difficult, incarceration lowers the likelihood that men and women will see marriage as a viable option in the first place. This premarital effect is apparent in the dissolution of relationships prior to marriage, even where children are present. Carla, the mother of David's son, Charles, for example, eventually tired of the time and energy that went into a relationship with David while he was incarcerated. The bonds of reciprocity only extend so far. Men in facilities where there is no employment are essentially dependent on their families to help them. For Carla, the obligations eventually became too much.

Carla's anger at the imbalance she perceived in their relationship was also common among many of the accounts of ex-girlfriends and ex-wives of prisoners. Most inmates do not earn much money and are unable to reciprocate the material sacrifices their partners must make. Girlfriends and wives often send money and care packages, accept expensive collect phone calls, spend money traveling to visit inmates, and support their children. For poor women, the marginal costs are quite high because they have less disposable income and time; as a result, incarceration has an especially corrosive effect on the relationships that poor women enter into.

But the imbalance is not only material to them; they also felt it to be symbolic. To visit inmates, partners also have to make significant personal sacrifices and accept a lot of stress. To visit, most must drive, ride a bus, or fly many miles, wait in line, be strip-searched, and so on. Inmates, generally, make lesser sacrifices (some are strip-searched and in maximum security facilities, some are required to wear shackles to visitation). Families, especially romantic partners, also feel the symbolic imbalance in the way phone calls are structured: while inmates can call collect when they need emotional support, girlfriends and wives always have to wait for the inmates to contact them. As David's wife, Sandra, told me, "You just feel it when something happens. You know, you need to call them, to hear their voice, and you can't do anything about it. You don't know if they, like, just have forgotten, or maybe they in lock-down, or what. But I feel like, it's like, it makes me feel helpless."

And, of course, having children by multiple partners implies having unprotected sexual activity with multiple partners. Indeed, one of the hidden secrets of correctional systems is that they are often the largest physical and mental health care providers in any given municipality,[8] and one of the major health crises in nearly every correctional setting is the high rate of HIV infection. By undermining family formation, incarceration not only indirectly contributes to the spread of HIV and other sexually transmitted diseases, it also alters the emotional relationships of those who transmit the virus.[9] As Sandra, David, and Carla can attest, HIV infection alters one's whole worldview. Certainly HIV has not only angered but significantly injured Carla and, by extension, her children. Carla's outlook on life, as many in her family have noted, has become increasingly dour, coloring her interactions with others.

This raises an issue that many families have struggled with during incarceration: the extent to which each family member felt that others cared for them. During incarceration, many prisoners and family members alike regularly questioned the extent to which the other cared about them. By undermining not only the material ability of prisoners to reciprocate but also the sense of caring that inhabits reciprocal relationships, incarceration can increase the perception that individuals really do need to look out for themselves first, that others are inherently selfish, and that all relationships are inherently exploitative. While many wrestled with these perceptions and were able to maintain a trusting and caring relationship, others were not. The broader impact of that diminished trust is difficult to measure, but it may well outweigh all the material costs combined.

Chapter 7 Pulling Families Apart

When academics talk about families, they often talk about the harm that comes from familial disintegration. Many lament the lack of dedication to family they see in high rates of unwed mothers, absent fathers, and divorce. These debates take on a special tone when black families are the subject. Consider, for example, Orlando Patterson's prognosis:

> [I]t cannot be overstated that, in the final analysis, the problems [of the black family] can only be solved by Afro-Americans themselves. . . . Not only because it is Afro-Americans themselves, especially men, who now inflict these wounds upon themselves—through the way they betray those who love them and bear their progeny, through the ways they bring up or abandon their children, through the ways they relate, or fail to relate, to each other, through the values and attitudes they cherish and those they choose to spurn, through the comforting ethnic myths about neighborhoods, through their self-indulgences, denials, and deceits—but also because it is only they as individual men and women who can find the antidote to heal themselves.[1]

Patterson puts a positive Afrocentric spin on the conservative (white) message to black men: get a job, respect your wife, raise your kids, and you can save yourself. Patterson is undoubtedly right that individuals in impoverished, crime-stricken, and highly incarcerated neighborhoods can do a lot to help themselves. But there is something strangely myopic about this kind of encouragement. While it is true that individual acts make up our society, our social institutions have been grinding away at some social norms and steadily fueling others. Indeed, the historical and sociological data that Patterson and other researchers cite show just how powerful the influence of institutions like slavery, Jim Crow, residential segregation, welfare law, and other racially biased government policies has been on the shape of black urban families and the quality of family life.

Without discounting the sacrifices required to keep any family together, it is worth considering just how much we can attribute to the norms that Patterson and others imagine are specific to black Americans. Indeed, though rarely mentioned in discussions about family integrity or family values, there is considerable evidence that the last twenty years of mass incarceration has been pulling apart the most vulnerable families in our society.[2] Incarceration has dramatically altered the structure of families in this study in ways that traditional studies measure, increasing the number of single female-headed households and removing many children to the care of extended kin.

By the Numbers

Extensive research indicates that men, women, and children in poor neighborhoods value family no less than do other Americans but face considerably greater obstacles in maintaining familial integrity.[3] Among the foremost of those obstacles are incarceration and its consequences. Marriage and co-parenting are far less common and single female-headed households are far more common in areas where incarceration rates are high. In the District, for example, in neighborhoods where the male incarceration rate exceeds 2 percent, fathers are absent from over half of the families. Among the District families living in the areas with the highest incarceration rates, fewer than one in four has a father present.*

* Of the 6,181 families living in areas with the highest male incarceration rates (averaging 16 percent), 4,842—over 78 percent—of those families were without fathers. Figures are based on D.C. Department of Corrections and U.S. Census data. Unfortunately, the data do not distinguish between biological fathers and stepfathers. However, because women with lower incomes are both more likely to remarry and more likely to live in areas with high incarceration rates, it seems likely that not only are there fewer fathers present in areas with high incarceration rates but a disproportionate number of the fathers who are present are stepfathers. See CHANDLER ARNOLD, CHILDREN AND STEPFAMILIES: A SNAPSHOT, Center for Law and Social Policy (1998). The issue is a significant one because, as Cynthia Harper and Sara S. McLanahan have noted, controlling for income and other demographic factors, "while children in single-mother households, particularly those born to single mothers, have

The statistical data suggest that family structure is powerfully shaped by the experience of incarceration. While it might be argued, for example, that it is not incarceration but differences in income or education that affect family structure, controlling for these other variables in a regression analysis shows that incarceration has a statistically significant and independent relationship with family structure. Using census data, the results of the analysis are striking.

TABLE 1. The Relative Impact of Incarceration on Father Absence

	Standardized Coefficients	Coefficients	Standard Errors
Constant	0.127***	1.26	0.000
Male unemployment rate	0.024	0.070	0.108
Median income	−0.164***	0.000	0.000
Average educational achievement	−0.410***	−0.099	0.018
Gender ratio	0.109***	0.000	0.000
Race (black = 1, non-black = 0)	−0.001	0.000	0.047
Male incarceration rate	0.190***	2.157	0.506
R^2		0.446	
Observations		576 block groups	

Note: Analyses using 1999 D.C. Department of Corrections and 2000 U.S. Census data..

In this analysis, as indicated by the relative size of the standardized coefficients, the influence of male incarceration is highly statistically significant and large in magnitude, second only to the relationship between educational levels and father absence and accounting for nearly twice the variance that community gender ratios do. It is also interesting to note that in this analysis, after controlling for incarceration and other variables, race has no significant relationship to father absence.

An examination of the relationship between incarceration and father absence in different income groups, shown as three fitted polynomial

---

higher chances of incarceration, those in stepparent families fare even worse." Cynthia Harper and Sara S. McLanahan, *Father Absence and Youth Incarceration,* Bendheim-Kenny Center for Research on Child Well-being, Working Paper 99–03, 33 (1999).

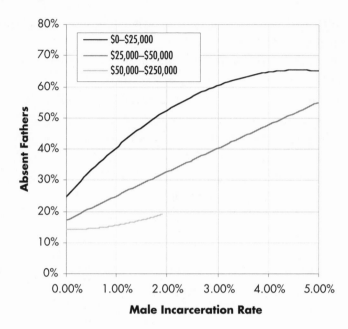

Fig. 9. Incarceration, father absence, and median household income. Analyses using 1999 District Department of Corrections and 2000 U.S. Census data.

lines in figure 9, illustrates the extent to which income may mediate the impact of incarceration on family organization.

For all three income groups, where incarceration rates are at their lowest, father absence is fairly similar: occurring in fewer than 25 percent of households with children. As the incarceration rate increases among lower-income families, father absence increases at a far greater rate than it does among middle-income families, among which father absence increases at a greater rate than among upper-income families. (Note that no upper-income census block group has an incarceration rate of over 2 percent.) So, as the incarceration rate increases to 2 percent, the percentage of families absent fathers in upper-income neighborhoods climbs about 5 percent; in middle-income neighborhoods, it climbs about 15 percent; and in lower-income neighborhoods, it climbs over 25 percent. The commonsense implication of this is that poor families not only are exposed to incarceration more often but are far more likely to be broken by it.

Beyond the Numbers

These statistics begin to indicate the corrosive power of incarceration on family structure. But the data do not tell the whole story. The failure is, in part, a matter of the limited reach of the data–something that might be cured with a more detailed survey. For example, these statistics fail to capture a significant portion of the influence that incarceration has on nonnuclear familial structures. There simply are no census data on the strength and number of nonhousehold ties that individuals have. The statistics also fail to account for the out-migration of many children who are sent to live with extended family. As a number of studies have shown, a significant portion of the out-migration from the inner cities during the last twenty years has been that of children and parents returning to the rural and suburban areas where some of their extended families remained during the in-migration of the previous twenty years.[4] So, as times get hard and families struggle in the cities, some of the consequences are borne by relatives elsewhere.

More importantly, these statistics cannot tell us the extent to which the variables influence one another. The relationship between incarceration and father absence runs both ways and is arguably cyclical. Children like Davida and Charles, made fatherless by incarceration, are not only more likely to be abused, to live in poverty, and to burden their extended family but also more likely to be involved in the criminal justice system themselves,[5] contributing to a cycle of abuse and neglect across generations. And while the considerable costs of incarceration and incarceration's effects on gender norms do contribute to family fragility, precisely how much is harder to say.

Most importantly, however, the statistical data fail to capture the meaning of family life and its dissolution for family members. What is it about letters, phone calls, and gifts that sustains relationships? Why do marital vows keep wives with their husbands despite the economic costs? When Derek sends his daughter a gift, it is more than a transfer of material goods; it is a display of care and concern that demonstrates the enduring significance of their kinship in his absence. This is why, as Marcel Mauss and so many others have since pointed out, our identities and relationships are intermingled with the exchanges we have with one another; gifts and letters help to establish and maintain social relationships that give life its meaning.[6] Capturing the meaning of a child's relationship with his or her father is no mere statistical undertaking.

That meaning, as the children themselves tell it, can have dramatic consequences in their personal lives. Londa's daughter makes it plain when she withdraws from her friendships and fails in school. So does Davida when she describes the happiest day of her life as one spent with her father, talks about being sexually abused while he is incarcerated, and describes secretly how she sells her body so that she and her grandmother can stay together and stay in touch with her father. So does Charles when he is severely beaten by his mother's boyfriend, takes to stealing cars, and thinks about being with his father in prison.

Marital contracts and spousal exchanges are also meaningful in ways that evade statistical abstraction.[7] Establishing and sustaining long-term trusting relationships—relationships where the balance sheets are never fully closed or disclosed—helps people to get through hard times financially and emotionally. But they can exert a strong normative pull on those who are in them, spreading the harsh realities of addiction and incarceration far beyond criminal offenders. The meaning of family to Londa is powerful; but, given her fifteen-year struggle with her husband's addiction and her unrelenting desire to achieve the middle-class dream for herself and her children, that meaning came with a heavy price. Before asking whether, in hindsight, she was wise to bear the costs of that commitment, we might ask what the costs (both public and private) would be were she and others to decide that their commitments are too heavy to bear and withdraw their support, concern, and care.

None of the women and few of the men I interviewed expressed a negative attitude toward marriage; instead, most had marital ambitions but low expectations of achieving them.[8] While there are many factors involved in the increase of divorce and out-of-wedlock births over the last thirty years, the people I interviewed generally described marriage as not only a desirable goal but a serious commitment. Indeed, many wives of prisoners said that they would have left their partners had they not been married to them.[9] David's current wife, Sandra, for example, told me that what has held them together through his three most recent incarcerations is "the fact that I took my vows." For her and for many wives of prisoners, as she says, "marriage makes a big difference. The marriage is probably holding us together."

While some commentators describe the inner city as a socially unstructured domain,[10] the lives and choices of the family members in this study appear to be highly structured–just not in ways that they or other Americans find particularly appealing. Indeed, the choices of families in the neighborhoods where incarceration rates are highest are far more constrained than are those of Americans whose lives are richer in material and social resources. But there is nothing *intrinsically* different about these families that sets them apart. While every family is unique, on the whole the families in this study are families like most others, adapting their lives, their reasoning, and their behavior to the social institutions that structure everyday life. The question that we as a society have failed to ask in a meaningful way is how years of steadily rising criminal sanctions have shaped family life. In this regard, the experience of families in our nation's capital is instructive.

Many of our policies–particularly our criminal justice policies–presume a lack of interest in family life. Listening to these families, it becomes apparent that these policies not only draw from the mischaracterizations but go a fair distance toward enforcing the same stereotypes that contributed to their creation. Criminal justice policy currently does this by separating black men from their families and placing them in the nonfamilial and noncommunity space of the prison and, at the same time, placing profound burdens on the female relatives of prisoners by increasing their individual responsibilities to family–enforcing the stereotype of the black woman as the solitary center of black families.

The irony of this is that harsh criminal sanctions are generally viewed as necessary because of the steady erosion of family life in America.[11] Many policymakers and analysts point to the dissolution of the traditional family as driving increased criminality among poor, urban, and minority populations over the last four decades.[12] The accounts of these families suggest that policymakers have closed the circle, developing criminal sanctions that effectively undermine family life in precisely those communities where families are the most fragile. The heavy hand of our criminal law thus appears to be accelerating the loss of social connections that usually inhibit criminal activity, thereby exacerbating the very normative problems it is intended to correct.

Part III Exchange

Lives are mingled together, and this is how, among persons and things so intermingled, each emerges from their own sphere and mixes together. This is precisely what contract and exchange are.

—Marcel Mauss, *The Gift*

Exchange . . . is moral conduct and is so regulated.

—Marshall Sahlins, *Stone Age Economics*

Accountability, a concept at the heart of get-tough sentencing reforms, has taken on a different meaning for Barbara. She lives in a small apartment in a housing project near the Maryland state line in Northeast Washington, D.C. Her nephew, Davone, violated the terms of his parole for a previous heroin distribution charge and is, as he has been for most of the past decade, incarcerated. When Davone's mother passed away, caring for Davone's son, Junior, fell to Barbara. While she loves him dearly, she is upset about the mounting costs of caring for her nephew's child. He was born with significant medical problems, including bone deformities and reduced lung capacity. He now wears special shoes that help correct his gait and is on a number of medications:

That shelf there, the top shelf alone, is full of medications for Junior. Then he has the machine, the nebulizer machine. Then you have to buy medications for the machine, because it's different from the aerosols and the pills and all. I applied for help, but you don't always get what you apply for. I got a Medicaid card for him, but that only pays

80 percent and then you have to pay the rest and you run your bill up so high until you just have to stop going to the doctors or you have to stop going to therapy because you can't afford to pay it. And you have no means of paying it.

When Davone was out of prison, she could persuade him to help support his son; he would buy groceries, clothing, and school supplies—though, she says wistfully, this year "he got arrested before he could get all of Junior's school supplies." It's not that Barbara thinks Davone shouldn't be punished—she, like many family members I spoke with, insisted that "if you do the crime, you do the time." What upsets her is that incarceration has reduced his responsibilities instead of forcing him to meet them. "He doesn't do a thing in there. They take the bread-winner out of the house, and the family has to go out and scuffle and get it on their own." The state, holding Davone accountable in one sense, is holding him unaccountable in another—and there are millions of families like his who are feeling the consequences.

The next four chapters examine how incarceration shapes the material conditions of family life. The stories of three families—the first dealing with an arrest, the second with a long-term sentence, and the third with repeated offenses extending over a decade—begin to illustrate the broad array of material consequences that can accompany incarceration. More importantly, however, they help us to see that the economic effects of incarceration cannot be separated from its social effects and that the repercussions of incarceration reach more deeply into the substance of family and community life than standard accounts of the criminal law suggest.

Chapter 8 Arrested: Edwina & Kenny

Edwina grew up in Alabama in the 1940s and 1950s, the daughter of a domestic worker and a factory hand. She recalls herself as a simple girl with simple parents, and most of her family agree, adding only that she hasn't changed much. She married her high school sweetheart, but, she points out, "we didn't really meet at school–it was at the church our families attended." Fairly soon after they were married, she became pregnant. Their son, Kenny, was born in 1957. Around Kenny's fifth birthday, Edwina recalls, "his father was drafted and we left for Fort Myers and then Fort Belvoir."

It wasn't long after the move that Kenny had a sister and Edwina and her husband began to have serious fights. "We just didn't see eye-to-eye," she told me.

> Well, you could say we just parted ways. He got kind of violent, and I was thinking about the children. I sent them back down to Alabama so I could get myself situated, which was very hard for a female in the city to get a place of her own. I was working part-time for A&P and in the school system cafeteria. My mother kept 'em about one year, then they came back to the District.

She was working at the A&P during the riots when the store was burned to the ground. "I couldn't draw unemployment, so I went to D.C. General Hospital as a nurse's assistant to have some income. But as the kids was getting older, and it wasn't like it is now–I had to work seven days straight before I got a day off and the hours was horrible–so I left that." Luckily, a girlfriend knew of a day job doing data entry for the Army. "A 'key puncher'? I said. 'Sure!' I jumped at that." That was followed by a series of promotions that eventually led to her supervising all of the data entry personnel in her division, the job from which she would retire in 1998.

By that time her son, Kenny, had had a daughter and two sons of his own. Kenny had sole custody of his sons because their mother was, as he put it, "in the drug life."[1] Kenny let the boys visit their mother when they asked to do so, but over the years they asked less and less as her addiction made her life and her living arrangements increasingly unpleasant. "Let me put it this way," Kenny told me, trying to give some indication of his boys' relationship with their mother. "Their mother no longer remembers their birthdays, and to a kid, that signifies. I used to try to remind her, but it just became more trouble than it was worth."

For several years leading up to her retirement, Edwina and her son had been carefully planning her return to her hometown in Alabama. Although Kenny and his two boys lived with her in the District, most of Edwina's relatives still lived near where they had grown up, and she was eager to return to a simpler life in the company of kin. "I've been away since '62, and I have got plenty of friends [here], but it's not like family, especially when the holidays come and you can't spend holidays with your family." Finances were also an issue, for although Edwina had, with Kenny's help, paid down most of her mortgage, her pension was small. "And," she noted, "by me being retired, it wouldn't be quite as expensive in Alabama as it is here."

Her primary consideration in relocating, however, was her mother. "My mother's coming down with Alzheimer's, and that would be closer for me to help my sister care for her. [We take turns caring for her], and it's very confusing for her, because once she gets situated here [in the District], then it's time for her to go back [to Alabama]." Living in the District also meant a lot of travel for Edwina, her mother, and her sister, which was proving to be expensive and tiring as well.

To supplement her pension she planned to sell her house. Her son, Kenny, had a job as a computer technician at a local TV station that paid reasonably well. He was able to help her with her expenses while she helped him to care for his children, and, when he moved in five years ago, he began helping her with the mortgage. His extra income helped to buy groceries and cover whatever bills she had trouble with, and she was proud that, in the family tradition, Kenny was working "in the computer field."

Kenny often worked at night, and Edwina was happy to spend time with the boys. But even when Kenny had been between jobs, she liked having him and the boys around:

> When he wasn't working, I didn't have to worry about those boys. He got them up, he fixed their breakfast, he washed their clothes, he'd see that they went to school. And like I tell people, "Y'all don't understand. Money is not everything. Sometimes it's what people do that means much more to you than giving you that money, because once you spend that money, you can't account for it." . . . He got his children up, he washed 'em, and not only that, you know, he would help around here in the house and clean the house.

Edwina hoped that Kenny and the boys would move down to Alabama with her. Kenny had spent part of his childhood there and enjoyed the family as much as she did. They also thought that, as the boys got older, country life might do them some good. Managing two preadolescent boys in the city was already proving challenging, and they worried about how, even with supervision, they would shepherd them through to adulthood.

Edwina's story is the quintessential American story—not from rags to riches but from very little to a little. The child of an illiterate factory worker and a housemaid, she moved to the city, overcame adversity—including an abusive husband—and raised her two children. When the mother of her grandchildren became addicted to crack cocaine, Edwina stepped in. When her mother became ill, she and her sister were there to care for her. She was ready to move back home to the bosom of her family, a move that would have placed her at the center of the great return migration now taking place from black inner-city neighborhoods to rural southern towns across America.[2] It wasn't a story of unadulterated triumph, but it was a story of love, family, and modest success.

"I Broke the Rules"

"That seems like a long time ago," Edwina tells me, looking around at her house, now in a state of disarray. "You know my mother was visiting when it happened, and we had just been getting ready to try to sell the house. We were just packing up and taking her to the airport." Late in the summer, while Kenny was returning from a trip to a convenience store near a relative's house in Southeast, a stranger came up to him and demanded a cigarette. When Kenny declined, he was first verbally and then physically assaulted by the man.* Kenny had recently started carrying a knife with him on the advice of his father, who thought the neighborhood was dangerous; he stabbed his assailant and, when the man collapsed, ran away. Two days later he was arrested and charged with murder; he had stabbed the man through the heart and killed him. A woman with whom Kenny was talking prior to the attack identified him as the killer. Kenny admits that he stabbed his assailant but argues that it was in self-defense. After six months of waiting, he is still unsure when his trial will occur or what the outcome will be.†

Edwina recalls her son's arrest as among the worst experiences in her life: "When I got here, they had handcuffed him, and he was wanting me to find him some shoes and some pants. They were waiting on me to bring a pair of jeans, so after I couldn't find no jeans, they just

---

* Kenny's account was supported by testimony and physical evidence presented at trial.
† Though the family is uncertain about Kenny's chances, they believe he has a good case and are happy that his lawyer seems both competent and hardworking–a rare stroke of luck with court-appointed attorneys. Judges often assign cases to underpaid and overworked attorneys who take court-appointed cases to make money for their own private practices. However, because the compensation for court-appointed cases is usually low, some attorneys take on far more cases than they can responsibly handle. The result, as many inmates and their families attest, is that the attorney's first priority becomes looking for the quickest way to settle a case rather than fully and fairly representing their clients. And, generally, the quickest way to settle is to make a deal with the prosecutor and cop a plea. Kenny's attorney, however, while court appointed, was from the District's public defender's office, considered by many to be staffed by the best public defense attorneys in the nation.

took him on out. And that just, when they handcuffed him, that just does something to you."*

In some respects, Kenny's predicament is fairly straightforward: he killed a man and is paying the price. This is fairly close to the standard legal model of "just deserts,"[3] and Kenny does not take issue with it as it relates to his situation:

I broke the rules. You can't just go and do what I did. That's what I'm trying to tell my sons now. I grew up thinking that if someone hit you, you hit back. But if you hit someone, that's assault. If you pick up a stick and hit someone with it, that's assault with a deadly weapon. Now I know the rules, and I'm gonna make sure, very sure, that my boys know them too. Follow the rules. Otherwise, you break the rules and you get put in jail–that's justice. . . . You may say you want justice, but justice is not what you think it is. Justice is what the law says it is.

Among the offenders and family members I spoke with, very few suggested otherwise. Many criticized the operation of the criminal justice system or felt that their own case was exceptional for any number of reasons, but few actually challenged the mainstream understanding of justice and punishment: we, as a society, agree on the rules and, as individuals, must follow them; if we do not, we are punished. Far more than excusing criminality, urban blacks overwhelmingly feel that the courts are not harsh enough with criminal offenders.[4]

Indeed, what many liberals miss when they advocate on behalf of

---

* Police often arrest suspects at night or in the early morning, when they are likely to be home with their families. As a result, many are taken away with whatever they happen to be wearing, and in the summer this can be underwear or, in extreme cases, nothing at all. The shock of the arrest combined with the image of one's naked or nearly naked father or son being led away in handcuffs is particularly upsetting to family members who have experienced it. As one mother told me:

You know, the worst part about it was–and I still don't like it and every time I think about it, you know, it hurts me real bad–is that when they come and get my son that morning, it was my son, his girlfriend, and they had a small baby up there. They come in my son's bedroom and got my son, the police did this now, they go in my son's bedroom and get my son out, get my son out and he doesn't even have any clothes on at all. They was going to take him outside with no clothes on!

criminal offenders is that those living in our inner cities are victims of crime far out of proportion to the rest of the population. (Recall that, while incarceration in the District is double the national rate, criminal victimization is ten times the national rate.[5]) The notorious under-enforcement of the law in impoverished urban neighborhoods has led to a sense of abandonment and the regular violation of traditional social contracts.[6] Many of the families I spoke with were very distressed about the level of criminal activity in their neighborhood and the lack of police presence there. As one woman told me, "The police are just too scared to come here. You can call them, but they're gonna take their time because they don't wanna get caught up in what's going on." As Elijah Anderson has noted:

> In many working-class and impoverished black communities today, particularly as faith in the criminal justice system erodes, social behavior in public is organized around the code of the streets. Feeling they cannot depend on the police and other civil authorities to protect them from danger, residents often take personal responsibility for their security. They may yield, but often they are prepared to let others know in no uncertain terms that there will be dire consequences if they are violated. They tend to teach their children to stand up for themselves physically or to meet violence with violence.[7]

Indeed, this worry about lawlessness is precisely what prompted Kenny's father to urge Kenny to carry a knife. And one might imagine that being accosted by a crack addict after midnight on a dark city street in a dangerous neighborhood is precisely what his father had in mind when he did so. One need not minimize the tragic loss of life to note that the loss is at least partly attributable to a broader context of distrust and fear in the inner city.

Civil abandonment of the inner city does not extend to police protection alone. Kenny's victim was, arguably, also a casualty of his addiction—an addiction that led him to commit a string of property crimes and assaults like the one he attempted against Kenny. It bears repeating that one of the reasons why crime rates remain high in the District is that an estimated sixty-five thousand residents are in need of drug treatment and well over 80 percent cannot be placed because of lack of treatment facilities.[8] Combining under-enforcement of the law with what can only be described as dismal prevention policies and programs, the District and many other troubled cities have created the conditions in which situations like this—an encounter between individuals who are some amalgam of addicted, impoverished, fearful, and armed—will occur.

It is not hard to see how, as individuals are increasingly confronted with circumstances that punish ethical decisions, a slow accretion of norms of violence and distrust is inevitable. Kenny agrees, however, that none of this absolves him. Liberal excuses for criminal conduct belittle the moral character of those living in the inner city who struggle to do honor to their conscience in an environment where doing so means leaving themselves open to serious harm. But while it provides no excuse, understanding the social context of crime does help give some indication of how the cost of moral behavior can be lowered and how real progress in the war against crime can be made.

Family Problems

Edwina decided to stay in the area "until Kenny is out and situated." She had the boys and, while it would be far less expensive to care for them in Alabama, thought they needed to be near their father. Unable to afford retirement, she found a part-time job at a staffing agency for nursing homes. At the age of sixty-two, she is responsible for the care of her two grandsons and her granddaughter, Tasha, Kenny's daughter from a previous relationship, who recently moved in after having a baby of her own.

Adding to her difficulties, Edwina fell and injured her knee after Kenny's arrest, and she has had a good deal of difficulty getting around as a result—something that makes caring for the boys especially hard: "It's hard to keep after them, and I just can't keep the place like I want to. That's another reason I need Kenny back is that he did all that when he was here. I never had to keep on the boys because he would handle them."

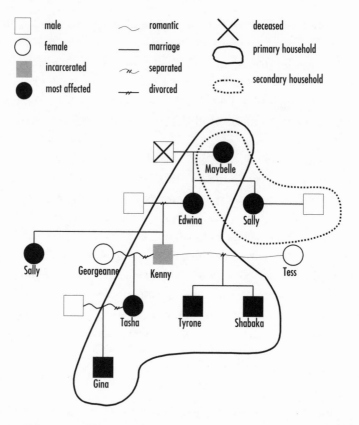

Fig. 10. Edwina and Kenny's family. *Note:* The heavy black line indicates the members of Edwina's household, though her mother, Maybelle, is only a part-time resident and, now that Kenny is incarcerated, he is no longer present either.

Edwina's and Kenny's greatest worries are about the boys. They are getting to be the age where Edwina and Kenny both feel they most need a father figure. Kenny had signed them up for basketball camp the year before and had been spending a lot of time with them. Their father's absence has had a significant impact on the boys' behavior. Kenny worries about this a good deal:

Sometimes they get mad because I'm not there. I can sense they're getting a attitude even when I talk to 'em on the telephone. Usually, they're very well mannered, you know, and like, it's that they display this attitude when they can't have their way or something is out of the norm, then they show up for attention, and I can see it. My mother, now she does as well as she can, but she's a grandmother to them, so she spoils 'em. They start to think they can just get away with things, you know, just skimping by on their homework or talking back.

Of the effects that incarceration may have on the boys, the hardest one to gauge is also the one that worries their father and grandmother the most: the stigma of their father's imprisonment. A story in the local paper appeared to suggest that Kenny had stabbed the victim because the man wouldn't give him a cigarette, effectively reversing the facts and making him out to be the initial aggressor, a point he adamantly denies. While Kenny does not defend his actions, the story, he feared, would have repercussions for his boys.

They printed my case in the paper, and oh, man, I may never forget it. I was talking to my daughter on the phone, and she said, "Daddy, they got you in the paper." And it really made me look real, like I was, like, a vicious person, and all I could think about was that people would identify my family, my mother, and the church members, and, you know, the people she was working with on her job, and how they would look at her, right? And she said she ain't even worried about that, but I know sometimes they keep it, like, hush-hush. "Where Stevie at?" You know? "Oh, he's gone to Alabama." They don't want anybody to know that you in jail or anything like that.

That's what I worried most about, because people read that and the next thing you know, "your daddy's a murderer!" And when you're alone in your cell, that's what you think about. I cried a lot over that story, thinking how they will grow up and what it will do to them.

Kenny may not fit the stereotype of the ruthless sociopath, disconnected from kin and community, that most would imagine when reading about him in the local crime blotter. But he is not, as he told me, without blame.

Of course, I feel terrible about it. But I was raised that if someone comes at you, you don't back down. That's not right, just that's how it is. Now a boy is dead because of me, and my boys have to deal with the fact that their father is a murderer behind bars. I'm not proud of it.

In fact, no inmate whom I spoke with claimed to feel pride in being incarcerated. While there are undoubtedly some inmates who do feel this way, even the youngest and least abashed drug dealer I interviewed expressed shame and regret.*

The Boys

Edwina was worried about the boys seeing Kenny in jail, but she also felt that they needed to see their father. They wanted to know where he was, and she did not feel she could resist telling them much longer. She told Kenny that he would have to tell them over the phone what was going on, and, eventually, she convinced him to let the boys visit.

> I told him . . . "I just want the boys to see you, and they need to see you." The only problem I have when I go see him is the youngest one–he gets upset and he wants to know, "Why you can't go home with us? How much longer you gonna be here?" You know? . . . Because they had a bond between them where they were very close to him, you know. It was Daddy, Daddy, Daddy. . . . They keeps on saying–I think it was just last night, the youngest one asked me, "Grams, how many more years Daddy got to do?" you know? And I say, "I don't know." I say, "We just praying every day that it don't be too much more longer." And then they worry about, you know, how old they're gonna be when

* As one young man related:

> I mean, every time I talk to my family on the phone, I can hear it in their voices that they want to cry. Then sometimes they do break down and cry. . . . That's why I don't really like to call them all the time, because it gets to me. It gets to me very deeply. And I have to stay focused. I have to stay on track, because I'm on the path whereas though I'm doing what I have to do to get out of here and me listening to them grieve and all that on the phone, it kind of, like, break me down. And it kind of, like, knock me off balance and have me very depressed. So, I kind of, like, you know, I might send them a card every now and then or a letter. "I'm doing fine. I'm okay. Tell everyone I love them" and stuff like that. And, um, you know, that'll be that. 'Cause I have that respect. I don't want to send them through too much pain. Which I've already done. I want to try to, like, end it, you know?

he comes. I said, "Regardless of how old you are when he comes, that is still Daddy. Your Daddy still has the right to tell you what's right and wrong."

The boys are acting out and their schoolwork is suffering, but the effects of this stigma run deeper. They rarely invite friends over to the house now and have withdrawn from many of the social relationships they had at school. Kenny doesn't believe the boys talk to anyone about their family situation. "The boys, no, they don't speak to no one about it. My family wears it more as a badge of shame. It's not like we're proud, so we just keep it to ourselves." Edwina agrees. "No, I don't think they'd tell a person. They get real quiet when people talk about fathers."

Social Costs

While parental incarceration and the stigma associated with it are difficult for any family to confront, many practical and material consequences compound the problem for families and children. Having lost a major provider, Kenny's family finds it difficult to make ends meet and is quickly losing many of the practical and symbolic rewards earned by years of hard work.

Looking more closely at Edwina and Kenny's family ties, it becomes clear how the impact of Kenny's incarceration has been borne not so much by him as by his family. Like most incarcerated men, Kenny is a father and, like most incarcerated fathers, an active family member.[9] Moreover, like most inmates, Kenny was employed prior to his incarceration. Nationally, approximately two-thirds of inmates are employed during the month before they are arrested, and over half are employed full-time.[10] Kenny's case is also typical in that he not only drew from but also contributed to a number of familial resources, benefiting both himself and others.[11] Kenny had been one of the primary caretakers of his children, had helped his mother with mortgage payments, and had contributed to his niece's college education at Howard. As Kenny related to me, it was often the things he had never thought about in connection with incarceration that made it so difficult for his family:

> They're trying to fix the house up to get it ready for sale and things of that nature. It's slower now because I'm not there to do the work. So, you know, you have to try to find the income to do this or to do that. . . . Because by me being the only man—I'm from the South, and you know, you're the man, and you're supposed to take care of all the females—and there's just a lot of things around the house that goes wrong, and you need somebody there to take care of them. I fix the car, and I fix all the plumbing and, you know, and when nobody's there and nobody has finances to pay a person to come in and do that, it becomes a strain when you have to find money to fix things.

Though it may surprise many who are accustomed to accounts of socially disconnected offenders, this perspective was the norm among the prisoners I spoke with. As Kenny put it:

> Look, in here, I'm pretty much provided for. Sure, it's a bare minimum, but I have food and shelter and plenty of time to pray and reflect. I don't even have to work if I don't want to. It's the rest of the family that has it hard. Some of the guys in here act like they have it rough, but in truth, it's their kids that have it rough and their parents or their baby's mother that has it rough.
>
> When they don't talk to the families, it's not that their families cut off, it's like they cut their families off, and it's mostly shame. The things you was doing when you were out there before, you know. There were really times you wouldn't listen to nobody and you couldn't see what you were doing. Now, you're in here where you have nothing but time but to reflect back over your life, and you think of some of things you did to your family members, you know, and you just feel ashamed. "How could I do that to my mother or my sister?" And you see it every day in here.

Instead of selling her home and entering retirement, Edwina has found herself caring for Kenny's sons, assisting his daughter, and helping make up the part of her niece's tuition that Kenny used to provide.

She hires a babysitter when she has to, and the children's maternal grandmother helps out once in a while, but it has been disruptive and costly. To make ends meet, she has taken out a second mortgage on the home that was her nest egg for retirement. "You just have to hope something will work out," she says, "but it's not easy."

When I ask Edwina what she needed her second mortgage for, she looks around. "I don't even know where it all goes. The boys, my grand-daughter, the house, just everything was piling up." After a moment's reflection, she adds, "It's a good thing we had the house, though, or I don't know how we'd manage." Pulling out receipts from a recent trip to the mechanic, Edwina describes her shock at the cost; Kenny had always repaired her car for her. "He used to work in an auto shop," she told me. "He definitely could have repaired that car for a lot less." Kenny concurred: "It was a brake job, and that's just–I could get new calipers for about twenty dollars a piece and do it myself. It's a lot of things like that. They're trying to sell the house, so yard work, digging up trees, repairing the wall where they broke it, all that stuff you can't do while you are incarcerated."

Kenny's primary concern has been getting to trial quickly so he can get out, something he felt was the likely outcome of a trial because he believed he had acted in self-defense. The man he stabbed, it turned out, was known around the neighborhood as a crack addict who aggressively panhandled. With further testimony from local residents and a witness to the incident confirming his version of events, Kenny felt his case was a good one. But while Kenny waited for trial, his mother's life was put on hold. "Everybody is sticking around, you see, to see what was my outcome going to be." In the meantime, Kenny's family is struggling to make up for his lost income, for the cost of his collect phone calls and commissary purchases, and for the cost of replacing the assistance he provided.

Kenny's case shows what can happen when a family first encounters incarceration. Within a month his family was feeling the effects of his absence, and after six months of his arrest the effects were extensive. Even in this brief period, Edwina has had to take her house off the market, return to work, obtain a second mortgage, and assume increased responsibility for the care of Kenny's children. While she bears most of the burden, the effects extend through many family ties—to her ailing mother and the sister who looks after her and to a cousin trying to find college tuition.

The very relationships that sustain families in the course of everyday life can also drain them in times of crisis. While it is common for family members to help one another out in times of need, the long-term, open-ended reciprocal relationships that family members have with one another can, as they have in Kenny's family, spread the impact of incarceration so that it touches far more than those imprisoned. Were this something that few families faced, it might be overlooked. But our criminal justice system is pulling millions of families into its orbit, slowly draining them of emotional and material resources. While Kenny's case shows some of the short-term consequences of incarceration, it also begins to hint at the longer intergenerational issues that mass incarceration raises. The next chapter looks at a family experiencing the incarceration of several family members over the course of a decade.

Chapter 9 Doing Time: Lilly & Arthur

Lilly is fifty-one. She was married with three children by the age of nineteen when her husband left her. A single parent without a high school education and functionally illiterate, she has worked as a beautician, a construction worker, a cook, a daycare provider, and at a host of other odd jobs to support her family.

Her oldest son, Arthur, is thirty-three and has three children of his own: one son, Arthur Jr., now seventeen, and two daughters, Renika and Lawanda, ages fifteen and thirteen, respectively, the younger of whom has cerebral palsy. Like many prisoners, Arthur relies on his family for support in many ways: not just emotional support and acceptance but financial assistance and the care for his three children. Lilly is Arthur's closest family connection and provides the most emotional support and monetary assistance to him, though his sister, Cheryl, and his great-aunt, Roseanne, also help out. Lilly also helps to care for Arthur's children.

Arthur has been incarcerated since the age of eighteen for beating a man in a fight over a girlfriend. His son recounts the story this way:

> He went up there to see a girl and, in the process of him seeing the girl, the people jumped him. They jumped him one time, he let it go. He told his brothers, "Naw, it's all right, it was a fair shake. Boom! One of them tried to hit me, I hit him, beat him up, and they jumped me, and I left. That was that." But then he went back up there, and, like, they ain't say nothing or do nothing. Then he went up a third time, and they jumped him again. But this time they put him in the hospital, so his brothers and them was, like, "Man, when you get out, we gotta go take care of

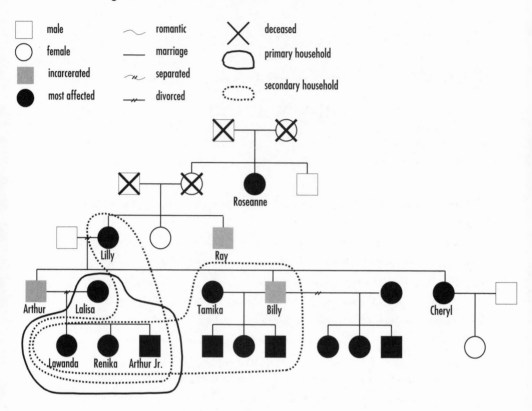

Fig. 11. Lilly and Arthur's family

them, because they, they're playing around." So then they went back up there. Then they got to fighting or whatever, and then my uncle Ray* pulled out a gun, and it was, like, "Man, I ain't fighting no more!" Boom! He just started shooting. And then once that happened, they went home.

Arthur was arrested and, when he refused to identify his uncle as the shooter,† the prosecutor decided against cutting him any deals. The

---

* In many families, family members call extended relations by names that imply closer ties. Arthur Jr. calls Ray–his father's mother's brother–his uncle.
† While the victims knew both Arthur and his brother, they were unfamiliar with and unable to identify his uncle.

judge sentenced him to eight to twenty-four years.* The conviction was for assault with intent to kill. Arthur is serving additional time for an assault while in prison, which he claims was in self-defense.[1] He has just successfully appealed additional charges for an altercation with a guard but has another year before he is eligible for parole. Arthur was held in the D.C. Jail during November and December 1999 while his appeal was heard but is now being held in a privately contracted facility in Youngstown, Ohio.

Prison Worries

Arthur's incarceration has taken an emotional toll on Lilly. While she can be upbeat and optimistic (often unrealistically so), she often cries and becomes depressed thinking and talking about her son. While difficult to measure, the pain of losing a loved one to prison is the most palpable cost to many relatives. When I asked Lilly to describe what it was like to have a son in prison, she told me,

> It's like a loss. It's a loss that if you ever had something, a favorite something, and you lose it, that's how it is for me. I got him, and I'm glad I got him, but I miss him tremendously because I can't talk to him all the time. Just not knowing if he's okay, you know, something could have happened to him. No words really can describe it when you take somebody away, and they're not dead. You can talk to them sometimes, but it's a big miss. It's a big part of your life, of the kids' life, the family gathering. My son used to play Santa Claus. We haven't had a Santa since then. He would put on the outfit, and my sister would be the elf. My sister's husband put the Santa Claus outfit on and the kids just started crying. And my son was helpful to everybody. He was a helpful person. And that's what's missed. His kindness. The way he was. That's the main thing.

---

* Arthur Jr. doesn't hold it against his father's uncle: "I love him dearly. I ain't changed. It was, like, he protecting his family. How can I expect him to sit there and let something happen to his family?"

To this feeling of loss is added what she often refers to as her "prison worries." When I asked what she worries about, Lilly described the various problems her son has had while inside:

> He was beaten over the head with a pipe, and when he protected himself, they gave him more time. And then there's the guards. He's got a skin condition and needs medical showers. Well, the guard wouldn't bring him, so he lit some paper on fire outside his cell, as protest. The guard turned the extinguisher on him. All those chemicals made him sick for weeks with breathing problems. Then they dragged him to the shower and put a fan on him to dry him. This is in winter. They tryin' to kill him. That's my worries.

Lilly produced affidavits from other inmates and guards describing these events in detail and a letter promising an investigation. After she tells me about the various injustices she believes he suffers on a daily basis, from hidden beatings to segregation and denial of visitation, she begins to cry, saying that she is afraid to say or do anything because she fears her son will be mistreated as a result. Her son's experience while incarcerated may be more complicated than Lilly knows or describes. But her anxiety is real and persistent, and she feels powerless to help.

Family Tension

As incarceration places additional demands on the extended networks of kinship that sustain people while outside prison, it can result in heightened tensions as well. For example, Arthur's incarceration has created problems between his mother and other family members. Lilly has lost respect for many of her kin, who she feels ought to do more to help Arthur. When asked if her relationship with the rest of her family has changed since Arthur's incarceration, Lilly told me that her siblings avoid talking to her because she reminds them of what they are not doing.

> If you got family members that don't participate like you do, it will be a conflict, and that's what it is for me. I just tell 'em the way I feel. "You running to church and you got your own people that need you. Only the good Lord knows the way it will come out in the end, but it looks to

me like you should start with your own house before you try to clean up everybody else's house."

My family goes to church every Sunday, and they go to church two and three times during the week, and they don't take the time to go see my son or my brother, but they call theyself family, and they don't like it because I say that to them. I tell them, "It hurts to know that don't nobody go see him." I mean, I was brought up that family was supposed to be important

I have to hear, "Well what did he do for me? He's costing me more now than when he was outside on the street." They tell me, "Oh, he used to help me out," but that's it. They promised to write and send money, but that's it. They started out visiting and sending money, but the longer it is, the less it is. It's a dedication when you got a loved one that's incarcerated. It is a dedication. They too busy, but it's their own flesh and blood.

Lilly is upset because her kin have, in essence, begun to see her son as no longer deserving of the kind of open-ended relationship in which participants can call upon one another according to their needs.[2] "That," she asserts, "is what family is about. It's what you there for." Lilly sees that what is being lost–both to her son and to the rest of the family–is not just time or money but, in a real sense, the family itself. She knows that her son has been demoted in the eyes of other family members, and it is something she cannot stand. She chides them for giving to nonfamily when "one of their own" is in need, but her son has been prevented from reciprocating for so long that, until he can do so, he is, in effect, afforded less consideration than the strangers his relatives help through their church.

Keeping the family intact is something that Lilly works on every day, as she encourages her grandchildren to write to their father and regularly includes them on phone calls from him.[3] The reason for her efforts, she tells me, is simply that her son and her grandchildren need each other:

From the time that he knew that the girl was pregnant with his first child, a son, and the boy was six months old, I gave my son–I won a case–I gave my son a hundred dollars, and my son spent the whole hundred dollars on his son. . . . That's how much he loved him from the beginning. The daughter, she was born with cerebral palsy. She was born weighing three pounds. The nurse, when I went to the hospital, the nurse told me she had never seen a father come to the hospital and take care of a baby better than the mother did. She said my son stayed at that hospital 'til his daughter came home, more better than the mother did. They were shocked. But he loved his kids. And see, that's expensive, living on a fixed income, going to see them, because you got to keep that family for them. They need their daddy.

When I asked her what it was they needed from their father, Lilly stopped for a moment, then told me:

> *Lilly:* It's always the love of that male. We can't give them that. We can only give them female. We're not men. It's impossible. It's impossible. And they miss it. Their behavior. They talk about him, but the behavior problem–the big kids are having behavior problems. My granddaughter, she's like, okay, a boy can say: "I like you." And she'll say, "Oh I got a boyfriend." Why? Because he say he like her. It's like she starving for male affection. That's what it is. All of them girls is . . . they starving for it. For male companionship, male bonding. Why else would a young girl, seventeen, [visit] the doctor's office for infections? And I try to tell her, "Honey, because you give a person your body don't make them love you."
>
> *Donald:* Are you saying that your granddaughter is sleeping with whoever her boyfriends are because she misses her dad?
>
> *Lilly:* Yep. That's what I believe. It's that she thinks: "Well, I'm accepted."[4]

There is substantial evidence that father absence does significantly increase the risk of early sexual activity for girls, although researchers are not entirely sure why. Authors of one recent longitudinal study found that father absence is "so fundamentally linked" to teenage pregnancy that its effects are largely undiminished by such factors as whether girls were "rich or poor, black or white, . . . cooperative or defiant in temperament, born to adult or teenage mothers, raised in safe or violent neighborhoods, subjected to few or many stressful life events, reared by supportive or rejecting parents, exposed to functional or dysfunctional marriages, or closely or loosely monitored by parents."[5]

This is not to say that these other factors do not influence early sexual activity: income in particular is also strongly and independently related to teenage sexual activity. But this raises troubling questions about the role that incarceration plays in the cycle of teenage pregnancy, single motherhood, and economic hardship. The United States has the highest teenage pregnancy rate among Western industrialized nations. Moreover, teenage childbearing is associated with a host of subsequent problems, including lower educational and career achievements, health problems, and inadequate social support for parenting.[6] Extensive evidence demonstrates that family structure has powerful effects on the economic welfare of families,[7] and, as we saw in part II, the effects of incarceration on family structure are robustly harmful.

Arthur is aware that his family—particularly his children—are experiencing significant hardship in his absence. The worst times for Arthur are when he starts thinking about his kids growing up without him. While some guys are able to "get into their time"—that is, do their time without thinking too much about the outside world—Arthur often can't believe that he has lost his relationship with his children's mother and that his kids are growing up without him. Arthur Jr. describes how his grandmother spends hours on the phone trying to calm his father down:

[My grandmother] be like the whole soul right there for that side of the family. She be trying, you know, to keep stuff intact 'cause sometime. . . . He used to call her and stuff, and it'd be, like, he about to kill hisself, or he about to kill all the guards and break out, and she would try and keep him under composed, 'cause he, like, he used to call her saying, "I can't believe my kids will grow up without a father, so I got to get up outta here." And she was, like, "Wait 'til you come up for parole." He come for parole, and they set him back. They were, like, he ain't going. So that's when he used to start talking crazy, and my grandmother talked to him or tried to get my uncles to come and see him.

Arthur Jr. was also quite critical of other family members for not wanting to help his father–something that he sees as selfishness.

> Most of the time, my uncle would be, like, "Naw." He ain't trying. He ain't trying to go out there to see him. . . . It's just stupid stuff. Stupid stuff. Like, one day I called my uncle and I asked my uncle to go because I was, like, "Man, it's about to be Father's Day again. Let's go out there." "No, no. I'm checking with my girl." That was that. Then my grandmother, she'll tell me to call my grandfather. My grandfather would usually be busy because he be on the road, so that'd be that. Out of the whole family, a handful of them be supportive. They'll start off, but they didn't wanna finish up.

The extended family's withdrawal of support over the years visibly upsets Arthur Jr., as it does Lilly. When I ask him whom he turns to now when he needs help, he says, shaking his head, "Nobody. Me, myself, and I."

Arthur Jr.'s and Lilly's efforts to bring even loyal family members to visit Arthur are further frustrated by the correctional system's handling of visitors. Indeed, most family members I spoke with could rattle off a list of what they consider to be needless indignities suffered during visitation, the most common of which is flat refusal of entry on any number of grounds but which often extend to cavity searches and the offhand insult. As Lilly recounted:

> The grandmother went to see him, and they wouldn't let her in because she had on a sweatshirt that was the wrong color. Can you believe, a sixty-three-year-old woman, and they wouldn't let her in. And she didn't want to go in the first place. So there I am, that's what I have to deal with, a family that doesn't want to go see their own in prison, and who would? But I got to try to bring them because he needs them, and the kids need him. And that's what I got to deal with. They stop you at any time, nothing you can do. Don't matter you're his mother, grandmother, whatever. And they search you like you nothing, very embarrassing. I don't need to tell you that it's not very private, and the ladies is searched in the worst ways.

The need for security is clear, and, as Lilly admits grudgingly, it is probably necessary to search every individual in a "thorough fashion" to prevent the smuggling of weapons or drugs into a correctional facility.* However, this does not void the humiliation that she and other family members experience when visiting facilities and makes visitation a ritual experience of degradation for many relatives.†

Often it was not the attitude of correctional staff but the details of security practices that many felt were demeaning. One woman I spoke with who had often visited the prison as a city official was shocked by her experience after her son was arrested.

> For years I'd drive past, got out of my car, and see these people out there. So, to actually have to experience this was a nightmare because the very first time that I went to see him was hard enough because, you know, I just didn't want to have to do this. My very first experience with this I was out there in this long line. I was outside for about two hours, okay? And then suddenly I'm standing there and I'm saying, "Gosh, this is what these people go through." So, I'm standing there

---

* I have heard detailed descriptions of how drugs and weapons are commonly smuggled into facilities, generally with the tacit or full cooperation of a corrupt member of the correctional staff. What upsets so many of the family members is not so much that they are searched but that not everyone is and that the standards vary from day to day. In particular, many family members feel that guards are responsible for the majority of contraband inside the facilities and should be subjected to the same procedures.

† Many family members whom I spoke with did feel that they were disrespected by prison staff, but some developed a rapport that served them in the long term. By demonstrating respect for correctional officers, some women were able to build up reserves of goodwill that came in handy when they encountered a problem. As one woman told me,

> Those guards down there loved me so much that even when another female did come see him, they stood at the window the whole time. They was waiting for him to touch her or anything. And a girl did keep trying to touch him, and he kept scooting his chair back. When I asked him about it he said, "I finally said 'You know what? You've got to go. I'm gonna tell you just like this, 'cause the last thing that I need to really do is [for it] to go back to my wife [that] some woman was there with her hands all over me. She ain't gonna hear nothing else. She ain't never gonna come back.'" All the guys kept teasing him, saying that, you know, I wear the pants in the relationship. But the guards on that block had respect for me and him both.

saying, "This is ludicrous." You know, they take people through all these changes. You stand in this long line for two hours, and for the life of me, as many times as I visited him there, I still couldn't figure out why it took so long. But, anyway, you go, you stand there, you wait. Even in the wintertime, okay? People outside. People are out there with babies. And you know what? It's thirty degrees out here! Why is this line outside? That whole process is madness! There's something wrong with this. You know, it just—something about it is not right. It's not right.

Megan Lee Comfort has described the many "ceremonies of belittlement" that families face during visitation and their effects on women's perceptions of self.[8] As Comfort describes, women who enter into prisons as visitors, regardless of their social status outside the prison, are often marked as "disgraced beings" by prison security procedures and staff.[9]

The fact that so many security procedures are, by their very nature, intrusive, distrustful, and disrespectful helps to explain why so many family members view visitation as stressful and degrading. But there is also something about the nature of the stigma that families bear that heightens their sensitivity toward these procedures. Indeed, visitation is a time when visitors are made keenly aware of the "contagious" nature of criminal stigma and the threat of their being labeled with all the stereotypes that incarceration brings.[10]

Can't Nobody Be My Father

Arthur Jr. is ambivalent about his father, alternating between forgiveness and anger over his own feelings of abandonment. "I never got to do a father-son moment with him. I never, ever got to do father-son stuff with him like go to the movies, go go-cart riding, go shoe shopping, and stuff like that. I never got to do none of that with him." Remembering the times that he was able to see his father, he recalls being upset when his father attempted to play the paternal role prevented by his incarceration:

He used to be asking me questions like "What's going on in the world? What you doing?" I used to feel insulted. "Don't ask me that. You ain't there. I understand it ain't your fault, but if you ain't there, how can you help me? You right here. You can't help me. No matter how much you try, you cannot help me. I'm out here on my own." But then when they started shipping people out, they started shipping people, like, to Ohio and places like that, we couldn't go all the way out there, so it was less talking. And he would call, and he'd be, like, "Man, I miss y'all. I wish I could make up for the time." But, like, man, you can't make up for no time. Time passes. Time lost.

While Arthur Jr. acknowledges that his father's incarceration has made the family's life harder in material ways, he is less concerned about the monetary issues than he is about the loss of human contact, the loss of his and his sisters' childhood with their father. When I asked him about the effects of his father's incarceration on the family, he told me he felt that the children have borne most of the emotional burden:

No matter what they do, they can't hurt him. They can't hurt him, they're only hurting us. 'Cause as a result of that, my little sisters came up without a father, I came up without a father. And without a father in the household, that's like having a half of your support, 'cause the male supposed to be the soul of the family, and that's like half of your support right there is gone. Now, your mother got to try to play mother and father, which she can't do. Now, some mothers like mine be saying they can, but they can't, 'cause all of the stuff that she could ever do for me, it couldn't compare. It's just crazy for her even to try to say she been my mother and my father. The only thing she did was be a mother. Can't nobody be my father 'cause he ain't here. He ain't here.

Arthur Jr. doesn't understand why his father's sentence is as long as it is. He has seen three people killed, and as far as he knows "nothing much was ever done about it." One victim, his cousin, was "killed in front of a police station–shot dead." The perpetrator was sentenced to three to five years, something that galls him since his father got a much longer sentence for a lesser charge: "Three to five! The system," he says pausing and shaking his head, "the system messed up. How you gonna kill somebody at point-blank range and get three to five?"

Dealing with the system, the system is just backwards. Some people will get past, and some people just don't. Some people just get a bad shake, and by that I'm saying, like, some people can go to jail for murder, and they come in three to five years, and there are others that go in for something less dramatic, and they get way more time, and it's just not right. It's like there ain't justice in the system.

Like many inmates and family members, Arthur's family feels that he should have done some time—he did break the law—but they do feel that there is something seriously wrong with the inconsistencies of the criminal justice system.

Arthur Jr.: Some things you just can't replace. Like money can't replace everything, and time is one of them, 'cause you know how when you go to school and they have father-son things, you just can't replace that. You can't even replace that with money, 'cause the time is gone. I'm grown now. It's, like, the cycle just repeats itself.

Donald: Why do you say that?

Arthur Jr.: Right after [my father was incarcerated], that's when my attitude just started going haywire, *haywire*! I wasn't always like that—when I was little, I wasn't. But as I got older that's when I started developing a real bad attitude. 'Cause as a kid you've gotta remember, all of this stuff happening, and I don't really know how to show my feelings. My first way was hit somebody in the face and knock them out. I remember one day I was playing a basketball game, and they just kept cheating. I just, I just, phew, I went and beat them down to the ground.

That's when they started giving me them little pills and told me if I ever feel like lashing out, just take one of them little pills, and they just calm my nerves down, 'cause the stupidest thing would get on my nerves—the stupidest thing. Then [my grandmother] took me to the doctor, and he was, like, he gave me some little pills to control my temper. But at first nobody couldn't control my temper. If I was in a room and they started talking some mess, I'd kirk off. . . . Or when somebody would try to come to step to me, like, all of that rage, mad about that, mad about this, and I'd just kirk off on them. I just hurt them real bad. I remember one time I put this boy in the hospital. I broke his face. I broke his jaw and his nose.

So, while Arthur Jr. doesn't plan on following in his father's footsteps, he feels that he could have and quite easily so. But he has his medication and, as he reminds me, the lesson of his father to keep him in check. Now that he's eighteen, he knows that if he were to get into a fight, "they're gonna give me a record off the top . . . and I can't get rid of it, so I just try to stay out of harm's way."

As many criminologists have noted, one of the best predictors of involvement in the criminal justice system is the incarceration of a parent.[11] Among the reasons usually provided is that the child emerged from the same social setting as the parent or that the parent modeled the criminal behavior for the child. Both are plausible, backed by significant studies, and echoed by statements of other families.[12] But Arthur Jr.'s story suggests two other reasons why parental involvement in the criminal justice system may increase the likelihood of incarceration. First, he feels considerable generalized anger about what he perceives as the injustice of his father's lengthy sentence and the injustice of his own and his sisters' suffering.[13] Second, he feels that he has been largely left to his own devices in figuring out how to handle life as a teen.

Sometimes I get the feeling if I had a father figure around coming up, some of the stuff that I went through I probably wouldn't have went through. Like my going places by myself, because your mother can't go everywhere with you. I mean, and places, like when I used to go to the basketball court, 'cause I was playing basketball I'd go there. Like in one instance I was at the basketball court, and this dude was, like, "Man, I'll give you a hundred dollars to take that over there." I was, like, "A hundred dollars?" And so I was, like, "From here to here?" And on Paine, the basketball court where he was talking about, it wasn't even a block; it was, like, a couple of steps, and it's over. So I went from there to there, and I got a hundred dollars.

I ain't actually set down and realize what I was doing, 'til I was, like, "Damn! He just gave me a hundred dollars." Then I went home, and my grandmother was, like, "Where you get some money from?" And I was, like, "Some dude on the basketball court, he just told me to take this over there and I took it." And she was, like, "You sure?" I was, like, "Yeah." She said, "Let me see the money," and I showed her the money. And she was, like, "Boy, you could have got yourself in some trouble!" I was, like, "I ain't know. Ain't nobody never tell me." And, like, I'm gonna go, "Oh well, what's in the bag?" I'm on the basketball court, we're playing. It's supposed to be my friend. I ain't know the tables was gonna turn like that. I seriously sat down and thought: "I probably wouldn't have had to go through that door if my father had been around, 'cause I would have knew." But you ain't never think it could happen, 'cause ain't nobody never tell you about it, 'cause you don't got that male figure to sit down and tell you this can go on.

Without help from his father, Arthur Jr.'s mother couldn't afford to buy him new clothes for school or provide spending money to hang out with his friends. When he would ask for something, she'd just say, "Get a job."

She always figured that I was supposed to be making my own money. Basically, what I'm saying is she try and put me on the scale whereas though I was already a man. Once I hit about thirteen or fourteen, I was supposed to be making my own income, so I was, like, "Man, I got to get me some funds. She ain't giving them to me."

So, he started earning money on the street, though, as he said, "it weren't legal." He knew he could get in trouble, so he sought out his father's mother again.

So then I went to my grandmother, and my grandmother was, like, "Instead of doing that, it'd be a better way." And I was like, "What'd be a better way?" And that's when she took me down to where she worked and got me a little job down there. But at first I used to stay on the block. But the point was if I would have got caught doing it, it would have been something different, so she got me my first legitimate job.

Without counseling, medication, and the concern of his grandmother, Lilly, Arthur Jr. might well have been through the juvenile correctional system and into the adult one by now. How good a father Arthur would have been had he not been incarcerated is impossible to know, but clearly his absence has been keenly felt.

A Parent All Over Again

Lilly has her own set of personal problems. She walks with a cane because she suffers from chronic back pain that runs down her left leg ("my disability," as she refers to it), a physical problem her doctors tell her is aggravated by stress and hypertension and one that she is certain is as bad as it is, at least in part, from the stress her son's incarceration has caused her. It is not uncommon for many of the older relatives I spoke with to talk about the way stress has contributed to their health problems, a bit of folk wisdom about the relationship between stress and health that has received significant scientific support in recent years.[14] Back pain, strokes, heart conditions, migraines, and depression, particularly among older participants, are commonly included in descriptions of health problems caused or at least compounded by the stress of familial incarceration.

The problems that Lilly and other relatives of prisoners face are difficult to negotiate. They know that their anxiety about their incarcerated relatives and their frustration with the bureaucracy of the criminal justice system are hurting their mental and physical health, but alternative coping strategies are not clear to them. If they believe the sentence is unjust, the appropriate reaction is anger and frustration, something that is debilitating in the long run. To react otherwise would run counter to a powerful instinct to show loyalty to their family member and would be to signal that, in their minds, justice was being done. So, to give expression to their perception of injustice, family members have to accept the emotional and physical costs of holding on to and living with their anger and frustration.[15]

Lilly's criticism of her extended family highlights the tensions that arise between family members over incarceration. While Lilly is critical of family members who do not demonstrate what she feels is adequate concern for her son, the costs of showing that concern are significant in time and emotional energy. For those already struggling to make ends meet in less than ideal living environments, the added burden of an additional nonreciprocal relationship can be great. While she chides her relatives for not doing more, Lilly doesn't deny that being there for her son and her grandchildren is taking its toll on her:

> It seems like I'm always rippin' and runnin' these days, just to make ends meet. I've got my back and my blood pressure, but I still have to get out to the church to get my groceries to help feed these kids. They have all kinds of expenses, medical bills, shoes. You just can't believe how much shoes costs for these kids. But it's a burden like you a parent all over again, but you're ready to retire and you watching your money go. My money's all gone now. I thank God for the church with those groceries. But living week to week, it just keeps you stressed out.

Lilly's Other Son

The issue of childcare for Arthur's children has also required extensive negotiation. Initially, the mother of Arthur's three children, Lalisa, visited Arthur in prison and depended a good deal on Lilly for help with the kids. When she found another boyfriend, however, Lilly was less inclined to help her out. Lalisa works full-time as a beautician and struggles to make ends meet. Although she is their primary caretaker, Arthur's extended family often cares for his three children in addition to their own. Arthur's brother, Billy, lives with his girlfriend, Tamika, and works several odd jobs for friends of the family that pay under the table. While Lilly and Arthur's great-aunt, Roseanne, do help out on occasion, generally on weekends, the burden of childcare also falls on Billy and Tamika.

This is particularly difficult, as Billy has had trouble with the law himself and is struggling to find a job in the formal economy. Billy already faces many of the difficulties that await Arthur, should he be released, most of which stem from the social stigma of a criminal record. A former drug dealer, Billy pleaded guilty to a murder he didn't commit to avoid the long sentence he would get for a third drug offense.*

As Lilly relates the incident, it becomes clear that she was shaken by the experience of Billy's case as much as by Arthur's.

The lawyer came to me and told me that he had to plead guilty. I had—me, a mother—had to make my son say he was guilty for shooting when we knew that he really wasn't, but we had to do a plea bargain because this is what the lawyer said, because we're uneducated and we don't know. But I know it was not right. I know my son didn't do the shooting, but I knew that she said if I. . . . She said she could win that case, but she would lose the other case, and if we put all both cases together, the judge would give my son four to twelve, and the judge gave my son four to twelve. And in two years, my son was out. He lied and said he shot. . . . The judge knew he didn't shoot, because when the judge asked him what type of weapon it was, how far was he from the shooter, he didn't know anything. He didn't know anything because he wasn't even there. He copped a plea, and that's something else about the system. He copped a plea for one thing, because he did another thing. His lawyer told me that they would give my son twelve, I mean, ten to thirty years for selling drugs. I didn't want him to go ten to thirty years, so we had to tell a lie and say guilty. You see what I'm saying? I mean, you can see the right and wrong of it. Because like I said, by me not even having an education, I still have the common sense God gave me in letting me know that it hurt to tell your child to tell a lie and say he did that. It's on record that my son did the shooting, and he didn't.

While Billy's choice seemed like the lesser of evils at the time, the murder rap has proved a serious impediment in his subsequent efforts

---

* The murder was actually committed by Billy's uncle, Ray, who is now serving time for another murder. Billy was faced with the choice of ten to thirty years for a third drug offense or four to twelve for murder. He pleaded guilty to manslaughter, the drug charge was dropped, and he was released in two years. This appears to be a not uncommon occurrence; police and district attorneys are under tremendous pressure to "solve" murder cases in D.C., and exposés of the mounting unsolved murder cases in local papers have been met with rapid resolution of what appear to be an improbable number of cases.

to enter the formal economy. Explicitly denied apartment rentals and work in the private sector on the basis of the gaps in his employment record that he must explain as stints in prison, he regularly voices an opinion that reflects a personalization of the general effect of carrying a criminal record. Describing what he considers to be a social conspiracy against black men, he reflects: "They want me to sell drugs, but I can't do that cause I got my own kids now and my brother's kids. So I work. For what? Minimum wage sometimes. You know they want me back in prison, but I'm not going. I resist that path." Tamika has a good job at an insurance company and is able to get by with the help of her family, but it is not easy. "It's the bills, it's the kids, it's work, all of it just gets to me. I thank God I have family to help."

While Billy has gained much from the support of his family, relations with his former wife are not always good. Billy's ex-wife is generally disliked by his family for having left him for another man while he was in prison. The icing on the cake for Lilly was that, after her new boyfriend left her, she began receiving public assistance, which mandated state-involved child support from Billy. Though he often cares for the children and buys them clothing and food, the state required him to pay child support, which he failed to do. Failure to pay child support violated the terms of his parole, and he was rearrested.

Ironically, the children were staying with him when his warrant for evading support was served, and they watched as police handcuffed their father and led him away. His family was understandably upset, as Billy was unable to assist his current wife or family at all while he was in jail. After spending a month in jail awaiting trial, Billy was released with the help of his ex-wife, who realized that she would get nothing from him or his family while he was incarcerated.

> She dropped it. She wasn't aware that it was gonna go down like that, and she dropped it. She ended up having to come to court, and we got it all taken care of, you know. I ended up having to pay nothing. They just took time out of my life again. That, you know, that's where they were wrong on that one. But, they did it, and it's a done deal.

This was a particularly difficult time for Tamika, who was forced to turn to family for more than the usual help. As she said, "You know I hate to ask, because none of them have monies, but I really had no choice, I couldn't just not feed the kids."

Billy's children have been told that their father's incarceration was unjust, particularly his conviction for a murder he didn't commit. In some ways the adults in the family feel this helps them cope with what might otherwise be a more shameful status for their father. However, this understanding also leads them to believe that the criminal justice system is corrupt, to have little respect for police or government, and to fear that they are also at risk for similar unjust treatment.

Direct and Indirect Costs

As a result of Arthur's incarceration and Billy's trouble with the law, Lilly has experienced a number of practical financial difficulties. Reviewing Lilly's various expenses related to Arthur's incarceration, it is clear that her worries about money are directly related to her son's imprisonment. She lives on a fixed income of $530 a month, a good portion of which is spent on Arthur. "Lord, just look at my phone bill," she exclaims, pulling out her bills and canceled checks from the last year. "You know the only people this helps is the corporations." One of the more unpleasant surprises for many families is the high cost of phone calls from prison. Inmates can only call collect, and additional charges for monitoring and recording by the prison phone company add up quickly; indeed, many families have their phones disconnected within two months of an incarceration.

Perhaps the most costly regular expense that families complain about is phone charges. Most correctional facilities contract out phone services and profit by doing so. Phone companies compete with each other for the service, but not by providing lower prices; the key criteria that phone companies compete on is how much revenue the service will return to the Department of Corrections or the private corrections company. Because phone conversations are often time limited, many families are required to accept several calls to complete a single conversation, with connection charges applying to each call. While there are no data on overall phone costs for D.C. inmates, the costs are high locally and nationally, as several news accounts have noted:

> In Florida, where the state prison system collected $13.8 million in commissions in fiscal 1997–98, a legislative committee found that big prison systems in 10 other states took in more than $115 million in the same budget year. New York topped the list with $20.5 million. In Virginia, MCI gave the state $10.4 million, or 39 percent of the revenue from prison calls. Maryland receives a 20 percent commission on local calls by inmates, which must be made through Bell Atlantic, and gets 42 percent of revenue from long-distance calls, all of which are handled by AT&T.[16]

Rather than risk another disconnect and a subsequent hefty reconnect fee, many families block calls from the prison because they cannot bring themselves to say no to the collect call. In an arrangement that is not unusual, Lilly is the main conduit for all her son's calls; because no one else will accept collect calls from prison, she patches him through to whomever he needs to talk to.

> That's the main thing I have to make sure I keep going. It's for him and his kids to keep the contact. That's why it's so hard for me. I have to pay for a three-way on the telephone so I can hook him up with the kids, hook him up with the lawyer. That's what I'm always doing, hooking him up. That's like six dollars a month extra, too, for the three-way.

Families with loved ones incarcerated out of state have shown me years of phone records that average well over $200 a month.* Lilly's most recent bill is just over $130, with over $100 of it going toward prison calls, about average for her since Arthur was transferred out of

---

* For example, calls from some out-of-state prisons cost ten dollars per ten minutes. Families try to time their calls but are often cut off after ten minutes and then accept another call from the incarcerated relative. Five calls a week quickly become two hundred dollars a month.

state five years ago. In effect, prison-related phone costs have taken up 20 percent of her total income.

Lilly also spends money on regular visits to Ohio–every three months or so now, though when she was younger and in better health she would visit every month or, when he was in the District or Virginia, every week. For each visit to Ohio, her mother, her aunt, and her sister pool resources for car rental, food, and a motel for a two-day trip. There are also the regular postal money orders and the twice yearly gifts allowed at the prison that are sent by Lilly, Arthur's sister, Cheryl, and Arthur's great-aunt, Roseanne.

Accounting for Incarceration

Arthur has been incarcerated for just over the average time served in D.C., about eight years. Before Arthur was incarcerated, he was a contributing member of a familial social network, but for years–indeed most of his children's lives–he has been a drain on that network, and, as his less loyal kin have distanced themselves from him, his closer relations have had to pick up the slack. These are far from trivial matters, as none of Arthur's contributing relatives earns more than twenty thousand dollars a year, and any sacrifice for them is a large one.

The financial costs of Arthur's incarceration to his family tallied in table 2 include only those costs that were clearly identifiable and sim-

TABLE 2.   Direct Annual Expenses Related to Arthur's Incarceration

	Lilly[a] (mother)	Billy (brother)	Cheryl (sister)	Roseanne (great-aunt)	Other Family	Total
Telephone	$1,200	0	0	0	$200	$1,400
Travel	$200	0	$200	$200	$200	$800
Money	$480	0	$240	$240	$180	$1,140
Gifts	$100	0	$50	$50	$240	$440
Childcare[b]	$1,580	$1,200	$120	0	$6,000	$8,900
Total	$3,560	$1,200	$610	$490	$6,820	$12,680

[a]Includes costs that Lilly covers but that other family members help with. These costs are not included under other headings.

[b]Reflects out-of-pocket expenses (e.g., for baby-sitters or professional childcare), not time spent.

ple to calculate. There are a number of additional expenses that are difficult to quantify, such as Arthur's lost income (he was employed full-time prior to his incarceration), the value of his assistance around the house, stress-related medical expenses, and what now amounts to years of effort to aid him in his legal battles by a host of friends and family members. While the monetary costs might not be hard for some middle-class Americans to bear, the costs are clearly substantial given the limited resources available to Lilly.

The costs to families like Lilly's have been largely absent from discussions about incarceration. Unfortunately, these costs bear down disproportionately on families that are least able to absorb them. When states collect tens of millions of dollars from collect phone calls to prisoners' families, they disproportionately burden poor and minority families that are struggling not only to keep their families together but also simply to keep their heads above water financially. When these families lose income or the childcare that the incarcerated family member provided, the loss is often substantial.

As significant as they may be, in the end, the financial sacrifices of Arthur's family don't compare with the less tangible difficulties the family faces. When Lilly says, "It's like a loss," she is describing the emotional investments that people make in relationships. The "big miss" is not the money. The small favors that people, especially family, do for one another cannot be reduced to cash equivalents because, even when they take the form of lending money or other material goods, they are, in a much deeper sense, about the relationship itself. As Arthur's son says, "you can't even replace that with money."

As we began to see in the case of Lilly's younger son, Billy, the costs of incarceration often extend well beyond the prison sentence itself. The next chapter examines the difficulties that families face as, all too often, incarceration becomes part of a lengthy and draining cycle.

Chapter 10 Cycling through the System: Zelda & Clinton

Clinton is one of thirteen children, although he is in regular contact with only two of his sisters and is close only to the younger, Zelda. He has one daughter, Janet, and is still close to her mother, Pat. Janet recently gave birth to a baby boy, whom she named after her father.

Following a long string of drug-related arrests and prison terms, Clinton was paroled two years ago, and he moved in with Zelda. After twenty years of selling drugs on the street, both saw his release as an opportunity for him to go straight. He had previously stayed with Pat, but the neighborhood where she lived presented too many opportunities to become involved in hustling again. Of the families described so far, theirs inhabits the economically most marginal neighborhood, one in which incarceration is especially prevalent. In this respect, Clinton's story is comparatively typical.

Hustling from an Early Age

While most of their siblings were raised in Virginia, Clinton and Zelda spent most of their childhood with relatives in the District. After Clinton was born, his parents hit financial difficulties, and, when their fourth child was born, they sent Clinton, then five years old, to live with two of his mother's sisters in D.C.

Clinton's extended family had troubles of their own. The older of his two aunts was blind and diabetic, the younger was an alcoholic, and together they had responsibility for their elderly, housebound grandmother. The only person with whom Clinton remembered developing

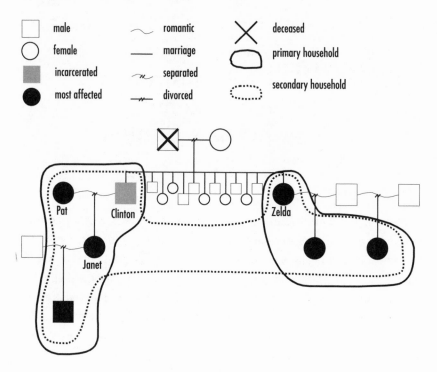

Fig. 12. Zelda and Clinton's family

a significant relationship was his uncle, whom he began to see as a father figure during his first few years in the District. In Clinton's mind, the decisive turn in his life was his uncle's arrest for a murder when Clinton was about eight years old.[1]

Largely unsupervised by his two aunts after his uncle's incarceration, he came and went as he pleased, quickly getting into trouble:

> I was in Simmons, Simmons Elementary, and I got to smoking marijuana. . . . and one thing led to another, you know. It's like, once I got high off of it . . . whatever the guy said to do, I was ready to go do. And I graduated from Simmons, and I went to Terrell [High School, though I didn't graduate from there.] I started playing hooky at the age of eight and started smoking marijuana, and I wanted, I wanted to go stay with my mother and my father, and, you know, I felt ostracized.

Clinton started his relationship with the criminal justice system early and has been in and out of correctional facilities since he was twelve. He managed to parlay his first arrest at the age of eleven into a short return to his family in Virginia, which he remembers vividly:

> The officers caught me, and they [sent me to] Junior Village was what it was called, and I stayed there for about a week. Then I got the longing for being home. I missed home, so I ran. . . . I left and I came back home, and my aunt and them sent me to my Mom's and them, so I felt better. . . . So when I got in school my grades got to picking up—I had more focus then. My focus was broken by being in Washington, but when I got back there, my focus was better because I felt better. I felt good. I was back with my family, my sisters, and my brothers, and my mother, and my father, so I felt good.

While it may have felt good to be with his family, for his parents it meant another mouth to feed and more expenses than they could manage, so they sent him back to D.C. at the end of the school year. As he told me, even though his mother and father explained that it was a financial decision and that they still loved him, "at a young age . . . you're not concerned about that." Instead, he felt the sting of rejection. Thinking back on his return to D.C., he told me, "I just couldn't maintain a focus, a concern for myself, because I felt as though my parents didn't have a concern for me."

Back in the District, things went from bad to worse. Throughout his teens, Clinton sold drugs and spent time in and out of juvenile facilities. At the age of nineteen, he was able to land a job at an emergency shelter for the homeless. Because all his previous arrests had been as a juvenile, they were expunged from his record, and he thought he might make a clean break.

Hoping to beat the odds, Clinton started making plans for applying to become a police officer, a lifelong dream of his: "See, I had these fantasies, and that's what I wanted to be. I had moments when I used to just see how the crimes and everything—I said, 'If I was a police officer, that wouldn't go down.' . . . So as I got older, I wanted to be one." After people on the job site found out that he had a record, however, Clinton began to get snide remarks about his criminal past, and some co-workers began to complain openly about his being hired. Pretty soon he was told that he wasn't needed.

He found another part-time job right away. "I went and got to working at Columbia Maintenance, because I started with the CETA [Construction Education and Training Authority] Program, and that was pretty good, but I couldn't get hired permanent." The pay was low, there were no benefits, and he saw little opportunity for advancement. Clinton, like many people trying to enter the workforce, found that part-time work, while available, had many drawbacks.[2]

Into the Adult System

Frustrated with his lack of income and prospects, Clinton was considering what to do next when his mother died while giving birth to his youngest sister. Clinton returned to the streets again at the height of the heroin boom in the United States, doing what he felt he knew how to do best: sell heroin. By his mid-twenties, Clinton had a rap sheet, and he and Pat had a daughter, whom they named Janet. By Pat's and Janet's accounts, Clinton was a good partner and father. The new drug laws hit the books in the early 1980s, though, and he found himself, at the age of twenty-seven, at the beginning of a six-year minimum sentence for distribution in Maryland.

Six years is a long time, and Clinton decided early on to try to cut his time and to turn his life around. He started "programming"–participating in whatever educational or job programs were available–and taking on a new attitude about what he would do with his life. He credits his change in attitude, at least in part, to the different approach to corrections that he found in Maryland.

> [Compared to the District's facilities] the Maryland system is very professional–I'll have to admit that. And they're very respectful. . . . You want a skill, we got this. You want education, we got this. . . . And it makes you want it. . . . Whereas opposed to I may have had that attitude, "Man, anybody mess with me, I'm gonna do something to 'em.

They violating me!" Now I got a responsibility. And you done obligated yourself to that responsibility, and you like it. You get to studying more, you get to focusing more, so when a guy you would normally jump on when he says something, now you go ahead and ignore him. "My fault." It's not your fault, it's his, but. . . . you're letting him know, "Man, I don't want no trouble." See, because of the fact that when you get something that you want, you tend to want to hold on to it. And each time that I was programming, that's how it was.

Repeat offenders are keenly aware of the differences between correctional facilities, and there is considerable agreement on the social atmosphere that characterizes the various institutions.

When prisoners talk about the characteristics of a prison that they like or dislike, they often sound like middle-class family men talking about a neighborhood they'd like to live in or a company culture that they appreciate. Federal facilities are described as quiet, professional, and productive. The most common complaint about them is that they are often far from home, so that inmates lose touch with their families. State-run facilities run the gamut, depending on who is in charge and the history of the facility. Central Facility at Lorton,* for example, is often described as "summer camp for criminals," filled with corrupt and inept officials. While these types of facilities offer an opportunity to interact with friends and family, this is combined with in-facility violence, crime, and seemingly arbitrary enforcement of rules and regulations that change frequently. Private facilities often combine the worst of both worlds: usually located in distant states but staffed with underpaid and undertrained correctional officers. The ideal prison for most inmates is one where the staff and management are professional and consistent and where prisoners can obtain drug treatment and job training and can maintain some contact with family.

Clinton, like many inmates, was interested in more than just getting an education. He knew that the parole board would look to see what he had done while incarcerated and was hoping to impress them with his

---

* Central Facility, now closed, was the largest D.C. correctional facility.

achievements. As he described it, at first he was serious about his programming not because of the value of the education in and of itself but because it would help him when he faced the parole board: "At first I wasn't so serious about learning, but I was serious about my freedom."

Clinton's involvement in programs also made a difference to his family. As he told me,

> [In Maryland,] when you go to school, they know you don't got time to work at a detail, so they [paid inmates a dollar a day while they were in classes]. So you go twenty-one days, you got twenty-one dollars. It helps. It's not a lot, but it helps, and especially if you're really concerned about your education, you're not really concerned about the finance. And, say if you go to auto mechanics, they give you forty-five dollars. If you took up printing, I think they were giving them fifty-five to a hundred dollars a week, and this helps to better their skills, and then while they [are in the program] it helps them focus. Now, you don't have to worry about no money, you know you're working and getting money. You're earning while you learn, and that was lacking in the D.C. Department of Corrections, which they called it the "D.C. Department of Corruption."

While Clinton had been relying on help from his family to buy basic toiletries and clothing while he was incarcerated in the D.C. system, the twenty-one dollars a month he made in the Maryland system attending classes allowed him to provide those things for himself. His relationship with Zelda, Pat, and Janet improved because he didn't have to ask for money when he called them, so he felt better about staying in touch.

Clinton never earned enough to send money home, having chosen the educational route, but it was not unusual for men, particularly parents, with good jobs on the inside to send home extra money. Clinton describes the case of a friend he served time with:

> A friend of mine, he has a daughter, so he was sending home a hundred dollars every month. So that hundred dollars is helping his daughter, and she, the mother, would take the hundred dollars and go buy her some little clothes, and she'd come down and he would feel

pleased. She was four years old. And it made him feel good that he was able to do something for his daughter while incarcerated.

This perspective on the value of a prisoner's gainful employment to his family during his incarceration is one that was shared by nearly every family member I spoke with. In particular, those who were caring for one or more of the prisoner's children emphasized the burden of raising a child without assistance from the father.

The importance of some assistance from prisoners to their families is not simply financial but also symbolic. By sending money home, fathers are able to give material expression to their love for their child and the child's mother. As one mother described it to me, the hardest part of coping with the incarceration of her children's father was bringing up the children alone:

> Doing birthdays for my kids by myself. Inviting children that come with their father and their mother, seeing the two parent, the two parent thing. Even now for [my daughter] with her classmates, for her it sometimes becomes difficult when she goes on a field trip and I come along, and some of the children have their mother and their father come along. Or the first day of school, I'm the one that shows up, and it's not her father and me, it's just me.

But because her husband was incarcerated in a federal system, he was able to send home a little money to help out or to buy some gifts, and this made a huge difference to her and her daughters. "Even though it's not a lot of money, being able to send fifty dollars home, or being able to save up enough where he can send a hundred dollars home is a lot. It means a lot to them. Whenever my daughters really needed something, he'd try to help."

The issue of prison labor is a controversial one, however, and with good reason. Although the symbolic and material benefits of sending money home are readily apparent to families of prisoners, the line between employment and exploitation in a prison setting is often difficult to discern. With African Americans disproportionately represented in the prison system, many critics feel that the use of labor echoes earlier types of exploitation once exercised within the institutions of slavery and sharecropping.[3]

Indeed, prison labor during the last few decades has resembled something like indentured servitude in some states. While federal law prohibits domestic commerce in prison-made goods unless inmates are paid "prevailing wage," the law doesn't apply to exports. As a result, in Texas, California, Oregon, and other states, inmates often work for pennies an hour on products that are then sold overseas. As the same woman told me:

> Now I have heard, or read, how different items are made by people in prison, and companies are selling the stuff. I don't know where the money is going to, whether the money is going back into the prison, because I know that the prisoners are not getting paid. If the prisoners are doing that type of work for companies, I think the companies should be paying a fair wage. . . . if they did pay them, like, six, seven, or eight dollars an hour for the work that they're doing, maybe they do give [the inmate], like, two dollars, and the rest of it goes to where it needs to–whether it goes for child support or a [victim compensation] program or whatever. That's what they really need to do instead of paying them less money and then making all the profit off of it.

Drug treatment, job training, parenting classes, and actual employment can help families by allowing or even forcing offenders to meet their obligations. But, as Clinton explained, where a minority of the prisoners have access to these programs, they can present prisoners with a serious dilemma. On the cell block it becomes immediately clear who is "programming" and who is not, and those who are have more to lose. To begin a program in the correctional setting is thus not only a matter of making an effort to better oneself or to please the parole board, it also gives other less scrupulous inmates leverage. When Clinton had his belongings stolen out of his cell, he was sure it was because the thief knew he was motivated to go home:

> They felt that, being that I was a programmer–that I was trying to go home and I wasn't gonna let nothing stop me from going home–they

felt as though there were certain things they could get away with. I think that a separation needs to be drawn between people that program and don't program, 'cause, see, that's where being taken for granted comes in. If you take a person that you see that's not trying to program and put him around people who are programming, you're designing catastrophe is what you're doing.

Mixing various populations–a practice avoided in federal facilities but something prisons in the District and many states often do–can have deadly consequences, even leading to riots.[4] Still, Clinton felt that his education was important enough for him to continue because it would help him find employment when he returned home.

Zelda's Story

Zelda, seventeen years Clinton's junior, was three when her mother died. She too was sent to live with her extended family. Her childhood was, as she described it, "rough." Physically and later sexually abused by men in her extended family, she ran away at the age of sixteen, then found out she was pregnant. "It was hard, very hard. [I was staying] on the street, basically, then with my sister's foster mother. And then I eventually went to my godmother's house before I had my child, and I got help once I got there, but my first child passed [soon after she was born]."

Zelda's boyfriend at the time was badly affected by their daughter's death. He went "crazy," she told me. "It's bad for him. . . . He was a good father, but [because of his mental breakdown] we just broke up. I see him and talk, you know we're still friends." Still, she says, even though it was years ago, "mentally, he hasn't been the same since she passed away." Without anywhere to go, she tracked down Clinton, who had looked out for her when he was not incarcerated. When she found him, he had just been released from prison and was living with Pat. Clinton and Pat took Zelda in, and ever since she has seen Clinton as her protective older brother and Pat as her adopted mother.

Zelda looks back on that time as the period that turned her life around. For two years, from 1988 to 1990, she lived with Clinton, Pat, and her niece, Janet, rebuilding her sense of who she was and what she would do with her life. As she told me, "Ever since, that's who I've been with as family." In 1990, however, Clinton was again arrested and charged with distribution, and Pat was forced to move in with her sister. Zelda moved into a local shelter, where she met up with an old boyfriend and became pregnant again. Her relationship with him was, as she says, "unhealthy–and I'll just leave it at that," so she didn't stay in touch with him after he was arrested a few months into her pregnancy and hasn't told him about their daughter. She believes he is still serving out a lengthy sentence.

Zelda has had another daughter since then, but the father disappeared before finding out she was pregnant. She found an apartment, stopped dating altogether, and struggled to raise her two girls on her own. Her apartment, on the fourth floor of an older project, something that looks like it's been scraped hard by time, is small but sufficient. Projects in other cities are large, but in the District they vary greatly from row houses to large multibuilding complexes. Zelda's is somewhere in the middle, a single five-story building on a barren strip of road near the highway that runs through the District. Looking at it the first time, I thought it might be abandoned, but most of the windows were intact and the door seemed functional.

Zelda doesn't let her daughters walk around the project alone. Her experience of abuse is one of the things that makes her especially devoted to the care and safety of her own daughters:

> You know, I just don't want to take them or let them go through the things that I've been through when I was growing up. . . . I don't want them to have to be abused. . . . I just keep them here. I know they're safe here. I keep them close. [crying] I let them know that I do love them, always. I've been doing okay. I'm just trying to make it.

Many of the single mothers I spoke with struggled with a feeling of inadequacy in their role as a parent.* It hasn't been easy for Zelda, because neither the fathers of her children nor their families are pro-

---

* In extreme cases, the mothers I spoke with described suicidal ideation on a regular basis and connected this with their self-perception as a poor parent:

viding support. When I ask why the family of the father whom she could locate isn't helping, she explains that it is because she doesn't want to introduce her daughter to them just for support:

> I know his father stays up on Kennedy and Georgia, but it's, like, how can I go to him and introduce him to his granddaughter, someone who he has never seen, so, you know, it has been kinda hard. . . . I let her know that he does stay up there, and she has been asking to go see him. And I always tell her, "Yeah. Well, I'll take you," but, you know, I just can't pop it in on his father that this is his granddaughter. And I don't want him to think that, well, I want something from him, because I don't, but I would like her to know the other side of her family. It's just been hard.

Without the involvement of her children's fathers' families and unwilling to return to the extended family that abused her, Zelda relies mostly on Pat.

Pat, Janet, and Janet's baby son live together in a small row house, part of an expansive Section 8 housing development in Southeast. I had trouble finding Pat's house at first. Her neighbors looked concerned and came over to help. "You know where you going? I don't think this is where you want to be. This isn't a good place to be lost." When I told them I was looking for a house number, they shook their heads and asked who I was looking for, then pointed to the row house. Most of the numbers, it turns out, have been torn off the doors, so that the address I asked for was fairly useless. Approaching the house, I wonder how police and emergency services are able to locate buildings and serve residents in the neighborhood. As both Janet and Pat told me later, the lack of good police and emergency services is one of the major com-

---

I don't care if I die, really, it would be peaceful, really. I know you think that's crazy, but that's how I look at it. His father need to get out here soon and take care of him, because I can't do it. I mean, I'll want to see him, I'll see my son again, but . . . [crying] . . . but I'm not a good mother. If [his father] had never gotten locked up–if he wouldn't have never gotten locked, [my son] wouldn't have went through what he had to go through with me. I ain't always made the best of choices. God forgive me, but it is all I knew. Sometimes, I just can't do it no more.

plaints that residents in the area have: "Police never come here. They have shootings all the time, but I think the police is scared, truly I do."

The neighborhood is notorious for its amount of drug-related crime, including shootings nearly every night: "It's bad here at night; you can't really go out because of the shooting. We just, kinda, stay inside. The police come here for little stuff. It takes them forever if somebody was getting hurt, somebody was shot, you know."

When I ask Pat and Janet how they are dealing with Clinton's incarceration, they talk mostly about the emotional impact:

> *Janet:* Well, my mother's been right there whenever he was in, so it really has affected her–and like if I might cry or something, she'll cry too. She always says, "I'm lonely" or "I miss him" or something like that.
>
> *Pat:* Janet doesn't talk about it much. [To Janet] Well, I don't know. I guess the hardest part is being lonely and him being there. And like I say, I get in my little spirits dropping without him. But that's part of my whole thing being here by myself and not having him here.
>
> *Janet:* It's hard when your father is in. Like, I remember we had stuff at school, like plays, or, you know, one time they had a father and daughter dinner. I didn't go. Just stuff like that. Seeing other kids there with their mother and father made me wish that I was not there at the time.

There are financial consequences as well. Janet was trying to stay in touch with Clinton, but the phone and travel expenses were difficult to manage: "The calls now, you know, and spending money getting back and forth. Time, because of how much time you spend. It becomes a real burden." Pat also noted that even minor contributions from Clinton did make a difference. "Not that I depend on him, but his little monies do help. Like when I had to move–because he was helping with rent, then he got locked up."

Released

Clinton was released last year and moved in with his sister. Things started out well for them. Clinton got a job at a department store where a friend worked, and, while it didn't pay much, it was enough while he looked around for other work. With two children, Zelda's annual income from public assistance (PA) is $4,656. Even with the money she made cutting hair on the side, after rent, food, and the phone bill, she had little left over to buy her growing daughters shoes, clothing, and school supplies. Her brother helped out with these expenses while he had his job, often making the difference between having a phone and not. "I was on PA. So he would pay my phone bill, take my kids shopping, give me a little money here and there to buy something for myself. So he helped me out."

In addition to providing some financial help, Clinton also helped out by picking up the kids or taking them out on weekends while Zelda cut hair. That worked well for about six months, until the store where he worked closed and his income vanished with it. He applied for a number of jobs, but no one wanted to hire him. He blames his lack of success in part on his candor about his criminal record, something he is up-front about because of his previous experience of being "outed" at his first job:

> I couldn't lie. I feel as though that if I lied and the next thing you know it came out, it's embarrassing. I can't be on a job and then when you work a job, and you get used to the job, you get competent at that job. You and your peers start to clicking together like a family, you start to liking the peoples on the job you're associating with. Man, this is your second family. And all of the sudden, the man walk in one day and say, "You're fired. We have to terminate you because we found out that you had a record and you did not mention it on your application."

Whether his lack of success had to do with his record or with something else, his experience is one that many ex-offenders related. For Clinton, his lack of employment shook his confidence in his ability to earn a living by any means other than hustling:

> You do everything you can, and when it gets so bad that when you go and apply for a McDonalds job and you don't get hired, now that's really bad, and McDonalds used to hire everybody. Six dollars an hour.

It shows. . . . Even at times I would go over to the market over there in Northeast off Fifty-sixth Street and try to help people–try to work around the loading dock areas and everything. I'd get there. They'd tell me, "We got enough."

The loss of his job and his inability to provide for any of the people in his family the way he used to while he was hustling weighed heavily on him. He was seeing Pat often and wanted to help pay for her expenses.

I was staying with my sister [Zelda]. She's a younger sister, and she always wanted me to come stay with her, because, you know, I'm her older brother. I used to always look out for her and take care of her when I was coming up, so she felt obligated to that. But I would tell her that I might not get another job right away, but I'm gonna keep trying. But I felt good, 'cause I know I got this, I'm looking at this degree. I'm looking at these certificates. All my accomplishments, all of the things I achieved while I was in there, and I think about how I eventually pursued them to achievement, so I feel good. So when I go and apply for a job I'm feeling good. Then when it get around to about the fifteenth or twentieth application and no one calling, now I go into a slump. I don't have no finance. My family keeps giving me money. Then, now, they short, 'cause they're saying that the bills is catching up on them because they have to provide for me.

He also knew that Zelda was having difficulty supporting herself and her two daughters, let alone her now unemployed older brother. After a few months without pay, he went back to his old neighborhood and decided to start hustling again, telling his family he'd gotten work as a day laborer. Many unskilled laborers pick up work on a daily basis at places like the market in Northeast that Clinton visited. However, there are generally more workers than jobs, and the regulars are usually picked first because they are known to the employers. A recent crackdown on day laborers in the area caused a minor furor, as the only source of legal income that many men felt they had was effectively cut off.[5] For Clinton, it was untenable that he should be a burden to his family.

See, it's. . . . just certain things just don't sit right with you. If you know you accomplished a certain degree, you feel as though "I'm supposed to be able to give my child some money from working on a job from the experience that I learned." And it's like going backwards, because every time I would sit there and look at that [college] degree and look at all of my certificates, all of my accomplishments, and look at 'em—I was outstanding in English. English was one of the best, one of my major subjects, and it was my best subject 'cause I loved it. And even in American literature I was pretty good—so I would look at [my degree], and it made me feel good. And then when I looked around [after losing the job at the clothing store] and said, "But I can't get a damn job!" Back to basics. And what that does, it makes you resort back to what you do best—what you feel as though you do best, what you know, and that is to break the law. . . . You know, even though you can try and try and try and try and try not to, there you are.

Clinton got an education—even an associate's degree—while inside and a job, however brief, when he came out. So why did he return to hustling? For Clinton, despite his family's desire for him to stay straight, it was the feeling of obligation to them that weighed on him and made him decide to look for "easy money." But even while he made good money selling drugs, he felt bad about that too: "I started selling drugs, but then, when I started to take the proceeds from that and go give them little things, buy them little things, I didn't feel good about it, because I knew I was not doing it right."

Related to these reasons are, of course, issues of identity. Clinton and other offenders insisted that they felt that part of the meaning of fatherhood was supporting their children. In fact, a number of them used precisely the same phrase: "Right or wrong, I do what I have to do to provide." Again and again in interviews, criminal offenders like Clinton tried to square their dependency on relatives with their conception of their proper role in their family and in society.[6] Humility was something that, in the face of prolonged unilateral dependence, both offenders and their family members felt stretched into humiliation. The social and moral questions related to the economic concerns that many families confronted as they grappled with incarceration were, as with Clinton and his sister, often more significant to them than the facts of material hardship.

Clinton is like most petty drug dealers—no gold jewelry, no fancy cars, no automatic weapons.[7] There is little of the popular fantasy depictions of drug dealing in the lives of most young men in the inner city who join the informal drug economy. Instead, their lives consist mostly of hanging out in dilapidated public housing, living with family or scraping by with just enough money for food and rent, occasionally attending church or a family picnic, and thinking vaguely about how they can leave the street life but never seeing a clear path out. Despite his unease with his return to hustling, it gave Clinton cash to help out his family, which they dearly needed. For Clinton, the idea that he had supposedly been "rehabilitated" made him shake his head, thinking about his return to hustling:

> What settles in the mind is this: Your tax dollars paid for this education that I have. It paid for these vocational skills that I've accomplished, but they're not amounting to a damned thing because I can't get a job with them.*

Within a few months of his return to hustling, Clinton was rearrested.

Let's be clear: Neither Clinton nor anyone in his family ever suggested that drugs should be legalized or that drug dealing should be considered a legitimate means of obtaining an income. Clinton knew it was wrong and hid it from his family for precisely that reason. These, after all, are the same drugs that lead to the nightly shootings that force his own daughter inside every night and make over half of urban blacks afraid to walk in their own neighborhoods after dark.[8] What is striking about Clinton's account and the accounts of other offenders is

---

* Clinton's point provides a useful supplement to the work of William Julius Wilson. Wilson argues that, as formal sector jobs disappear for young men, they are more likely to enter the informal economy, including illegal trafficking in drugs. WILSON, *supra* note 14 (chap. 3). What Wilson does not account for, but is clearly a major concern in many poor urban neighborhoods, is the effect of incarceration both on the employment prospects of ex-offenders and on the available labor pool for prospective employers.

that they did not give glib justifications for the offenses or attempt to legitimate criminal activity. What these offenders gave were accounts of the profound costs–personal and social, financial and moral–that they pay when they do or do not choose criminal activity. It is a messy and emotional calculus that incarceration enters into–in ways that most policymakers utterly fail to comprehend.

Inside, Again

Financially, Clinton's reincarceration has had significant consequences for Zelda. She had been depending on Clinton's added income and assistance with her daughters. Although Zelda was clear that she never wanted him to sell drugs again, she acknowledged that, since the two fathers of her children were not helping her to raise them, her brother felt pressure to earn money to help her out. Zelda is not pleased that Clinton gave up on going straight, not only because she loves her brother and wants to see him free but also because she was depending on him to get a job and help out with the kids. Clinton had promised to take her daughters shopping for notebooks, pencils, and back-to-school clothes but was arrested just before the school year began.

Zelda knows that Clinton's commitment to help out is part of what drove him to hustling again. His desire to help his younger sister and her desire to provide a decent living environment for her children were both powerful and helped push Clinton back into the informal drug economy. Now Clinton's incarceration is forcing Zelda to consider turning to the family that abused her for help. "I don't like to, but I think some of them would help a little." This is particularly painful for her and gives some indication of the social consequences of financial difficulties. In times of need, people are often forced to make use of resources they might otherwise refuse. While this is probably true for everyone, most Americans have a far wider and far more attractive array of options than do people in Zelda's situation.

One of the most striking findings of recent research into the consequences of welfare reform is that, while an increased number of marriages remain intact, the price for some women has been increased exposure to abuse.[9] The reason for this is that, by removing material resources from the lives of poor mothers, welfare reform has forced them to make use of other sources of support that are available to them, usually family and friends. While in many cases this is an effective way of spreading the added burden of child support, it also has forced some women to maintain or reopen relationships that they had left with good reason.

Incarceration can produce a similar effect. For many of the women I interviewed, the choices they felt they were left with were extremely limited.* Zelda's case is analogous to this except that it wasn't simply her material resources that were diminished but her pool of available social resources as well. She is left with two undesirable options: returning to her abusive family or making do on her own.

Now, instead of receiving Clinton's help, Zelda is working extra hours to send him money until he gets a job inside. The private prison he is in prohibits receiving personal items through the mail; underwear, undershirts, soap, toothpaste, toothbrushes, antifungal powder,† and deodorant must all be purchased at the private canteen operated by the corporation that owns and manages the facility. The prices are high, but inmates have no alternative.

Perhaps most significantly, Zelda feels that, even if she had to reach out to her extended family while Clinton was outside but unemployed, she wouldn't be nearly as fearful about doing so with him around. Clinton is not just a material resource that she has lost but also one of her

---

* More typical examples of this pattern involved reliance on abusive boyfriends or ex-boyfriends for support while a current partner, brother, or father was incarcerated. As one woman told me,

> In January I was with one of the abusive guys I was with, and he gave me money and bought [my son] stuff. It was my boyfriend but I didn't like him, but I needed him for a reason to–I needed him to buy my son his stuff. So I dealt with. Did what I had to do. [My son] ain't have no Christmas last year. He had it in January last year. He had it had in January this year. . . . I always end up getting a boyfriend and then they'll be somebody abusive. Then I have to deal with their problems and what they throwing at me.

† In the correctional setting, foot fungus is a significant problem. Several inmates told me about the importance of obtaining and guarding one's own cosmetic products. "In this type of environment you got people coming from the street. . . . they got all kinds of fungus because they been smoking crack."

closest friends, the person who she feels can understand her complicated family situation best and who will protect her and her daughters
when they need protection. Collect phone calls from Clinton's facility
cost a flat rate of nine dollars for ten minutes.[10] Although Clinton limits
his calls to one a month, the cost is still more than she can afford.

When I last see Zelda, it is late winter and fairly cold for D.C. Pulling up
to her apartment complex I can see that the downstairs door has been
broken open since I last visited. She didn't sound well over the phone,
and I am worried about her but don't feel there's much I can or know
how to do for her. She is still waiting for her brother to be paroled but
is less hopeful since he was denied parole and shipped out of state.
When we start talking she tells me she feels tired and that she doesn't
leave the apartment much any more, "just to shop, really." During this,
our last, interview, she seems exhausted and overwhelmed. While talking, she slowly lowers her head into her hands and stares through her
fingers at the floor, speaking more and more quietly until barely
audible. She spends most of her days dressing hair in the middle of her
living room and cleaning. The apartment is immaculate. She says the
reason she works so hard now is so she won't have to rely on her family; she's determined not to go back to them for anything. Her goal, she
says, is to save enough so her daughters will have what she didn't–"all
the things that they can have, you know, once it's over for me." When I
ask what she means by "over," she shrugs and puts her face down into
her hands.

Chapter 11 Material and Social Consequences

Many families of prisoners face significant obstacles in day-to-day life that are not directly related to incarceration. Many of the women I interviewed are, like Zelda, survivors of physical and sexual abuse, struggling against poverty and working hard to raise their children without much help. These are not troubles faced only by families of prisoners, but they are problems that they face disproportionately and with added difficulty. These are problems that incarceration, while not necessarily causing, compounds. For families with these types of problems, incarceration is not only far more prevalent but also more devastating in both material and social terms.

Material Exchange and Economic Concerns

While most accounts that relate poverty and crime generally describe poverty as driving criminal activity and thus involvement in the criminal justice system, families with these types of problems provide evidence that the relationship runs both ways and is arguably cyclical. Many inner-city families not only experience incarceration because they are poor, but they are also poor because they experience incarceration. In light of their experiences, standard correlations such as those shown in figure 13 take on a very different meaning.

One way—the traditional way—of interpreting these data would be to infer that people who are unemployed or have less money are more likely to engage in criminal activity. This is one of the main findings of William Julius Wilson's book *When Work Disappears:* "As many studies have revealed, the decline in legitimate employment opportunities among inner-city residents has increased incentives to sell drugs."[1] Indeed, this is

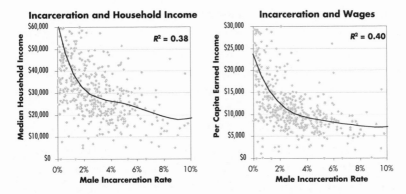

Fig. 13. Incarceration, household income, and earned income. *Note:* Plotted line represents best-fit polynomial regression. Data for incarceration rates over 10 percent not shown. Data from DC Department of Corrections (1999) and the U.S. Census (2000). Household income is the median household income for that census block, while per capita earned income is the income from wages or salaries for that census block divided by the population of that census block.

the explanation Clinton gave for his return to hustling heroin: he needed money and couldn't find work.[2] But the experiences of these families tell us that the reverse is also true: incarceration can significantly lower the income and increase the expenses of prisoners' families.

Like Kenny, over two-thirds of the incarcerated population are gainfully employed prior to arrest.[3] Even though family members sent to prison make, on average, poverty wages, the median household income is still lowered by the elimination of these wages. And because many prisoners are often a source of income in households prior to their arrest, the per capita income in that household, including unemployed, children, and elderly, is also lowered when they are removed. Furthermore, as was the case both with Clinton and with Arthur's brother, Billy, many ex-offenders find it difficult to obtain employment after release, and, when they do, their earning potential is significantly lowered when compared with that of nonoffenders.[4] The decreased family income is thus due not only to the removal of a wage-earning family member to prison but also to the lowered lifetime earning potential of that family member after they have returned from prison.[5]

But many of the most significant material effects of incarceration are far harder to measure than household income. Prior to their incarceration, many offenders I spoke with provided their families with non-monetary assistance–such as Kenny, who helped his mother with car repairs and house maintenance–the loss of which was often of material consequence.* The loss of childcare and eldercare was also among the most prominent concerns that families raised.[6] There are also costs related to maintaining family ties. Edwina and Lilly, for example, were left not only assuming many of the childcare duties for their sons' children but drawing down familial funds to support their grandchildren's relationship with their fathers through telephone calls and visits to correctional facilities, care packages, and so on.

More subtle than the immediate and direct material effects of incarceration, but perhaps more serious, is the cumulative impact these effects can have on familial wealth across generations. By depleting the savings of offenders' families, incarceration inhibits capital accumulation and reduces the ability of parents to pass wealth on to their children and grandchildren through inheritance and gifts. Indeed, incarceration's draining of the resources of extended family members in this study–particularly the older family members–helps explain why there has been so little capital accumulation and inheritance among inner-city families in general and minority families in particular.

This becomes apparent when we see not only how incarceration saps the savings of grandparents like Edwina and Lilly but how hard it is for someone like Zelda to save enough to buy her children school supplies, let alone provide for their inheritance. The disproportionate incarceration of black men like Clinton helps to explain why black families are less able to save money and why each successive generation inherits less wealth than their white counterparts.[7] Incarceration acts like a hidden tax, one that is visited disproportionately on poor and minority families; and while its costs are most directly felt by the adults closest to the incarcerated family member, the full effect is eventually felt by the next generation as well.

* Just as Edwina complained that she had to pay out of pocket for the basic auto work that her son, Kenny, used to do, many family members complained that they had trouble paying for things or making do without the assistance of their incarcerated relatives: everything from fixing a leaky faucet or broken door to providing help on moving day or in getting to the doctor's office.

The effects of this tax are profound. A recent study by Mark Joseph estimated the effects of incarceration on the lifetime earnings of offenders at over three hundred billion dollars—and that is limited to the age cohort that is sixteen years old today.[8] The full impact across the generations, while far larger, is also far harder to estimate. In light of the accounts of the families in the present study, however, it becomes apparent that these are costs borne *not* solely or even predominantly by offenders themselves. Moreover, the effects of incarceration, as the accounts of families in this study show, are far more expansive than the lost earnings of offenders alone. We know, for example, that phone companies and departments of corrections draw hundreds of millions of dollars each year from prisoners' families. We also know that a broad array of other costs—from childcare and eldercare to services to replace household help to travel and legal expenses—is borne by families. But because these costs are more diffuse and difficult to estimate, they are rarely discussed.

Viewed in this light, racial disparities in arrests, sentencing, and parole take on a broader significance.[9] For example, census data show that blacks typically possess only one-third of the assets of whites with similar incomes.[10] While this pattern is generally attributed to lower savings and inheritance,[11] this explanation simply begs the question of why savings and inheritance are lower—something that the concentration of incarceration in minority communities and its effect on capital accumulation help to explain. Incarceration, of course, is not alone in contributing to these disparities. Perhaps most obviously, the structure of our current welfare policies discourages capital accumulation by punishing savings with the discontinuation of assistance (a point made powerfully by Carol Stack in her still resonant analysis of families living in an Illinois housing project[12]). But incarceration compounds the effect.

Similarly, while about three-quarters of white American families own the home they live in, less than half of black American families do—again, a disparity that persists after controlling for differences in income.* And while it is readily apparent how diminished savings can

---

* While some of this has to do with discrimination, surveys of African Americans find that the down payment on a home is often the most significant barrier to home ownership and all the benefits that come with it. Home ownership, for example, confers

affect home ownership, Edwina's case demonstrates how increased expenses associated with incarceration can influence the capital value of home ownership in ways that escape most statistical studies: while Edwina's reported income increased as she came out of retirement in order to make up some of the additional expenses of raising Kenny's children, the value of her home was dramatically reduced when she took out a second mortgage in order to support her grandchildren.*

Familial costs can also decrease investments in what is often called "human capital,"[13] as moving to a better school district, purchasing an up-to-date computer, and attending college all become less affordable. For Kenny's niece, the loss of money for college tuition was direct; but the broader effect can be more subtle and indirect, as the general ability to engage in this kind of investment is lowered. Educational attainment is, of course, one of the best predictors we have for avoiding the criminal justice system, but the benefits of investing in (and the costs of neglecting) human capital extend well beyond crime rates. As investments are not made, the collective capacities of family members are limited, making the pooling of resources less beneficial overall.

Finally, it is worth noting that all the material effects of incarceration are particularly devastating to poor families because they generally have the highest *marginal costs*–that is, their above-subsistence resources are already severely taxed, so any additional expenses or burdens cut closer to the bone. That incarceration is concentrated in poor and minority communities, where members of the family's social network are less likely to be able to provide significant assistance, only compounds the problem. Here, then, are significant consequences not only for criminal offenders but for precisely those nonoffenders who have the fewest resources and are thus least capable of sustaining them.†

---

significant tax benefits on families and is the most significant form of investment for most Americans, one they traditionally pass on to their children.
* One family I spoke with described remortgaging and then losing their home in order to pay for legal counsel to represent their incarcerated relative. Another lost their apartment because they put rent money toward prison-related expenses.
† The demographic distribution of incarceration also helps to explain why many inner-city families feel like they are losing ground despite government reports that employment rates and income are rising among young black men, even among the poorest and least educated. According to a recent study led by the Princeton sociolo-

Social Exchange & Moral Concerns

A wealth of studies, following Carol Stack's work with families in Chicago projects in the late 1960s,[14] indicate that informal resource-sharing networks play a crucial role in helping poor urban families to cope with personal and structural economic fluctuations.[15] These studies demonstrate that networks of kin and substitute kin are essential to the ability of those who are otherwise resource-poor to survive hard times by providing both material and emotional assistance. While Stack's work was groundbreaking in the study of urban American society, it drew on extensive anthropological literature documenting the bonds of reciprocal exchange around the world across cultural and class differences.[16] As one reviewer of the anthropological literature on exchange noted over thirty years ago, the norm of reciprocity appears to be "no less important and as universal as the incest taboo."[17]

Why is reciprocity the "central moral formula for interpersonal conduct?"[18] Many of the benefits of informal reciprocal exchange networks are economic. The likelihood of any one person experiencing hardship during her or his life is fairly high, but the likelihood of everyone experiencing it at the same time is much lower; so long-term, open-ended relationships of exchange increase the likelihood that individuals will have someone to call upon when they are in need.[19] One can see how important this type of reciprocal exchange can be for people like Edwina, Lilly, and Zelda, who may not always have enough food to feed the children they care for or enough money to pay the rent. At one time, during Prohibition, urban "rent parties" served to turn this kind of social cost sharing into a marketlike interaction in many cities, though even these were normally conducted among trusted intimates.[20]

---

gist Bruce Western, decreasing employment and income disparities between whites and blacks, particularly those with less education and income, are largely explained by the exclusion of inmates (who tend to be poor, black, and less educated). Once the incarcerated population is included in these analyses, it turns out that unemployment has actually *risen* among black men and risen quite dramatically among young high school dropouts. *See* Western, Pettit and Guetzkow, *supra* note 4 (chap. 11), at 4 (arguing that the "rise in average wages doesn't represent a real improvement in living standards, but rather is an artifact of incarceration which is concentrated among low earners").

A second economic explanation for the importance of open-ended reciprocal exchange is that sharing what one has in abundance at any given time–whether that be money, food, or simply time and energy–makes sense because it can help others in need more than it can help the person who has it in excess of his or her need.[21] This kind of logic can move people to donate money to fight hunger in drought-stricken countries, but the pull is far more powerful when those with less are already part of one's own personal network of friends and family. People often simply do favors for one another–such as watching the kids, fixing a leaky faucet, or picking a child up from school. Indeed, within families and among close friends, these forms of assistance are so fundamental that they are often not even considered favors. Thus it is simply taken for granted that Kenny will help repair his mother's car and that she will help him raise his children, that Clinton and his sister will help each other, and that Lilly will help her grandson.

A third economic benefit of regular social exchange is the development of predictability and trust, which, in turn, dramatically lowers inefficiencies related to what economists call "transaction costs."[22] While it would be absurd, for example, for someone to exchange childcare with a complete stranger without many assurances and safeguards in place, parents frequently and even casually offer childcare to, or ask for childcare from, a close friend or relative. In healthy communities, this kind of trust is extended (though often in a reduced capacity) to the close friends of family members and to the family of close friends. These networks of trust allow people to enter into important relationships quickly and without the formalities associated with impersonal market transactions.

Looking at efficiencies that inhere in reciprocal exchange networks, one can understand why many researchers describe the stock of these social networks and the norms that govern them as social *capital.* By considering "the resources that emerge from one's social ties,"[23] economists and political scientists have been able to expand their analyses from limited considerations of material goods in formal markets to the flow of those goods through nonmarket relationships.

For all the material gains that relations of trust and reciprocity confer, however, the social information exchanged and the social meaning established are perhaps more essential still. It has long been a mainstay of anthropological research to tease out just how such networks help lend meaning to everyday life, shape moral concerns, and even give rise to political action.[24] More than utilitarian connections, they are generally *meaningful* in a richer sense than temporary and untrusting relationships serving only material exchange. The feelings that members of Kenny's family have, for example, about their relationships with one another and the significance that being part of that family gives their lives is at least as important as the cash they transact and the services they perform. By helping one another through hard times they not only participate in informal economic exchanges but also create viable identities and shared meanings. This is why anthropologists consider these networks and the norms of reciprocity and trust that inhere in them as so important: they are the ties that bind us together–not just materially but socially and symbolically as well.

One of the great puzzles of recent studies of urban life has been the attenuation of extended open-ended networks of exchange over the last three decades, particularly in poor and minority urban communities.[25] Regular and significant social exchange was widely documented among the urban poor in the 1960s and 1970s but with far less regularity during the 1980s and 1990s. One recent national study found that, by the late 1990s, these networks of friends and family were far less extensive among low-income, urban, and minority families than had previously been observed.[26]

Attending to the manner in which incarceration disrupts the economic and moral functioning of these networks can help to explain this decline. The first consequences that families of prisoners feel are often material, immediate, and substantial. The small measure of capital that Edwina had accrued over a lifetime of hard work, for example, was quickly transformed into debt that will likely extend well beyond her death. During the last twenty years, many women–particularly low-income and minority women–have found out the hard way just how much their love and care for a son, brother, or husband can cost them.

But a second set of consequences—ones that cannot be fully captured in economic terms—comes into play in the longer term. In the accounts previously described, while incarceration forces offenders to answer to the state, it also forces them to abrogate their familial and community responsibilities. As families feel the slow grind of unreturned assistance and care, social consequences can ripple out from the initial material failings.

In Lilly's story, for example, we begin to see that, as the material costs of incarceration accumulate, family members pull back from the relationships and norms that usually bind them together. Lilly and her grandson are distressed not only because their own lives are made more difficult as their relatives withdraw support but also because, in a deeper sense, they understand a refusal to help a family member in need as something more than an economic decision; for them it is also a social and thus a moral decision.

The accounts of these families, in which the burden of incarceration is spread through intimate relationships, thus not only bring us a good deal closer to understanding why measures of social capital have fallen so precipitously in low-income urban neighborhoods in recent decades but also show how little recent discussions about social capital tell us about the plight of inner-city families and communities.[27] While many commentators describe the normative aspects of social capital as promoting material well-being, they miss the way that public policy can turn these moral expectations and obligations against those who depend on them. Indeed, what is so striking in the accounts of the families in this study is how the norms of reciprocity and networks of exchange that are normally considered beneficial to families and communities turn out to be devastating for those who bear the brunt of current sentencing practices. Their stories illustrate the flip side of social capital—how normally sustaining relationships can drain and exhaust the very families and communities they are thought to benefit most.

This, then, is the tragic dilemma that families like Edwina's, Lilly's, and Zelda's find themselves in: give up the ties that bind them together or honor those ties and face further impoverishment. The effects of incarceration on these families are so damaging because there is no acceptable remedy that they can pursue. They can shoulder the burdens that accompany the incarceration of their loved one, suffering significant material hardship and emotional strain, or–an even less appealing option for many–they can withdraw from their social commitments, sacrificing the norms of trust and mutual responsibility that give meaning to their lives.

It is undoubtedly true that, as Edwina says, "money is not everything," and the accounts of these families begin to indicate how much many family members are willing to sacrifice in order to adhere to the norms that kinship engenders. But by tampering in such a forceful way with the ability of so many individuals to engage in basic moral behavior, we risk doing far more than inflicting an overly harsh punishment. Mass incarceration is pulling away the basic building blocks of social life itself. When individuals are pressed hard to withdraw their care and concern from one another, the effect is more than the impoverishment of individuals; as overincarceration increases the costs of caring relationships, the losses become moral, and in time it is our culture itself that becomes impoverished.

Clearly, life can be chaotic for families in the inner city, and incarceration can exacerbate that chaos. Sensationalist media accounts aside, this is not because these families are impervious to the value systems to which other Americans adhere. Most of the families I have come to know are painfully aware of the diminished status they are afforded because they are poor, because there is no husband or father present, because he is in prison, and because all these attributes bring them into close proximity with the ever-present stereotypes of failure and moral decay in modern America. As a result, information about incarceration is often carefully guarded by relatives. Part IV explores some of the consequences of these normative concerns and the role that stigma plays in shaping urban family life.

Part IV Silence

Oh Lord, trouble so hard.
Yes, indeed, my trouble is hard.
Oh Lord, trouble so hard.
Don't nobody know my troubles but God.

—Vera Hall, *Trouble So Hard*

[D]oes the stigmatized individual assume his differentness is known
about already or is evident on the spot, or does he assume it is neither
known about by those present nor immediately perceivable by them?

—Erving Goffman, *Stigma*

The preceding chapters have described the difficulties that families
of prisoners face. Their experiences are, one would think, more than
enough to prompt many to protest a regime of criminal sanctions that
punishes them along with criminal offenders. Yet, most told no one outside of the immediate family about their relative's incarceration and the
troubles they faced. Indeed, many were even hiding the incarceration
from extended family members.[1] The silence of these families is, in
many ways, counterintuitive. If incarceration in the District and in
many urban areas is the statistical norm, why isn't it socially normative
as well?

The collateral effects of incarceration on families and communities
are, as the previous chapters have emphasized, not only material but
deeply social. The chapters in part IV describe how the moral concerns
about criminality influence other aspects of familial and community
relationships. Perhaps the most unexpected finding is that the stigma

related to incarceration is visited on the families of prisoners as much as–if not more than–it is on prisoners themselves.[2]

This finding complicates recent popular and theoretical accounts of shame and criminal sanctions considerably. Over the last five to ten years, legal scholars and policy analysts have rediscovered social science and, more specifically, social norms.[3] It is a rediscovery that has had a significant impact on discussions about criminal law in general[4] and about shame and criminal sanctions in particular.[5] Politicians, academics, and prominent critics on TV and radio shows have discussed how we must restore the criminal justice system's ability to stigmatize and induce shame. Because many perceive contemporary urban culture as outside or resistant to the moral system of social norms they would like to promote, these discussions have gained considerable traction.

For example, it has been suggested that, in areas where incarceration is commonplace, there is little stigma attached to a prison sentence. Worse still, many fear that incarceration might even be taking on a positive connotation, an association with masculinity–"rite of passage" is the phrase often used in the press. As a result, many would like to enable the criminal justice system to stigmatize more effectively and induce shame more consistently and to thereby both express public moral condemnation and reduce the likelihood of offense. Shame and stigma emerge in these debates both as expressions of pent-up public disapprobation and as underutilized and cost-effective deterrents.

While it is encouraging that policymakers and analysts are interested in how law shapes social meaning and how social meaning shapes human experience and behavior, there is reason for caution. In discussing and promoting policies based on law's expressive function,[6] few analysts have actually observed the effects of the statutes that have been proposed and implemented. That is, those making the law and talking about it don't know whether the intended effects actually have happened or will.

The findings from the accounts in this book suggest that the symbolically harsh statutes that have been enacted to date do not correlate with their intended effects and that many of their consequences are not

only unintended but undesirable. Rather than simply deterring potential offenders from future crimes, the most significant impact of the
stigma related to increased incarceration has been the silencing and
isolation of families of prisoners, an effect that few legal analysts antic-
ipate.

Chapter 12 Missing the Mark: Louisa & Robert

Louisa and Robert are in their mid-thirties and are married with one son, Jimmy. Their small family, like many working-poor families in the District, is deeply religious. Aware of the odds against their staying together, family is not something they take for granted; it is something they have struggled to achieve. Ten years ago, when their son was three, Robert started using crack and was soon addicted, leaving Louisa and Jimmy for the streets. After being incarcerated and completing a drug treatment program, he sought them out, and, after a period of reconciliation, their family was reunited. For the next two years, they attended a local church and, in Louisa's words, "kept on the straight and narrow," both of them working full-time at entry-level jobs to try to save up enough money to make the down payment on a house.

Louisa looked beyond Robert's earlier abandonment and criminal activity, focusing on his return and recovery: "You know, unfortunately, we were separated. That happened. And when we reunited, he had to pay the penalty. I accepted his wrongdoing, because I just wanted our family to rejoin and reunite." Robert's criminal history cast a permanent shadow, however, as they both knew he was still wanted for a robbery he had committed during his addiction.

> He was telling me, "It's inevitable," because he did do it. He said, "Well, I've got a bench warrant out on me, and the inevitable might come." But he was running because he knew what it was like [in prison]. He didn't want to go back. And he wanted his life. So he got a job. We remained being a family. But he was always conscious. "Okay, we can't go that way. Too many police." Always being conscious, trying to avoid going back.

Robert cleaned himself up and stayed off drugs for those two years, got a job, started attending church, and–of great significance to Louisa– began praying with the family. Then, one afternoon he was pulled over for a traffic violation, and it was over.

For Louisa, her husband's arrest and reincarceration have been particularly hard in light of the changes she saw in him and the aspirations they had developed. They had the enthusiasm of converts for family and community life and had come to think of and present themselves as morally upstanding citizens and churchgoers. Because of this, Louisa felt the stigma of her husband's most recent incarceration all the more intensely. She began to avoid friends and family, not wanting to talk about Robert's incarceration and lying to them when she did.

> You isolate yourself because, you know, even though the other person don't know what you going through, you really don't want to open up and talk to them about it. You don't want them knowing about your business. Or it's a certain amount of respect you want them to have. I just don't like the idea of people knowing that he's incarcerated.

While Louisa is able to distinguish between her husband's actions and his identity (as she puts it, "he did commit a crime, but he is not a criminal"[1]), she feels others are unlikely to make the same distinction. As a result of her withdrawal, her old friendships have suffered and she has held back from making new friends. "I just stick to myself. It's a lot less problems that way."[2]

Louisa has a number of reasons to remain guarded. Concerned for her husband's reputation when he returns, she said, she hides his incarceration so that, "when they look at him, they won't slap all these labels on him and have to be afraid of him." She also feels the possibility of people judging her and her son. "It's how people look at you. The respect you want and they don't respect you because your husband is incarcerated."

Louisa is very wary of discussing the matter not only with her co-workers and church members but with other family members as well. She has told her family that he was reincarcerated because of a serious traffic violation instead of an armed robbery charge. It is a story that is, at least at first, believable given that a serious traffic violation would violate the terms of his parole.

> I don't talk to them. I evades the subject. They evades the subject. They, like, pleases me not to say anything about it. They pleases me not to question me about it. Every now and then my oldest sister asks, "Well, when is he coming home?" And I'll just evade the question—"He'll be home soon." She said, "Oh, well, didn't you say he had a traffic violation or something? Well, why are they keeping him so long for such small thing?" And I'll go and say, "Well did you go shopping and get the pink or purple blouse?" And they'll pick up. "Oh, she don't want to talk about that." That's how I keep it.

Many spouses and parents of prisoners I spoke with did not tell the extended family about the incarceration of a loved one or lied about the type of crime committed.*

Unfortunately, Louisa's withdrawal from friends and family has had an indirect effect on her ability to cope with her increased parenting duties, as she does not want to open herself up to discussions about her husband. As was apparent in previous chapters, families—and low-income families in particular—are often dependent on networks of relatives and friends to cope with poverty and hardship.[3] The fluid households and expansive exchange networks that these families maintain are, while not necessarily their own ideal image of family, adaptive necessities for making ends meet in the long run.[4] Perhaps the most significant consequence of stigma among families of prisoners, then, is the distortion, diminution, and even severance of these social ties.[5] Stigma related to incarceration is powerful, in part, because the families know that the same relationships on which they have come to depend can be turned against them, as social networks that provide resources are transformed into social networks of approbation. It is little wonder, then, that many family members carefully guard information about incarceration.

---

* Other family members explained that they withheld information from extended family for reasons varying from "I don't know what it would do to his aunt. She just thinks so highly of him." to "Somebody's business is nobody's business."

As a result, many family members are forced on a daily basis to choose between sacrificing the honesty of their relationships or the relationships themselves. The result can be draining and painful. Louisa, in addition to her concern about potential labeling by the people she knows, feels the pull of her evasion and deception at her own conscience. As Louisa describes herself lying, her voice quivers with disappointment in herself, and she begins to cry. While she does not want her husband to be branded a criminal, she does feel guilty about lying: "[I feel] terrible because I'm living a lie. I'm living a lie. I'm not normal. I'm abnormal. Being a God-fearing woman, I have to repent and ask forgiveness from the creator, from God."

While Louisa describes frequent crying, depression, and a growing sense of isolation from family and friends, Robert's reaction to his incarceration is strikingly different. As is the case with many of the incarcerated men I interviewed, Robert is coping far better with his incarceration than is his wife. While occasionally depressed, he more frequently feels angry at the criminal justice system that has incarcerated him, and his anger and indignation are voiced in political terms that help him cope. His ability to articulate this anger in terms of the race and class bias of the criminal justice system and the supportive network of offenders around him are both tools that enable him to reframe his punishment in terms that are less stigmatizing than they might otherwise be. In fact, he often receives sympathy and encouragement from other prisoners, who sympathize with his bad break and recognize him as a basically good and decent person.

Robert's ability to cope well is in part due to his perspective on the social and political context in which his incarceration takes place. In a letter, he laid out what he saw behind his own incarceration and that of many other black men in prison:[6]

Even though an annual study at the University of Michigan confirms that the overwhelming majority of drug users, abusers and sellers in America are white, even though the 1992 National Household Survey on Drug Abuse revealed that 8.7 million whites used drugs in one month versus 1.6 million blacks, the drug problem, which is an American problem has been conveniently depicted as a black problem. The war on drugs essentially is a war on black men, America's favorite bogeyman. Then in their misguided logic they attempt to deal with this problem from a perspective of criminality rather than a public health perspective; so countless numbers of petty drug users end up in penal institutions rather than treatment facilities where the problem could be appropriately addressed.

In 1990 thirty-two thousand more young whites were arrested for murder, forcible rape, robbery and assault than black juveniles. Even so, three hundred more blacks than whites were tried as adults. In 1991 more than 70 percent of young males arrested were white, 25 percent were black. Yet a strange thing has happened between arrest and trial: only 35 percent of whites were held in custody while 44 percent of the blacks were held. Racism? Of course not; more like an outgrowth from a durable and time-resistant bedrock of stereotypes.

While Robert makes greater use of statistics about the criminal justice system than most of the prisoners I spoke with, his general argument was a refrain that ran through my interviews with many inmates. Robert's ability to develop an explanation for his incarceration that extends beyond his own moral culpability is one of the things that has helped him to cope with his isolation from family and community.

Sticky Stigma

If Louisa is bearing the brunt of the moral burden for her husband's incarceration, the literature on stigma and shame give some indication as to why this is so.[7] First, stigma is, in many respects, "sticky"—associated not only with those who offend a social norm but also with those associated with them.[8] As the sociologist Erving Goffman has noted, stigma travels through relationships, tainting those associated with the stigmatized.[9] The implications for families of prisoners is clear: the stigma of criminality associated with incarceration marks them as well as the person incarcerated. One family member described what he considered to be the biggest misconception about families of prisoners:

"basically . . . that if there's one criminal, there's another, and another . . . a consistency within every family."

A second reason is that stigma is experienced in relation to the judgment or perceived judgment of a social group.[10] So, whereas Robert lives among other offenders, Louisa remains in the community and is subject to the attendant social pressures that apply there. While many offenders may experience stigma related to their incarceration, unless their offense is considered particularly disgraceful by their co-offenders (as in cases of child sexual assault) their experience will be mitigated by the tacit acceptance of their peers, at least while they are incarcerated.* This, as research across disciplines has shown, increases the self-esteem and functioning of those who bear stigma.[11]

Family members, on the other hand, live and work outside the prison setting and are exposed to the judgment of their neighbors, churchgoers, co-workers, supervisors, employers, and other community members. As a result, female members of nearly every family that I spoke with have experienced shaming and humiliation related to the incarceration of a loved one.

The women I spoke with recounted many specific instances in which they felt that they were looked down on by another person because of their family member's incarceration and countless instances where they worried about disclosure. Those who had a positive experience of acceptance and sympathy after disclosing the status of their loved one to a close friend or family member were able to cope better. Significantly, however, even these family members attempted to manage who knew and who did not. None had "come out" completely in their extended families and at church and work. For those women who are willing to reach out, increasing the number of people who know is not a "solution" to their problem but a mixed bag of psychological benefits and burdens, increasing the pool of confidants with whom they

* Of course, once they leave prison, the stigma of criminality is significant unless they associate with other ex-offenders, creating an incentive for them not to associate with "straight" society. But among the released prisoners whom I spoke with, their inability to earn a decent living and support a family was far more shameful than their criminality. So, the stigma of criminality leads to the shame of being unable to support one's children, to help one's mother, and so forth.

can remain unguarded but also decreasing the control they have over damaging information about themselves.

Female relatives of prisoners also bear a significant burden as a result of gender differences in their reactions to stigma.[12] While men and women can experience shame in many ways, and gender differences do not hold true in every case, there are gender patterns that are well documented in the clinical literature. Generally speaking, women are more likely to "attribute their success to others and to blame themselves for failure" and, when they do blame themselves for failure, "are more likely to make global attributions of failure than males."[13] As a consequence, they are more likely to experience shame than are males.[14] When women do experience shame, the most common sequelae are depression and withdrawal;[15] when males experience shame, they are more likely to respond by deflecting blame, by becoming angry, or by threatening violent action.[16] As a result, women relatives of prisoners, like Louisa, often internalize the brunt of the expressive function of punishment.

These normal variations in reactions to shaming also help to explain some of the unanticipated effects of incarceration, most notably, the sometimes defiant reaction of men to their sentences as well as the relative silence of their family members (particularly women), who often bear the bulk of incarceration's burdens.

Chapter 13   Problems at Home: Constance & Jonathan

Jonathan and Constance Smith have been married twenty years. They have six sons and live in a small house in a working-class section of Anacostia, in Southeast Washington. Anacostia is often described in general and unflattering terms.* Anyone who has spent time in Anacostia, however, knows that it is made up of many smaller neighborhoods that vary, often dramatically, from block to block. The Smiths' house is located in a residential section of one of the major thoroughfares in Southeast. The neighborhood resembles—at least the dozen or so houses that surround the Smiths—one of the small suburbs outside of the District: small houses on small plots surrounded by shrubs and trees on carefully manicured lawns. It is by no means a wealthy block, or even comfortably middle class, but neither does it fit the stereotype of urban blight that many people would connect with the level of incarceration found there.

---

* The local *Washington City Paper* recently took the *Washington Post* to task for their over-the-top characterizations of Southeast D.C.:

> [A recent story in the *Post*] described Ward Eight's main drag just as it is always imagined by those who never go there: bleak, depressed, and violent. Beneath subheads like "Death and the Avenue," the story had all the requisite Ward Eight touchstones: teddy-bear murder memorials, idle men, and empty storefronts. Reporter John Fountain wrote: "[MLK Avenue] is public housing, boarded abandoned buildings, winos and drug addicts who linger from dawn to dusk. . . . Bulletproof partitions in small corner convenience stores and carry outs. Iron bars on schools and houses of God. Sirens blaring. Poverty. Conspicuous young men on corners." The ward was described as a place where "poverty and peril sometimes gush like rainwater down a gutter."

Stephanie Mencimer, *When Hell Freezes Over*, WASHINGTON CITY PAPER, November 5–11, 1999.

Jonathan and Constance are both regular churchgoers and express the earnest aspirations of upward mobility that their house symbolizes, aspirations they managed to attain in steady, careful steps. The obligations they meet are not small. Constance works as a data processor, then works the "second shift" as homemaker,[1] shopping, preparing meals, and caring for the children. Jonathan works long hours as a bus driver for the city, is president of the PTA at the local high school, and devotes a good deal of time and effort to promoting education in their church and community.*

Theirs is a family with what are often described as "working-class values" and aspirations, values not generally associated with the inner city.[2] They both work at stable jobs that allow them to own a small house with a mortgage and two cars (even if the cars are old enough to be a bit unreliable). While the jobs are just enough to get by on, they provide the security and a sense of comfort that many families strive for. They are not wealthy, but they can provide a decent home and take a vacation once a year. They attend church often, usually more than twice a week, and are at every school function throughout the year. They are the type of family most communities hope to have, and they are conscious and proud of their reputation as such.

Like many parents, when their eighteen-year-old son Jackson was hanging around the house, they pressed him to go out and get a job. Instead, he moved out, staying at a series of friends' apartments. Constance knew he didn't have his own apartment, so she would drive around the neighborhoods where she thought he might be. One Saturday night, it was just starting to rain when she saw him. She stopped and picked him up and brought him back home. They went to church together the next morning, but again he insisted on leaving. As Constance explains,

> You know, I had to really come to grips with myself in reference to that he was eighteen. I had to let him go because, by law, I couldn't really

* Jonathan organized a number of educational outings for the school and encouraged his son to enter the Street Law program offered through the Georgetown Law Center, hoping his son might become a lawyer.

hold him, you know, so I brought him back home, and I said, "Well, I won't take you there, but I will pray with you and ask you to keep in touch with me, you know, when you do leave here. At least call me and let me know that you're okay."

So, you know, he left, and when he left, I mean, it was bad. I cried for hours when he left here. You know, I was frustrated. I actually felt like I wanted to run away from home myself, because I felt like my child is going in the street and he's not ready, you know. He doesn't have a job. He doesn't have a place of his own.

She and Jonathan now feel that if they had not pushed him, he would not have felt the need to leave. But having an adult child sit around the house did not suit their conception of responsibility either. At the time they felt bad about pushing him to do something with his life, but they also knew that he was not fitting into the life they had envisioned for him.

Jackson did not find work and was living off the goodwill of friends. As he described it, he felt he needed to do something to make some money and get an apartment. "It's just embarrassing to have no money and like that. When you're hungry you're mooching off people. Pretty soon you're not welcome. People start telling you, 'Hey, remember that money I gave you?' and asking you, 'When you gonna get some money?'"

Jackson borrowed a gun from a friend and held up a woman outside a convenience store. He was bewildered after he did it and wandered around for a while in a daze. He realized he was hungry and went into a store to buy a soda and some chips and was arrested almost immediately. He was one block from where he had held up the woman less than a half hour previously. His arrest was a shock to his family. As his father related,

That was a crushing blow. . . . It was horrifying, you know, to get that call from him that I didn't want to get, because I knew, I kind of knew, you know, when a kid, when they're not ready to go, but when they go out on their own, it was, like . . . he wasn't on his own, but he was out there, you know, just, I felt bad as a dad that my son had to call me and tell me that he was locked up.

Both Jonathan and Constance were devastated by Jackson's arrest. They felt that they had failed as parents and that their son's incarceration placed their family in a poor light. Where before they had been a proud, upwardly mobile family, they felt like all their hard work and careful parenting were now in question. As Constance described it:

> Regardless of what you feel like you've done for your kid, it still comes back on you, and you feel like, "Well maybe I did something wrong. Maybe I messed up. You know, maybe if I had a did it this way, then it wouldn't a happened that way."

Shame is the flip side of parental pride. Acutely alert to public perceptions that families—and parents in particular—are at least in part to blame for the behavior of criminal offenders, many parents of prisoners, even the elderly parents of adult prisoners, were quick to tell me that they "didn't raise him that way" and that they were not sure what went wrong.

With Jackson's incarceration, Constance and Jonathan felt the unflattering and omnipresent stereotypes of criminals in a new way—the daily barrage of crime and justice in the news and popular culture became a constant reminder of the stigma they themselves felt. As Jonathan noted, "Until your son, or daughter, or somebody that is close to you goes into the court system, it's another world. It's not another TV program that you can pick up a remote and just cut it off."

Constance and Jonathan could not face friends or relatives and kept to themselves. The retreat from social interactions was difficult for both. Jonathan struggled with alcoholism, a problem he associated with his desire to, as he put it, "bottle up" his problems.

> I think that for people who don't open up and talk sometime, those are the people that, in turn, end up with issues, personal issues, of their own. They may end up drinking, getting into drugs theirselves. . . . I want me a Singapore Sling right now! Because I know that that's gonna take the edge off.

Constance had struggled with depression for years and was nervous about relapsing, particularly as she felt that her family needed her more than ever. As a result of her past experience, Constance was, more than most of the family members I spoke with, alert to the precursors and symptoms of depression. Knowing what they are and escaping them, however, are not one and the same.

> I know what depression can do to you if you don't seek help right away, and I try to, you know, monitor myself and try and make sure that I'm not getting too out of touch with me as to where I don't realize that I'm not well, so to speak. Because a lot of times you feel like you can handle more than you can, you don't realize that you're at that breaking point until you break, and I broke before.

Soon after Jackson's incarceration Constance began feeling the old haunting low of depression during the day, while feeling sleepless and anxiety ridden at night. She and Jonathan began fighting, and one of their younger sons began having problems at school. As Jonathan described it, the entire family was upset about Jackson, but they were unsure about what they could do.

> We're tense and we argue whatever is going on. Initially, we will argue about him, you know, when we first, the pattern first started, you know, it would be a argument between me and [Jackson] about [Jackson]. Then it got to the point where when after Jackson got locked up, then with [his younger brother Jarod] starting up, it got to be an argument with me and [Jarod] about [Jarod].

Particularly hard for Jonathan was the almost immediate change in attitude and behavior he saw in Jarod, his next-oldest son. Jarod, previously a model student and the most well behaved of their sons, began having problems after Jackson's arrest. "They were like twins," Jonathan says, clasping his hands together. "He would always follow Jackson. They were always really close. You know, people would get them mixed up when they were growing up. He looked up to his big brother, right? When his brother got in trouble, his behavior went like this," said Jonathan, making a steep downward motion with his hands. "We started noticing trouble signs in him."

The children, especially Jarod, did not want to talk about Jackson's incarceration with their parents either and hated visiting him in jail. They stopped inviting friends over to the house, and their parents increasingly discouraged them from going out in order to avoid their getting mixed up with "the wrong kind of kids." They effectively isolated themselves from the rest of the world.

Jonathan and Constance no longer had to worry about discussing Jackson with nonfamily members because they had stopped socializing. Jonathan relates their reluctance to reach out to other people to a concern about perceptions of their family after Jackson's incarceration:

> Because if you see a child on the street and they're unkempt or whatever, the first thing I know that I see is, "Why did the mother let that child come of the house looking like that?" You know? I mean, you know, a lot of times even though it could be people that know you, but they may not know you very well, and they might not know how you are as far as the way you raise your family. They might think that maybe you did something wrong in why your child got in trouble and whatnot. So, you know, it, it made me feel like that.

It was not simply that Jackson had done wrong but that his criminality had cast an unflattering light on the entire family. As the father figure, Jonathan felt responsible for his child, even though his son was legally an adult. In this regard, incarceration can bring a sense of stigma that is related to a whole network of associations surrounding responsibility and respectability in the working-class neighborhoods of the District. While theirs is not the kind of family that is obsessed with their status in the neighborhood, they had always felt like good members of the community. They weren't rich, but they had the right values and worked hard—this simply wasn't something they could explain. For families like the Smiths that have worked hard toward their aspirations, and especially for families that have attained some measure of their goals, the incarceration of a close family member is a powerful secret.

The feeling is particularly intense when families both are close to poverty and hold a tenuous grip on middle-class status. The threat of downward mobility for these families is ever present. Living in the District, one need only walk a few streets south of the Smiths' house to witness what life could be like. Most parents ask themselves whether they are doing the right thing for their children. Families like Jonathan and Constance's are forced to ask themselves whether, despite having a son who is incarcerated, they are still good parents and good people. Whether they are able to convince others of that is not something they ever thought was open to question. They work hard, provide what they can, and hope it is enough. The weight of criminal stigma falls heavily on these families because the presumption inherent in the stereotype is that for them—a low-income black family in Southeast Washington, D.C.–criminality is not an aberration.

Stigma and Race

Jonathan and Constance's story touches on the complicated and often covert role that racial concerns play in the lives of the families of prisoners. Many ethnographers, Elijah Anderson most prominently in recent years, have noted the distinctions that individuals in the inner city make between licit and illicit behavior and norms. But just as most family, friends, and neighbors are capable of identifying and employing street slang and standard English in varying degrees, they are also constantly evaluating the qualities of the individuals and families around them. Thus, while most families in the poorest neighborhoods of the city are capable of switching between "decent" and "street" or "ghetto" modes of expression with alacrity, changing the quality of the identity that others assign them is far more difficult and happens far less quickly. Damaging information, these families know, will stick to them indefinitely.

Adults and children distinguishing their own families from other families often made moral distinctions, arguing that there was something that set them apart—or at least that should set them apart—from other families living in impoverished neighborhoods. While occasionally a family would be described as "ghetto," more often participants would describe their own family as distinct from "those families." When I asked people to fill in the unspoken part of that sentence—what distinguishes "those families" from their own—the answer was fairly consistent: "You know, always in trouble, kids running around wild, people drinking and drugging." When I asked people to describe the stereotype of the ghetto family, race was always a factor. And without exception family members, when asked about race and stereotypes, said that incarceration was part of the stereotype of the black family that they wanted to avoid.

Many black participants described in excruciating detail the daily reminders of being thought of as suspect or, worse, relating race to a host of negative experiences. Things that whites rarely notice–the smile that cashiers give them but withhold from black customers, store security who trail black customers, the differing tones used by store clerks when asking whether a white or black customer needs any help–are readily apparent to blacks in their everyday life. While numerous studies have demonstrated racial bias in the criminal justice system, there has not been corresponding attention to the ways mass incarceration has come to define blacks in the eyes of many white Americans–and, perhaps more importantly, the way blacks view themselves. Apparent throughout this study was the participants' keen awareness of how criminality shapes white and black Americans' conceptions of race.

While the link between racial stereotypes and mass incarceration may seem tenuous to some Americans, to the families in this study it was experienced as ever present, something they faced not only when shopping or trying to catch a cab but in the more personal spheres of church and work as well. For example, Ruth, whose younger brother is incarcerated, told me she would never discuss the matter with her co-workers or supervisor, something that she felt was linked to stereotypes about being black:

> You know, I talk to [my supervisor] about stuff, but not this. This was too much, and it definitely made, well, it was just harder to talk to him. He wants to know how my brother is. I just can't tell it to him. What does he know about prison?

When asked to explain why her white co-workers and supervisors would have trouble understanding her brother's incarceration, Ruth said it was not just incarceration but "everything." As an example, she described nights when she works late:

I tell my boss all the time, I say, "If you want me to take a taxi you go down there and flag one for me. I'm not going out there and stand twenty minutes for a cab when they'll run over me to get to you." . . . He's white and, see, he don't know the difference because he's from Seattle, Washington. He looks at me real strange, like, "What are you talking about?"

Given the "sticky" nature of stigma and the abundance of stereotypes about black families, Ruth wonders how her supervisor could possibly understand her brother's incarceration when he cannot even understand her difficulty with catching a cab. "His picture would be all wrong. He would just think . . . I don't know, but it wouldn't be good."

For many Americans, particularly white Americans, acknowledging race at all is seen as dangerous in almost any context—better to just ignore race altogether.[3] In this regard, many white Americans see incarceration in terms that are race neutral: if someone gets locked up, it is because they did something bad and broke the law. The logical corollary—that black people are bad more often than white people—is less neutral, however.

Many family members also pointed out that the stereotypes not only exist in white communities segregated from majority black neighborhoods but pervade African-American communities and culture as well and are as close as the next-door neighbor. "Blacks feel the same way about blacks," one aunt said, pointing up the street. "And right in this block here, the lady across the street over there, she does not particularly like any black folks, or many, in this neighborhood. She downgrades them. . . . and there are black people that will tell you they don't want to move where blacks are."

Arthur's mother saw race as a significant factor in keeping family members of prisoners from talking to one another. "People of color, they're so, number one, they're embarrassed. They don't want nobody to know that their family is incarcerated." The reason, she said, was obvious: "Well, if I would say my son is incarcerated, they would picture him as a killer, a cutthroat, a murderer, vicious. They would have come to that conclusion, number one, because I'm black. That's the first reason why they would come to it; they wouldn't even come to it if I was a white woman saying it." For her, the issue went beyond racial stereotyping by others to a deeper problem of racial self-disrespect that she sees affecting the ability of relatives of prisoners to speak openly about incarceration:

> All your life you been taught that you're not a worthy person, or something is wrong with you. So you don't have no respect for yourself. See, people of color have—not all of them, but a lot of them—have poor self-esteem, because we've been branded. We hate ourselves, you know. We have been programmed that it's something that's wrong with us. We hate ourselves.

Even in her nearly all-black neighborhood, she worried about what the neighbors would think: "It's hard, because, like I say, you understand and I understand, we've been labeled all our lives that we are the bad people."

The stigma and social isolation that these families face are bound tightly with the racial and class stereotypes of criminality, making the intersection of race and incarceration doubly devastating. Not only does being black mean that a person stands a greater chance of being detained, arrested, convicted, and the recipient of a longer sentence, as studies have demonstrated,[4] but when being black is combined with criminality, it means losing a fair measure of whatever social solidarity and support one's community might provide. In fact, survey data suggest that blacks, like most Americans, do not support many of the rights that protect criminal suspects. Few, for example, support the exclusion of evidence illegally obtained.[5] Since 1987, 80 percent of black respondents to the General Social Survey have felt that the courts are not harsh enough with offenders.[6]

Stigma, race, and incarceration are thus related in more subtle ways than common discussions of racial bias in the criminal justice system would suggest. The very problems that incarceration exacerbates—from diminished income to undesired single parenting—are deeply embedded in stereotypes of black families in America. These racially constitutive aspects of our criminal sanctions, the extent to which our criminal justice system continues to create the social construct of race and to reinforce our understanding of it, are linked to the stigmatization of black Americans in general. As families of prisoners confront incarceration, they also confront a widespread set of assumptions about their loved ones and about themselves, not only in the eyes of society at large but also in the communities where they live. For African Americans, the stigma of familial criminality is colored with racial and class overtones that make it particularly powerful.

The literature on what is called "stereotype threat" paints a disturbing picture of the consequences of stigma in hard numbers. Through a remarkable series of experiments, researchers have shown that, when members of a stigmatized group feel that their disputed ability is being measured, they perform poorly. Black students who normally test as well as white students, for example, show marked declines in test scores when they are told that the test is measuring their intelligence. They also test poorly when aware of another black student looking stereotypically "ghetto," something that they feel bleeds over into how others perceive them. And when they are in these situations, black students who are asked about their recreational preferences eschew stereotypically "black" responses like basketball and hip-hop.

Although domains such as the job site present situations that are less easily controlled and measured, it is not hard to see how these findings could be extrapolated to the work environment. As the next chapter describes, for many black Americans the workplace is an environment in which they regularly confront tests of their abilities and supervision by whites. But even where they supervise others or have black co-workers, the threat of being caught out as "criminal" or "ghetto" is ever present.[7]

Chapter 14 Work Worries: Tina & Dante

Tina is raising her two daughters and two of her nieces after their mother was diagnosed with schizophrenia. She rents a small row house that's part of a suburban public housing project just outside of the District. She is acutely aware of the value of education, and her children are all good students. She moved her family out of the District six years ago for her children's education. The housing project that she lives in is a small part of what is an otherwise fairly wealthy district, so the school her kids go to has excellent resources.[1] Although she works full-time in a furniture shop, selling upscale items she herself cannot afford, she is enrolled in a master's degree program in child development and hopes to use it to get a better job in education or public policy.

Tina's husband, Dante, was first arrested and charged for involvement in a drug-related shooting. Although he maintains his innocence, he refused to give evidence against the person he claims is responsible, and he received an eight-year sentence. Once incarcerated, he became politically active and was involved in a number of protests, two of which turned into prison riots, earning him considerable additional time. His case is currently being appealed, and his family and his pro bono attorney are hopeful that his original sentence will be overturned. If that does happen, the subsequent offenses will also be voided because they will have occurred as a result of a wrongful incarceration.

Despite his claim of wrongful imprisonment, Dante is philosophical about his incarceration. As he describes it, while he was not guilty of murder, he did commit many crimes. Prison allowed him to discover God through his Muslim faith and to join a community of serious and thoughtful men devoted to family, community, and justice. He believes his experience has made him a better person, father, and friend. Indeed, he sees the difficulties he has had since his incarceration as entirely distinct from his earlier criminal life, related instead to his political activism and the protests that he led while incarcerated. This perspective helps him to cope with his incarceration, and he is a strikingly confident person, despite his loss of autonomy.

Tina also appears confident. She speaks quickly and with self-assurance, and at first her manner suggests an optimism that is indefatigable. Her husband's incarceration for the last ten years, however, has taken its toll. Tina is proud of Dante, valuing him as a partner and a good parent to her children. In part because of her pride in him, she did not tell any of her friends at work about his incarceration. When he was first incarcerated, she was new at her government job and feared risking her security clearance. "I was at the Pentagon, so, of course, I didn't want them to know my business. So I would just always say he was in the military." Office conversation, however, is such that personal business is hard to protect.[2]

> Even though they didn't know he was in prison, they could tell the weekends that I'd seen him. It was hardest at the beginning of the week, 'cause I'd have seen him [at the prison and would be missing him]. So my friends want to know, "Well, when are you gonna see him?" You have to lie about why you're having a bad day. So they're like, "Why are you crying?" And I gotta lie.

At work, where people knew she was married but did not know that her husband had been incarcerated, her sense of loss was particularly acute. But added to it was also a sense of the stigma that her husband's status might carry. Many women described withdrawing from the casual friendships they made at work, always steering conversation in another direction when discussion of their husband, son, or brother came up. But this could be extremely difficult. One woman described how what under different circumstances would be welcome friendships were instead threatening and frustrating:

> See, I'm distorting the whole picture for them. And then I ran into a co-worker on the subway. "Oh! Where's your husband? How is he?" I

said, "You're always asking me about my husband. Why? Are you interested in my husband?" You know I have to evade that. Oh, and always guys ask me, "Why don't you and your husband come in to this restaurant? It's a nice restaurant." "Oh yeah. I'll tell him about it. We'll check it out." Lying.

The lies became difficult to maintain not only because they became more complex but because the stress of lying itself takes a toll. While hard to measure, this experience has clearly had an effect on Tina. The extent to which she feels hidden and withdrawn extends from friends and neighbors to her work and career.

Losing a Source of Support

While many people find that work is an important source of support in difficult times (in one recent survey, more people cited work as an important source of support than church or family),[3] the opposite is often true for family members of prisoners. Whereas other people at the workplace socialize together and include discussions of family in their day, many families of prisoners develop strategies to avoid any discussion of personal life, as it can lead to uncomfortable questions. What is for others in the workplace a significant strategy for coping with life's travails is turned on its head for Tina, who described her workplace experience as a daily test of evasion and boundary guarding, having the greatest difficulty with people when they are sociable and friendly.

Tina left that job at the Pentagon, she says, in large part because she could not handle the stress that came with maintaining the elaborate pattern of lies she used as cover. Her next job, working in an automotive services company, did not start out well either. After about a month on the job, she was promoted from sales to be trained as a manager. Just about the same time, she got some bad news:

One of my girlfriends called me at work. I'll never forget. She said, "You get the paper?" I said, "I'm at work. They always get the paper. I mean I'm at work, busy. I'm running the place. I'm, you know, manager trainee." She said, "Dante's in the paper–picture is on the front page. It was a riot down Lorton." I went in the bathroom. I sat in there for a long time. And I was reading it and crying.

She was able to collect herself and make it through the rest of the day, but she realized that she would not be able to handle coming in the next day to her job, knowing that her husband had been through a riot and trying to hide it from everyone. "I had not let anybody know my circumstances or my situation. And how could I go to them and say, 'Oh, my husband's locked up'?" Given that his picture was in the paper, she could only imagine their reaction: they might "say they're sorry, [but they'd] be looking at me like, 'Are you crazy? Why are you even with this psycho?'"

It is normal for employees to blur the boundaries of professional and personal life in the contemporary workplace.[4] The care taken to manage information about familial incarceration and the personal anxiety experienced doing so is, in this regard, related to the importance of the social aspects of the work environment in contemporary society.[5] Because the social setting of the workplace defines significant aspects of who people are and how they feel about themselves,[6] people's private lives are becoming integrated into the work setting–an integration that families of prisoners often view with great trepidation.

Life & Career on Hold

After a day off, Tina returned to work, but her husband's situation exacerbated a host of other job stresses that she struggled with every day. As she described it, she was "in a haze":

> It's hard being under that type of stress and you can't tell nobody at work. See, I hadn't been on the job long enough to feel secure or comfortable enough with anybody. I was their manager trainee at the company. I never even went far as managing at the job.
>
> And when I first got there it was really hard, because I was, like, one of the first women at this company. And what made it so bad [was that]

the guys laughed about it. They bet a wager that I wouldn't make it. Because, first of all, everything you do you have to do on the computer, [and] I was totally computer illiterate, okay, so I'm fighting with the computer. And certain days that you have lines all the way out the door of people. Being new on the job and then going through this, I'm not keeping my mind focused on what's going on, because at this moment I feel like crying. People yelling at me. Then I'm thinking about I ain't seen [Dante] in weeks. It just was a mess. So you know I'd get there okay. But I'd get there and by midday I was ready to just crack. And this job was, like, some days you had to work thirteen hours.

For many family members, the topic of familial incarceration can be particularly difficult to manage at work. The work environment is one in which most people attempt to present a positive identity and in which stigmatizing information is especially fraught. Many family members wondered aloud to me about what a co-worker would do with the knowledge that their husband or son is incarcerated. And, having worked long and hard to overcome the barriers to employment and promotion, they are understandably cautious.

Most are attempting to live and be perceived as part of the modern upwardly mobile middle class, even if their income does not place them in it. They are all too aware of the historically intransigent caricatures of criminal, dysfunctional families that lie behind many public discussions about our inner cities. Because of this, the stakes are high in terms of both perceived social identity and practical career aspirations. For Tina, the only solution to managing information about her husband was to leave for another job where no one knew she had a husband:

> You know, one lie becomes too many lies. I actually, I think I actually left that job because of the lies. Because I'm not that person. I'm, I'm straight up. My sister always say, "You tell too much," because I just can't do no whole bunch of lies, I can't even do it. So one lie leads to another lie, and I think I really left the job to start up fresh.

By starting in a new job, she was able to conceal that she was married and to actively avoid making friends with anyone at work. In this way, she thought she would not have to constantly reject or mislead the casual friends she made at work—something she had to do at her previous job. But that, too, had its problems. "You know, for the longest time I wouldn't even keep his picture up around here [her home], because someone would stop by and it's just obvious it's a prison picture."

As work becomes a larger part of American life, both in hours spent there and in the strength of social relationships that people develop there,[7] the experience of workplace stress and anxiety is a common one, and most people can relate to feeling insecure about how they are perceived on the job, both by co-workers and by supervisors. Most Americans take care to fit in where they work and to present themselves well—after all, a considerable amount in both material and social terms is on the line. For employees who are new, who are seeking promotion, or who feel insecure about their financial status, the desire to maintain a positive image at work can cause significant anxiety.

As each generation of Americans spends more time at work, there has also been a general trend toward integrating personal and professional lives. Colleagues are expected to seek social activities with one another[8] and to include family and home life in their daily discussions.[9] As one woman whose brother is incarcerated described it, for many Americans work is like a "second family." This daily mixing of personal and work-related discussions is an essential part of many workplaces and is particularly important to career success. Friendships and personal talk at work grease the wheels of workday interaction for most employees.[10] For families of prisoners, however, such discussions are a minefield filled with the potential for exposure.

Tina, like many of the women I spoke with, felt that her career was "put on hold" during her partner's incarceration. In our interviews, she describes crying often, a growing sense of isolation, and a recurrent sense of hopelessness. She feels terrible about her depression, which she believes has a negative impact on her children. It is, sadly, the awareness of her depression that brings a greater sense of guilt and lowers her sense of self-esteem. While there are times when she is able to feel almost normal, for her this means putting her husband out of her mind—not something she wants to do. She wants to adjust to the degree that she can, but she cannot really get over the idea that her family is not intact. For her, all their plans and hopes, including her job, are at a standstill.

> Our life is on hold. That's what I feel like. And being as though our life is on hold, I really can't spread my horizons without my husband. I accepted his wrongdoing, because I just wanted our family to rejoin and reunite. And all I ever do, Don, is hope that it's over. All I can do is hope and dream. When is it going to manifest? When is it going to materialize? They just gave him another hit [denial of parole]. What if they keep him for the duration of his time? What does that leave me as a wife?

Committed relationships require both partners to make sacrifices for each other. Husbands and wives often put a career move on hold for a while so that they can have a child, so that one or the other can finish a degree, or because a family member becomes ill. For many partners of prisoners, however, incarceration can be a repeated cycle of waiting for release, stretching their commitment to the limit.

Chapter 15 Depression and Isolation: Robin & Aaron

Robin, who is thirty-four and has two daughters and a son, married her husband, Aaron, while he was incarcerated. He has a mandatory release date in four years and will come up for parole once before then. They met in elementary school, but their families knew each other before that. After she finished high school and got a job, she found out that Aaron was incarcerated through a friend who, while visiting an incarcerated relative, saw Aaron's mother. At first Robin was hesitant to start up a relationship with a man in prison. She went to visit him a few times but was really just thinking of him as a friend.

> At that time, I'm like, "I really don't have the energy to put into this. This is a relationship that's very complicated because you're there and I'm here, and any relationship is complicated regardless, but I really don't have the energy to get involved with someone in prison. It's just not for me. I need something that's permanent." At that point, I was feeling like I wanted something that's permanent, you know? At that time, it could have been with anybody that I cared enough for, or they cared enough for me both ways. So I was, like, "I just, you know, and I don't know if I can handle a relationship of this magnitude because, again, you're not here." Even if it would have been just six months, that's a long time not to have someone to lay beside you or walk down the street with you, or things that we take for granted every day.

Eventually, though, she became closer with Aaron, and they developed a relationship that was close to what she had been looking for. While Robin had been secretive about his status, as she put it, "to the extreme," she had been able to confide in her sister, a daily source of sympathy and support. After four years of "dating" she was surprised when Aaron proposed. After talking things over with her sister, she decided to accept his proposal.

After they were married, Robin visited Aaron several times a week while he was located at Central Facility in Lorton, Virginia, half an hour's drive from D.C. After four years, however, Aaron was moved to a private facility in New Mexico and was locked down for reclassification.* Her sister's death soon after her husband's relocation was doubly devastating.

> They wouldn't let me see him to explain to him the situation about my sister. So I had to tell him over the phone. You know, he was really torn up at that point because he couldn't be there for me in no shape, form, or fashion because he was still in lockdown. So, he could barely even call.
>
> We didn't see each other for a whole year. And, you know, we had never been really separated since we had been together. And this was like almost four years of being together. And it was terrible. It was really terrible. And I stayed . . . I stayed down. I never stopped praying the whole time, but I stayed down a lot. You know, grieving for my sister and just, you know, for my friend that I had lost. It was just too much going on for me at that time for me to function like I should function.

Robin's case illustrates a problem that many women face, particularly when the person they are most intimate with is relocated out of state: the loss of companionship is added to the erosion of social supports, further isolation, and an increased likelihood of depression.

When Aaron was moved to New Mexico, Robin's income from informal child-care work barely paid the bills, making visitation nearly impossible. What money she made went to supporting her children and

---

* When an inmate is transferred to a new facility, it can take weeks or even months for the prison administration at the new facility to determine at what level of security to classify the new inmate. Facilities also have to assess any separation requirements. If two inmates have a history of violence and antagonism, then they should not be housed on the same cell block or allowed to come into contact with one another.

meeting basic necessities; traveling long distances was out of the question. She simply would not be able to see her husband. Alone and devastated, Robin just couldn't face life.

> It was starting to show in my kids. And they were like . . . you know, my daughter would lay her face on me and cry because I wouldn't get out the bed. "Oh, Mommy, please get up. Please get up. Please get up." You know, beg me to get up. And I couldn't . . . couldn't bring myself to get out of the bed. And my depression would just take over, you know. And I would pray, "God, please let me get up to be a mother to my kids," because I couldn't find the strength on my own, even when I tried it. I did get up, [but] I was still wandering to like this state of just zombie. You know, I was like a zombie.

The death of Robin's sister also illustrates how important social support can be: without her sister to talk to every day, Robin felt not only the loss of her sister and husband but also the effects of being left alone to cope. Her sister and she were close, in part, because her sister had been the only person in her family who was supportive of her relationship with Aaron. With her sister gone, she had lost a friend and ally. And, while depression after a death in the family is not unusual, Robin's struggle with depression was compounded by her sense of failure as a parent, Aaron's absence, and her lack of social supports.

A Vicious Cycle

Nearly without exception, the women I spoke with who were closest to a prisoner had experienced depression and related their depression, at least in part, to the incarceration of their loved one.[1] As previous chapters have described, family members often bear increased practical and material burdens as well, and these burdens often contribute to depression.[2] The clinical literature supports the fear that Robin and other parents share: that their children are likely to be negatively affected by their depression and withdrawal. A recent study, for example, estimated that children with parents who experience depression are eight times as likely to experience a childhood-onset major depressive disorder themselves and are at significantly increased risk of experiencing a number of other psychiatric disorders.*

Louisa, Tina, and Robin each described serious bouts with depression. After it became clear that Robert would be in prison for at least two years, Louisa described herself as often overwhelmed and depressed. She said she viewed the outside world as oppressive and wearing:

> It's stressful. You go through periods of depression. You go through periods of feeling alone. You cry a lot. You get depressed. You get dispirited. I cry a lot. A whole lot. Especially at night. And sometimes even during the day and on the weekend, I get this blue feeling that comes over me on the weekend, because me and my husband use to, you know, either go to the movie, or we use to do so much together. And we were so right, you know, we just so emotionally bonded and physically bonded that we would go sit down and play a game of Scrabble or play games together. You know, if we didn't have money to go out. It was just us—the family.

For Louisa and other relatives of prisoners, the loss of this sense of family is just as painful as the actual absence of their loved one. They have lost more than a person, they've lost a whole dream of what life could be.

For Tina and her family, depression hit home most acutely while she was working at the Pentagon, when her husband, Dante, was transferred to a private prison in Ohio, effectively ending their ability to see each other on a regular basis and dramatically increasing her phone bill.

> I went through it so bad when he went to Ohio, but I kept saying the whole time that I wasn't stressed, because I was still functioning. It seemed like everything because we all thought [his relocation] would be so temporary, so for the first couple of months you're doing okay. I mean, I struggled through school, because every week I was sick. And it's just. . . . Mentally, I was making myself sick.

---

* They are also five times as likely to develop an early-adult-onset major depressive disorder, five times as likely to develop a conduct disorder, and three times as likely to experience an anxiety disorder. Priya J. Wickramaratne and Myrna M. Weissman, *Onset of Psychopathology in Offspring by Developmental Phase and Parental Depression*, 37 J. AM. ACAD.CHILD & ADOLESC. PSYCHIATRY 9, 933–42 (1998).

During this time, Tina isolated herself at work and avoided discussing problems with her family. Alone, a single parent, a supportive long-distance spouse, an employee, and a student, she struggled to gain the level of control she normally maintained over her life but, for the first time, began to fail. She began to get sick frequently and developed migraines for the first time in her life. While she could force herself to do everything she felt she needed to do, the emotional strain began to have physical effects. "I started losing a lot of weight, and the doctor said why that was, I was having anxiety about our separation, because in our five years of being together, we had never been separated."*

> When he first went to Ohio, I started losing a lot of weight, so when I went up there to see him, he told me to pick up the phone. I picked up the phone. He said, "Look at you." He said, "I'm gonna tell you just like this," he said "As much as I love you and as much I want you in my life, this thing has taken a toll like the way I see you looking." He said, "I want you to walk out that door and don't come back in here. Get yourself another man, 'cause you're killing yourself." He said, "Look at you. You've lost weight, your eyes all sunk, you look terrible." . . . So I was, like, "I'm okay." He say, "You're not okay." You know? Because everybody else was telling me, "Look at you. You're losing so much weight, your face is so thin." And I'm, like, "I'm okay. I'm okay." That's what I keep telling myself.

Tina does not have the appearance or attitude of a weak or vulnerable person; she is determined and outgoing, careful to take care of herself and fight for what she wants. But there was simply no part of her life or her family that she felt she could sacrifice. For Tina, and for many women like her, struggling for her family was wearing her down, even if she was not going down without a fight. Even when women identify and want to work against depression, as was clearly the case with Tina, a combination of isolation and increased responsibilities can bring on stress in ways that are hard to manage.

---

* By "separated," Tina means that Dante had always been held in local facilities.

Chapter 16 Coping:
Murielle & Dale

Although many of the family members who were closest to prisoners struggled with stigma, isolation, and depression, most had also developed ways to cope. In many cases, however, their coping repertoires were limited, typically characterized by more avoidant strategies.[1] The most common coping strategies, for example, did not make use of extensive social networks or involve disclosing information about a prisoner's status. More often they were strategies that involved severing or diminishing relationships—with family, friends, or the incarcerated relative—or private strategies such as prayer.

Moving On

With all of the problems associated with maintaining a relationship with someone in prison, one might expect families to simply cut ties altogether. This was, among families in this study, surprisingly rare. While many family members did reduce contact with their incarcerated relative as time went by, they usually did not break ties entirely, and some actually increased their contact. Attending school or work was more difficult and friendships and family ties were often strained, but most of the people who were closest to the incarcerated family member from the outset did not cut their ties completely. Out of the fifty families in this study, in only two families did a relative who was closest to an offender completely cut ties after he was incarcerated, and when they did so, they moved to another state. This "starting over" method is one of the more radical coping strategies that a person might employ.

While few family members cut ties altogether, a more attenuated version of diminishing social relations with the incarcerated family member was common. Prison raises a number of impediments to maintaining close relationships. Murielle, for example, has been raising her two daughters on her own for some time. "Both fathers are incarcerated, both of their fathers. My oldest daughter's father has been incarcerated for the last sixteen years, and my youngest daughter's father has been incarcerated for the last thirteen."

Murielle was married to Dale, the father of her second daughter, for the first ten years of his incarceration.

> To be honest, I did not take and expose my daughter to that a lot, because I didn't want her to see the environment and I didn't want her to see her father incarcerated. What I'd learned to do with my first daughter when her father became incarcerated, I told her that he was away at school to make it a lot easier for her to accept, and if anybody asked her, you know, "Where is your dad?" "He's away at school." That pretty much worked for awhile, and then when the kids get older they become more inquisitive, and [they would ask] "Well, if he's at school, why can't he come home?" And the couple of times that I did take her down, she couldn't understand why. Both of them pretty much the same, the same attitude, and I guess it's the same with any kid. They want to know why they can't come. And when you get to that door and you have to say good-bye, they want to know why you can't get on the van or the bus. And they turn around with this look on their face. "Isn't he coming, Mom?" "No, he's not coming, he has to stay here."[2]

As Dale's wife, Murielle felt obliged to visit him; she divorced him, in part, because she didn't want her daughters to have to confront the criminality of their fathers so directly. For her, it was too much to manage both her own relationship with Dale and the threat of stigma for her daughters.

> Now that the marriage is over, believe it or not, Donald, when I called downtown last year to find out when the divorce became final, and the girl told me it was final on December 23, I took a deep breath and . . .

and it was almost as if a great burden had been lifted from my shoulders, because trying to be the wife of somebody incarcerated . . . it's like you are not just you, you are you and them, and you can't say, "That's not me. I'm somebody else."

As much as she was relieved to be divorced, she knew that she had really just made a transition into another kind of relationship with her daughters' fathers. She, like many ex-wives and ex-girlfriends of prisoners, still felt that it was important to keep her daughters' fathers involved in their lives. This was one of the most common sentiments expressed by women who had children by prisoners and one of the reasons many women stay involved with their ex-husbands and ex-boyfriends.

Murielle finds a middle ground that she and her daughters can manage, though it is not always easy and requires ongoing negotiations. She now pays for the collect calls from their fathers but has drawn the line at one call every two weeks.

From Sussex, Virginia, it costs you ten dollars for ten minutes, so it's a dollar a minute. So with Chriselle's father I had to put my foot down, and I told him that he couldn't call for awhile, because it became too expensive for me. And I told him, I said, "I understand that you want to talk to her, but you know, you're gonna have to find another way of doing it. Call Chriselle just to say hello and how-you-doing and then pick up the pen and write her. You know, she can write. She has very good penmanship. She's gonna have to start writing you, because it becomes so expensive, and the cost become so enormous that it takes away other things that you could be doing with your money." And that's what I told him. I said, "I'm not trying to be mean. I'm not trying to be the B-I-T-C-H in this, but I have to look out for my well-being and my children's well-being, because I'm the only source of income they have."

While Murielle has tried to maintain positive relationships with both of her daughters' paternal families, she still feels that the incarceration of her exes has limited her social world considerably, forcing her to guard against the stigma that attaches to criminality:

My friends for me are very limited. I don't have a lot of friends or associations at work, because too many people are in your business who
will turn it against you. . . . You've got a whole bunch of people that are
always trying to find out somebody's business, so I choose not to share
it, you know. And that's why I say, I have, like, few friends, period.

Many close relatives of prisoners, like Murielle, diminished their
social ties–both by avoiding friendships and by sharing less information within their friendships–for this reason. Although divorce has
made things easier for Murielle emotionally and financially, managing
the impact on her daughters is a difficult balancing act.

It's hardest, I think, around about the holidays. My youngest daughter
just celebrated her 10th birthday, and her father wrote her a letter, and
she read it, and she started crying. Holidays–Christmas and Thanks-
giving. I really see it now in Janise, you know. I used to see it in
Chriselle a lot. I don't see it in her that much anymore. But with
[Janise], I guess you can see the sensitivity in her, and she'll look at me,
and these big tears will be in her eyes, and she'll go, "Mom, I really
miss my daddy." I say, "I know you do." She'll say, "I wish he was
home." And I say, "He'll be home."

Many women are in the same predicament: they've moved on from
their former relationships but can't put them behind them entirely.

Claiming Innocence

Curtis and Liz, whose son John has been incarcerated now for over five
years, insist on his innocence. However, their insistence and that of the
other families that claimed innocence, is not something that has made
their lives any more peaceful. Liz gets right into the details of her son's
case, getting more and more worked up as she does. As she describes
her son's arrest, the trial, and the injustices she strongly believes have
been committed, her eyes get wider and her voice is raised. Curtis nods,
occasionally gesturing to remind her that she has left out a detail or that
he had something to say about an event when it happened. Finally her
frustration breaks.

So then you get in and you just talk to God. You cries out to God. And many a night, you know, I pull all my covers off my bed talking to Him. And, you know, "Why? Why me?" You know? Here I have raised seven children—seven! Five boys and two girls!—and then they grab my baby son. You know, I think lightning striking them is too good. Lightning striking them is actually too good for them, and I don't want nobody to die, because we all gonna die, but I just want them just to set down and think about "Would I want somebody to do this to me?" You know, that's what I want them to think about, but they don't think about that. . . . And my son ain't did nothing!

Liz strongly believes that her own stress and her husband's recent stroke and heart attack are related to her son's wrongful incarceration:

It was the trial that did it. I could see just looking over at my husband. We all cried, but he just got real quiet and looking sad. And he went back to work cleaning the church and school, and the minister did write a letter, but it wasn't a week before that stroke took him out. The stroke, his heart, my blood pressure. But I'm a keep fighting 'til I die for my boy and, God willing, I'll be alive when he come home. It just make me so angry.

While many prisoners and families claimed that a sentence was unfair or that the treatment of the incarcerated family member was inhumane, very few claimed innocence. From afar, asserting innocence might seem like an effective coping strategy—denying the premise of the charge and thereby undermining any potential attack on character or status—and a small number of women, most often mothers, did adopt this strategy. The relative infrequency of this approach was initially surprising, given the standard description of prisoner denials (as the character Red quipped in the movie *Shawshank Redemption,* "Everyone's innocent in here, don't you know that?"[3]). Why are family members so reluctant to make that claim?

There are a number of practical reasons why this might be so. First, family members quite often suspect or have knowledge of the criminal activity in which their relative was involved. With a large proportion of offenders convicted of drug-related crimes, many families consider incarceration a logical (if undesirable) result of a person's increasing drug use and the problems associated with it. Second, evidence presented at trial (where family members are often present) may undermine claims to innocence that offenders make.* For this reason, some offenders will ask their families not to attend a trial, even though their presence is (in most cases) considered to be helpful to the defendant during the trial and particularly during sentencing. Third, claiming innocence may actually add to the difficulties that the family faces.

Why would a claim of innocence make life *more* difficult? As with Liz and Curtis, there are a number of reasons why the few family members who did claim their relatives as innocent were more emotionally distressed about and involved in their loved ones' cases. The demand for

---

* There are also corollaries to this. One woman recounted to me how her daughter's father was arrested for raping a prostitute, possessing PCP, and a few other less serious charges.

> There was a carnival over at the stadium, and I think a lot of Chris's problems came from the fact that he was smoking drugs. I think at the time he was smoking angel dust or something . . . or lovely or something, or whatever they call it–PCP. He picked up a prostitute and took her over to the stadium, and they got caught by the park police, and the first thing that she said was the fact that he forced himself on her. So when the judge asked him did he accept the plea, because after talking to his mother and his sisters and brother, and then talking to me, he accepted. He said he would go ahead and accept the plea bargain. I'll never forget standing in front of [the judge], [the judge] asked him did he accept the plea bargain, and he said, "yes." He proceeded to explain to him an accepting of a plea bargain is an admission of guilt, and he said, "You have to show some. . . . Are you remorseful for the thing that you've done?" And Chris stumbled–I'll never forget that. He said, "I'm not sorry because I didn't do anything." And the judge said, "Well, then you can't accept this plea bargain."

Afterward, the attorney told her that Chris didn't want to let his family down. "And he looked at me, and he said, 'And especially you.'" Had his offense not been so shameful, Chris might have admitted guilt. But having his family present in the courtroom–a tactic his lawyer thought would help diminish the perception that the judge may have of Chris as a risk–backfired. Instead, the judge now saw him as unrepentant. He was sentenced to life with the possibility of parole after fourteen years.

practical action and intense emotional involvement that a claim to false conviction requires of family members makes claims to innocence very difficult. Those who feel their loved one is wrongly incarcerated tend to spend more time and energy working on behalf of their relative, a draining process, as anyone who has been involved with the criminal justice system well knows. Furthermore, working against a wrongful conviction continually highlights all of the issues that families feel about being categorized as criminal and the stereotypes that come with that label by placing them in direct contact with the criminal justice system itself.

Arthur's mother, Lilly, for example, told me that she was determined to fight against what she perceived to be the wrongful conviction of her son: "When that judge said, "twelve to thirty-six years," I told my son, I said, 'You'll be out in two years. We're gonna fight this.'" Her willingness to fight was directly related to her belief that her son's sentence was unjust: "Because I know that my family been railroaded. . . . People believe that everybody who incarcerated is guilty, which is not true, which is *not true!*" But her fighting the system has, she believes, made a mess of her life, straining her relations with other family members and aggravating her health problems.

Even when family members are willing to fight a conviction, their willingness to engage in the legal arena doesn't necessarily make them more likely to openly disclose their relative's status in other settings. As one woman related, she couldn't bring herself to talk to her doctor about her son's incarceration, even though she believed it was a major source of her hypertension.

I don't discuss with, you know, with nobody. No, [my doctor doesn't know] because I lied to her. She doesn't realize it. She just thinks that it's just my pressure is always up and stuff like that. No, I have not told her. I don't discuss this with anybody, because I'm not proud of it. You know. I mean even though I feel my son is innocent, and he is innocent as far as I'm concerned. I still . . . it's something that I don't want to discuss. I wouldn't discuss it with anybody. I don't want anybody to know anything like that.

While there may be many reasons for inmates to insist on their innocence, the benefits to family members are often outweighed by the
emotional toll that they bear as a result.

Reaching Out

While most family members had spoken to one or more people about
the difficulties related to incarceration, very few did so on a regular
basis. When they did reach out, it was often tentatively and with caution. Tina, for example, had been on the job at the automotive services
company for over a year before she told anyone at work. She and a co-
worker had become friendly through a mutual interest in religion. Tina
is a devout Christian, and her co-worker was studying to become a
minister. "So we use to always talk about spiritual things." Eventually,
she felt that he was trustworthy enough to tell him about her husband.
It took her all morning to work up to it:

> And he was married and a minister. . . . He said that he was scared all
> day long. He said, [here Tina pretends to be her friend, talking to him-
> self in a nervous manner] "Okay. We'll just go out to dinner and we'll
> just talk about it then. . . . Please don't let her be telling me that she's
> attracted to me." And we just sat there and cracked up. We had tears in
> our eyes. He said, "But I don't know, this might be even worse." He
> said, "So how are you doing with this? Because we always used to bet
> about . . . you know, everybody noticed that you wouldn't [flirt] with
> nobody, but we knew you wasn't gay. But we didn't know really what
> your story was." And I said, "Well don't tell the rest of them, because I
> really don't want them—everybody on the job—knowing."[4]

In the years since then, Tina has told a few more friends, but she is
still cautious and hides her husband's status at work. Tina is among the
most outgoing, forthright, and politically active family members I met,
so her caution is instructive. She feels that she has changed enough
over the course of her husband's incarceration to tell some friends and
relatives. "Still, you have to be careful about who you tell. I'm choosy
about that, still."

Her careful approach to disclosure and friendship is designed not only to guard her husband's status but also to guard against the many men who view her differently knowing that her husband is in prison. "Certain guys, you tell them, and then they come on to you even more. . . . ones that are just, like, 'Okay. This is my chance. He locked up–she *got* to get lonely!'" These men are half right–Tina is often lonely. But she would much rather avoid their attention, and she tries to carefully vet any person in whom she might confide.

After ten years, Tina has finally established honest and supportive relationships in her family and has found dependable and discreet friends whom she can rely on. Both, for her, are very important:

> And my mom and my sisters, and them, it's a good thing I had the support I had from them. And most of the women I deal with, their husbands are inmates as well, so it helps. It's like a support group. There's my hairdresser, her husband is locked up, and just about all the women I deal with, you know, on a close-knit basis, their husbands is a inmate, or their boyfriend, so it's easier to deal with.

It has taken Tina years to develop her network of friends, and it has not been easy.

One might imagine that their common difficulties would make women likely to befriend other women in similar situations, but even though prison visits put many women in close proximity to one another, these types of friendships are not easy to come by. When I asked Tina why more women did not become friends through visitation, she said that there were good reasons not to make friends or socialize at the prison. For example, when she stopped driving and decided to ride to the prison in a van of visitors, her husband voiced concerns.

> Now, after years of coming, I see why he didn't want me to meet some of the women, because they do get into a lot of "he said, she said." Okay, with what their ages are you would think they'd have outgrown that, [but] they have started a lot [of fights] between the guys, and you have some women that go down there and they man hop. Even though

their men are in the jail, and they go from man to man to man, and, of course, your man don't want you affiliating with such a thing.

There was surprisingly little conversation or socializing between visitors during the dozens of visits I made to facilities housing D.C. inmates. Those who did talk often drew critical glances or the less confrontational expression of rolling eyes from the other women present. As one wife said after visitation, "You know, that's one of the things I hate about visiting–I just don't like being around all those women that's down there."

Women who visited prison, and most of the women I spoke with had done so, were fully aware of the stereotypes of "prison ho's," and they were acutely aware of the disdain that many in their own families and communities felt for women who brought children into "that environment." One grandmother who was caring for the children of her incarcerated son-in-law told me:

That's why I don't take them babies down there. I don't know what the inside of a jail, prison, anything, look like. And I don't even want to know. I don't understand these women ripping and running to jails to see a man. I just don't understand it. No. And then when you constantly going to the jail. No, I can't see it. I just can't see it. But I have watched women rip and run up and down the road, running down there. When Woodies was downtown, running down to Woodies to catch that bus to go up and down that road to see a man in jail. I just couldn't understand it. And then when you start dragging kids with you, that's just sad. That's really sad.

In trying to understand why relatives of prisoners do not openly seek support related to the incarceration of a family member, it is worth examining one area where families find support mixed with approbation: in their faiths and in their churches.

Chapter 17 Faith and Church: Dolores & Lawrence

Dolores's son Lawrence has been incarcerated for four years, and, as she is quick to tell me, he is the first person in her immediate family to spend time in prison. Although she lives in what is generally considered to be a bad neighborhood near one of the oldest open-air drug markets in the District, her life gives the lie to the notion that inner cities are filled with people without a sense of community. She is an active member of her housing association, is an officer in a prominent local lodge, takes pride in her work in eldercare, and often describes her life in terms of its contribution to the local neighborhood. She, like many mothers, brags about all of her children—their careers, their achievements in school or the military, how close the whole family is. Her son's conviction and incarceration stunned her. When I asked her to describe the experience, she told me, "It just shattered my whole life."

Dolores's experience highlights the fears that many family members have about being associated with the criminal justice system and how important social standing is, even in neighborhoods that many would write off as stricken with not only physical but moral decay. Prior to Lawrence's arrest, a police investigator had placed wanted flyers around her apartment complex with his name and photo on them. A few of her friends helped her remove them, but she was, she said, "devastated" by the experience and the exposure. While she thanked the people who helped her, she never spoke about it again with anyone in her apartment complex. "It is very humiliating. . . . Friends of mine, if they ask me, 'How is the kids?' I say 'Oh, they're all fine. Everybody's good.' And I just hope that they don't never bring it up."

In many ways, her reaction to her son's incarceration is similar to those of the other family members described in this book, and she described the power of shame and stigma in her own life:

> I just wish it would go away. I wish it would be a bad dream. And I would wake up and it would all be gone. My boss asked me just the other day, "How's Lawrence? Does he still cut hair?" I said, "Mmm Hmm." Kept right on walking. And it hurts when people ask about him. And I have to lie. I cut myself from my lodge sisters. Normally during the holidays I'll have them over. And my family, they'd be here. This year I didn't invite anybody over, because they would notice.

When asked if she talked to anyone at work about her son, she was quite clear: "No, no, no, no. Never. No. I didn't want nobody to know. I would not want anybody to know."

The Diagnostic Power of Prayer

Like many of the other family members I spoke with, Dolores was managing to keep up appearances pretty well, despite her initial exposure with the police flyer. When asked how she coped with the stress of her son's incarceration, her answer was immediate: "Prayer. Prayer. That's it. That's all."

Dolores's reliance on prayer and faith is a thread that ran through interviews with many family members, few of whom failed to mention their faith as a resource and a supportive force in their lives. When asked how prayer helped them, most family members were able to cite numerous occasions on which prayer had given them some relief from anxiety and stress and had helped them to cope with all the difficulties they faced. Dolores was no exception. She recalled, for example, when Lawrence was first incarcerated, that she would lie awake at night, unable to sleep, and eventually sought a prescription for sleeping pills so she could get some rest. She found that prayer helped her to get to sleep and eventually give up the sleeping pills:

> Sometimes I'll cry because it'll suddenly hit me that my child is incarcerated. . . . And then when I get ready to go to bed at night or I'm in

looking at TV or something, it will hit me and I'll just start crying. Then
I get–I have my Bible–and I read the Ninety-first Psalm and then I'll
say, you know, then I'll pray. And then I kind of relax a little bit.*

Private prayer is a common coping strategy, at least in part, because the
alternatives are both painful and ineffective. Giving up on one's own
ability to influence the course of events through practical public action
is thus not simply a measure of faith but also a useful diagnostic tool,
indicating areas in people's lives where they feel that they have little or
no control and where attempting control would be draining, stressful,
or depressing. This is a negative reading of what is often a positive force
in the lives of many of this study's participants–but it is a reading that
is supported by many descriptions of the uses of prayer by family members.

One woman I spoke with, who, coincidentally, lived not far from
Dolores, described prayer in similarly emphatic terms. She had been
struggling with her husband's incarceration for nearly six years. While
she and her husband were able to visit often at first, even paying guards
so that they could have unofficial conjugal visits, he was eventually
moved to a facility in Sussex, Virginia, that has much tighter security.
She found that, after a while, she could not visit her husband anymore
because the prison setting made her feel claustrophobic.

When you go through those gates at Sussex, when they enclose you
into those two gates, it makes me feel claustrophobic, and I can't catch
my breath. And one time they had me in that gate for, like, five minutes
or more. . . . I was about to crawl up on those gates. I was, like, some-
how I was gonna get over those barbed wires even if I get cut with
them!

* Verses 1–3 of Psalm 91 (King James Version) read:

He that dwelleth in the secret place of the most High shall abide under the
shadow of the Almighty. I will say of the Lord, "He is my refuge and my fortress:
my God; in Him will I trust. Surely He shall deliver me from the snare of the
fowler, and from the noisome pestilence."

While there are many biblical and Koranic passages that family members relate with
incarceration, Psalm 91 and Psalm 124 are particularly common.

Even though she stopped visiting her husband, she found herself unable to sleep at night, thinking about her husband being on lockdown, during which all inmates are required to remain in their cells, sometimes for weeks. "I used to put myself in a cell and imagine myself being locked down, and I couldn't sleep." Adding to her sense of claustrophobia at night, she recently developed a medical condition that requires her to wear a compression wrap on her right leg. She manages to get through these times, she told me, by reading Scripture and singing hymns, "just to try to get my mind off of, you know, what's making me feel the claustrophobia."

While prayer is useful to her in this way, it also surfaced that others might view it as less beneficial. As she described to me, she used prayer to cope with medical problems in a way that would undoubtedly trouble many doctors:

> When I found out that this lump on my neck may be cancerous, I worried at first, and then I prayed. . . . And then I just . . . stopped thinking about it. I was, like, "Well, Lord, I know you promised me a long life, and I'm not gonna worry about it." . . . Then my boss just kept worrying. "Well, have you been to the doctor yet?" I was, like, "I'm not worrying about that anymore." And then I met somebody on the bus who told me his wife died from cancer in her throat, and I was, like, the Devil is trying to use that to make me start worrying again, but I'm not gonna worry. It's easier for me to have faith that this was healed than to go to that doctor and let them stick a needle in my neck. I couldn't . . . I just couldn't do it. I said, "I'd rather believe God. And if I die from this, then, hey, it was His will as far as I'm concerned," because I just couldn't go through with it.

Faith healing is a significant Christian tradition, but it is unsettling to find that faith can abet not only peace but resignation. What struck me in talking with her was that she used similar language to describe both her worries about incarceration and her use of faith:

> I'm just learning how to not worry so much about him and just leave it in God's hands to handle. And [my husband feels that this means that]

I don't want him, but I can't just . . . if I didn't have God in my life, I would . . . there were many times when he first got locked up that I just sat there and thought about ways to kill myself.

Neither she nor Dolores is a passive person. Seeing that they, both people who describe themselves as very determined and practical people, used prayer as their primary means of coping with what would otherwise be unbearable stress makes the point all the more significant.

It is a finding that is consistent with recent empirical studies showing that religious beliefs can help sustain people through hard times,[1] particularly African Americans. In a recent study of college students, for example, researchers found that belief in God's love for them was significantly more important than any other factor to the self-esteem of black students, something that did not hold true for white or Asian students. Another striking finding of this study was that this belief was strongly and significantly correlated with negative appraisals by others in society, again only among black students. This led the researchers to suggest that, in the absence of perceived approval of others, a belief in God's love helps to sustain the self-esteem of African Americans.[2]

Given the stigma, stress, and hardship that many families–particularly black families living in the poorest pockets of the city–face when a family member is incarcerated, it is not hard to see why so many cited prayer as a means of coping. Giving up control over incarceration allowed many to endure the shame and taint of criminality along with the profoundly difficult circumstances that incarceration can bring. It is significant, then, that prayer, often the only strategy left when all others have failed, is by far the most common form of coping among families of prisoners.

Complicated Relationships with Church

Given that a large majority of African-American families in the District have a family member who has been incarcerated at some point, that a large majority of these families find some measure of comfort in their faith, and that most are active members of one or more congregations, one might expect the local church to be a place for support and solidarity on the issue. For the most part, however, this is not so. When I asked Dolores about how her church had been supportive of her, for example, she made a clear distinction between seeking help from God and seeking support from her church:

> When I go to church on Sunday, we laugh, we smile, we shake hands, and you know. And they know me by seeing me on Sunday. But other than that, they don't know me. . . . No, I don't . . . I . . . no, no, I don't discuss [his incarceration] with nobody other than my immediate family.

Lonnie, Dolores's grandson and a nephew to her incarcerated son, concurred with Dolores's perceptions of church community life. Growing up in a poor but deeply religious community, church was a nexus for discussion of moral issues. So while Lonnie sees the value of a spiritual connection with other people and of the deep self-reflection that can come with spiritual life, he also understands the threat implicit in the daily discussions at church. As he described it, "The church is the biggest gossip hotbed in the world." Mentioning anything in a church setting is thus seen as an act of public disclosure and carries the tensions and the weight of that type of disclosure.

> I've seen heated situations come out because someone wasn't supposed to say something to someone in church, and it happened, and it just blew up real bad. . . . Basically, someone being incarcerated, I mean, it's news. It's just like the television. . . . What's gonna get the headline? The headline is gonna get the person that has killed twenty people. It's the same thing within gossip circles. The gossip that little Johnny got a 4.0 grade point average is not gonna spread as quickly. . . . And with churches being a place where you are judged, definitely judged by your actions, by any and all, well . . .

Describing himself as now "not religious but spiritual," Lonnie cited this as one of his reasons for leaving the church.

Dolores, Lonnie, and the rest of Lawrence's family are not alone in keeping familial incarceration a secret from their congregation. Many know firsthand how painful disclosure–even in an ostensibly forgiving and supportive setting–can be. Louisa did finally come to trust one woman at her church. "I felt she would understand because we used to pray together." The next time she encountered the woman in church, however, the woman called out, "How that jail bird husband of yours doing?" The importance of acceptance at church, and the unexpected public disclosure from a person she trusted, made the incident particularly painful.

> It hurt my feelings to the point, I said, well that's just the reason why I don't tell nobody else. That's just the reason why, 'cause they can make fun of you. They can say things to hurt your feelings. Being sarcastic. You know. People do stuff. They're mean. You know. I don't want other people calling him an "old jail bird," "ex-jail bird," "ex-offender," you know? "Once a jail bird always . . ." I don't want that. So the less they know, the less critical they can be. And people are mean. They say stuff to you. Disrespect you. Don't care about your–don't even consider your feelings. Or you being human. If they know the truth, they rub it in your face.

Louisa's experience of censure did not drive her from her faith; quite the reverse. She believes all the more strongly in the sustaining power of prayer. But her experience of faith is now less communal than it used to be, having become a far more private matter.

But most family members do not need to be humiliated in church to understand that faith and public censure are not mutually exclusive–indeed the social organization of church life often defines the relationship of one to the other. For this reason, church is a setting in which many families in the District are made keenly aware of the tension between collective celebration of faith and the possibility of moral censure. As one woman responded when asked if she could turn to church members for support, "Church? I wouldn't dare tell anyone at church."

The ministers I spoke with about this issue were surprised by the statistics indicating that many of their congregants' families probably had a member who was involved in the criminal justice system. As one minister told me, "People don't really come to me about that as much as you might think. Now, they could if they wanted to, but I suspect it's hard for them to talk about." Why would it be hard to talk to a minister about this? Many family members gave me a response similar to this one given by one mother of a prisoner:

> The reverend would be the last one I would go to. He gonna get up there in church and tell everybody. I wouldn't dare tell the reverend that. I had a friend who was over in D.C. Jail–and I went over there to visit this friend, and my girl–me and my girlfriend–so she said to me, she said, "Belinda, there's the reverend." I hid from him so he wouldn't see me because he would have gone to Sunday service. "Yeah, I saw Ms. so-and-so in the D.C. Jail yesterday." No. Uh-uh. Because he's going to get up in church and tell it. Yep.*

It was not so much that the minister would be unsympathetic–just the reverse. She thought that he would be far more sympathetic than the rest of the congregation. Those who attend church regularly know that, along with the many positive aspects of faith that can be found there, there can also be a competitive relationship between members that encourages emphasis on the positive and admirable aspects of one's family life and discourages disclosure of less seemly details.

While churches have long been seen as havens in the African-American community, they are also considered to be moral and spiritual guides, and both ministers and members of congregations help to develop what Cathy Cohen has termed the "indigenous constructed image of 'good black Christian folk.'"[3] The relationship of families of prisoners to African-American churches is one that must be considered in light of the roles that these churches have historically been called on to play: "The dual and contradictory legacy of the African-American church is that it has been among the most important instruments of African-American liberation and at the same time one of the most conservative institutions in the African-American community."[4]

African-American churches are put in a bind: they are expected to

---

* Ironically, her church is led by the Reverend Walter Fauntroy, one of the most politically active members of the District's clergy and a tireless activist for prisoners' rights. I don't think that this reflects poorly on the good reverend but rather indicates the power of the stigma that family members feel.

maintain the cultural capital that they currently have both within the black community and within American society at large, while at the same time they are expected to console and reach out to those who are associated with the worst stereotypes of black culture. To the extent that the church confers a collective identity on its members, the actions of a single member or family are seen to reflect on the entire community. Because church life presents people, families, and communities with an opportunity to put their best face forward, those involved are alert to the stickiness of stigma and the possibility of being associated with others who have fallen from grace. This sense is only heightened by the preexisting concern about racial stereotypes. Members of black churches may be able to control or explain their own behavior, but they are always at risk of having others behave in a way that sheds a poor light on them by association.

Added to the social threat of stigma are the more personal and practical feelings of local congregants. As the minister of a larger church said when asked about the role of black churches in supporting families of prisoners:

> You have to understand, many of these people are victims of crime themselves. It's not just that prisoners come from their neighborhoods, they're in prison for committing crimes in their neighborhoods. That's what prison reform activists don't get, and what I have to keep explaining to them. In my congregation people are crime victims, so sympathy for criminals is hard to come by. Even if it is their neighbor or even their own family member.

Indeed, in the services at local churches, there was a strong mixture of both concern for those less fortunate and a call to personal responsibility. It is this call to conscience that made black churches a logical place for civil rights activism in the last century and that maintains the position of moral legitimacy from which ministers and congregants can address both the black community and the rest of the nation. However, this claim to high moral ground also contributes to a powerful silence around the issue of incarceration as it relates to people's personal lives.

Chapter 18   Social Silence

One often hears in policy circles that incarceration no longer works because inner-city communities are places where shame has no hold.[1] One can only assume that most participants in these discussions have had little direct contact with the families or communities they are discussing. Stigma and incarceration interrelate in aspects of family life that are generally hidden from public view. A woman ashamed that she is giving up on her marriage, a son ashamed of his father's addiction, a daughter ashamed of selling her body to pay her grandmother's rent– these are things that don't make headline news, that are absent from stories of what prison and street life are "really like." Far from being unconcerned about criminality, familial integrity, and honesty, families of prisoners wrestle with each of these issues every day in settings they often perceive as hostile and unforgiving.[2] They are not shameless; they feel the stigma that accompanies not only incarceration but all the other stereotypes that accompany it– fatherlessness, poverty, and often, despite every intent to make it otherwise, diminished love.

The silence of these families constitutes, in its own way, a negative language that is closely related to and charged by our positive acts of political discourse and law making.[3] Descriptions of this kind of social silence are rare because people–whether they be politicians, social scientists, or judges–are usually more interested in speech and acts than in the negative field of silence and estrangement against which they occur. But the stories in this book–both the local, personal stories of the individual families and the broader stories told in policy and law–are constitutive of a silence that is, in its own way, meaningful.

This kind of silence–the kind that an increasing number of poor families live within–undermines the relationships that, as Mauss described nearly a century ago, are essential to any community. These are the relationships that create shared meaning through care and indebted-ness. Those estranged from these relationships suffer not only materi-ally; they are, in a sense, devalued as humans. There is a repression of self experienced by these families in their silence. The retreat of a mother or wife from friendships in church and at work, the words not spoken between friends, the enduring silence of children who guard what for them is profound and powerful information–all are telling indicators of the social effects of incarceration. As relationships between family or friends become strained or false, not only are people's understandings of one another diminished, but, because peo-ple are social, they themselves are diminished as well.

There is another kind of repression in this silence, one less direct and less obvious, that is conveyed by the stories that these families tell. This is a repression of public thought, of our collective imagination. It runs through public debate about urban families and communities, sub-merged and barely noticed. It takes form in the sense many have that these families are hardly families at all, that there is little we could do to damage them as they barely exist as families to begin with.

By forcing out of view the struggles these families face in the most simple and fundamental social acts–living together and caring for one another–this broader social silence makes it seem as though they sim-ply are "that way": broken, valueless, irreparable. It is a silence that underwrites the same policy choices that create these same stereo-types. This form of social silence is, so to speak, deafening–the less we hear of their problems, the less we are able to understand or make sense of what we do hear because we have no context in which to place new information. The problems of these families are so difficult to address, in part, because we know so little of them. Our collective fail-ure to understand the injuries that our social institutions inflict upon them continues to prevent us from doing the justice we intend.

Conclusion Looking Ahead

By employing incarceration–the bluntest of policy instruments–as the primary response to social disorder, policymakers have significantly missed the mark. The very laws intended to punish selfish behavior and to further common social interests have, in practice, strained and eroded the personal relationships vital to family and community life. Crime cannot go unpunished. But by draining the resources of families, by frustrating the norm of reciprocity that inheres in family life, and by stigmatizing poor and minority families, our current regime of criminal sanctions has created a set of second-order problems that furthers social detachment. Incarceration cannot replace the strict enforcement of long-term mandatory drug treatment, public housing programs that move poor families out of the ghetto, employment opportunities that provide for those who remain, and well-considered family welfare programs for those who are unable to find employment.

The concern here is only partly material. Where individuals can commit to each other's well-being, they are better at surviving the unpredictable fluctuations in their personal fortunes because they can rely on one another in times of need. But the lesson of a century of research is that material life is integral to other concerns–concerns that are equal, if not paramount, to material wealth. The ability to be of use to one another is what gives rise to the normative world people live in, providing not only material sustenance but also identity and a sense of what matters most. As the law forcefully shapes how individuals relate to one another, it also alters many of the most meaningful aspects of their lives. In evaluating our laws, then, the question is not merely whether and for whom they are enriching or impoverishing but how they shape the way we as individuals and as a society view one another and ourselves.

By punishing the commitments they have to one another, incarceration not only impoverishes those in vulnerable families and communities but makes them more wary of commitments in general. The well-documented decline of trust in urban America is not solely the result of blunt criminal sanctions, but the accounts of families confronting incarceration show us how significantly sanctions can transform personal relationships at home, at work, in church, and in school. The decline in the ability of those in fragile families and high-imprisonment communities to care for one another is ultimately more troubling than their decreased abilities to care for themselves. As they come to trust and rely on one another less, they come to assume that there is less that they can safely share with or expect from each other.

Law also shapes perceptions and identities at a broader level. By weakening the ties that bind poor families together, criminal sanctions join a host of other social policies that practically enforce the stereotypes of inner-city families. And because these families are, for historical reasons, predominantly minority families, these policies harden the racial lines that divide our society in particularly stigmatizing and destructive ways. The negative cascade of policy effects over the last half century has moved many to view the dissolution of poor inner-city families as a foregone conclusion—and to view the state's role as replacing rather than shoring up the bonds that hold them together.

Both of these transformations and the losses they represent are moral and, in the deepest sense of the word, cultural. What we have faced in the urban crisis of the last fifty years is not, as some argue, a "culture of poverty" that our policies must correct. Rather, what is occurring is more aptly described as a slow but steady impoverishment of culture itself. In this respect, the example of incarceration is largely a negative one; but the accounts of these families also indicate that a more constructive approach to public policy is possible. Rather than viewing the state's role as regulating individual behavior through force, these accounts suggest the more profitable approach of encouraging the informal obligations that inhere in families and communities and enabling individuals to meet them. If the real concern is the unraveling of social commitment that feeds criminal behavior, the criminal law is conceptually the last–and probably the least effective–tool available. A more pragmatic approach would look elsewhere, rethinking, for example, public housing programs that concentrate the worst off in our society into already vulnerable neighborhoods, welfare policies that punish marriage and domestic partnership and undermine capital accumulation, market incentives that drive employment opportunities out of low-income neighborhoods, and educational opportunities that correlate all too tightly with historical inequalities.

This does not mean either that the criminal law is ineffectual or that it has no role to play. As the accounts in this book demonstrate, the criminal law is powerful, indeed. But the thin theories of human motivation that have been used to justify the expansion of human captivity would also have us imagine the law as far more precise, predictable, and limited in its application than in actuality it is. In addition to serving as a deterrent and giving expression to public anger, our criminal law has also levied a heavy tax on already impoverished communities, strained and broken many families, and brought the powerful force of stigma to bear down on millions of noncriminal citizens, citizens who are disproportionately black and disproportionately poor.

The single most important reform that can be made in the criminal law is the strict and universal enforcement of long-term mandatory drug treatment for all drug offenders. We now have a decade of studies that demonstrate that drug treatment works when it is mandatory, of high quality, and of reasonable length. Surely, if we can construct the world's most extensive penal system, we can do poor families and communities the service of enforcing a graduated system of drug treatment sanctions that involves family members.

Most Americans sense that their criminal justice system is failing them. Liberals, concerned about equality and individual rights, complain that poor and minority communities are disproportionately affected by a biased criminal justice system. They speak in the language of equality and rights, proposing increased protections of the liberty interests of offenders and complaining about disproportionate minority incarceration. Conservatives argue that incarceration has become too easy, failing to instill a sense of responsibility. They speak in the language of moral accountability and propose harsher sanctions. Both are partially right: our current regime of criminal sanctions injures poor and minority families and communities disproportionately while at the same time failing to hold offenders accountable in any meaningful way.

The failure of our criminal law stems not from a lack of concern about liberal or conservative values: most Americans share a fundamental interest in equality under the law and individual accountability. Rather, its failure stems from a fundamental misapprehension of the social world, one that obscures the relationships individuals have with one another. By conceptually stripping individuals of their most common and fundamental commitments, policymakers have imagined that they can transform poverty-stricken neighborhoods through the sheer force of the sanctions imposed.

But if we expand the scope of our inquiry from the isolated individual to the relationships they inhabit and the debts they owe one another, a different picture emerges. In this picture we see individuals in families, struggling to forge moral commitments and live up to them. This perspective presents social disorder as more complex and far more challenging. The question that this perspective requires us to ask is not merely how to punish or deter offenders but how to encourage and strengthen the bonds that make families possible, give life to community, and ultimately determine the character of our society as a whole.

Postscript

People are resilient, all the more so when they are part of caring families. The families in this book, for the most part, live on, making the stories I first wrote about them seem like the necessarily dated verbal snapshots they are. I continued to revise the accounts for some time, but finally I had to draw the line and end the story. Without attempting to describe the details of their lives to any great extent, I want to share a little of what has happened *en route* to publication.

Perhaps the most surprising story is Kenny's. Sentenced to ten to thirty years for voluntary manslaughter, he appealed and won a retrial. Although both he and his attorney believed that he could have prevailed in a new trial with a claim of self-defense, the plea's offer of a reduction to time served and an immediate return to his family was too great to resist. Making up for the years when he was awaiting trial and filing appeals, Kenny is now studying computer systems management and spending his free time either with his boys or with church groups. "They're doing much better now, behavior-wise," he tells me. "And because I'm in school and studying all the time, we all study together now in the evenings, so they're doing much better in school." Edwina, of course, is happy. "It is a blessing," she tells me, "to have him home again." Kenny has the same wide grin and honest manner, and although he seems happier than he did in prison, he also seems more weighed upon. His family still faces considerable debt, and Kenny, as of yet, has no job. While he hopes to work as a systems administrator in a year or two, he faces a long road before the mortgage and credit card bills are paid off. But, he tells me, "I like planning for the future, so we'll get there."

Other families have had harder times. Lilly's grandson by her youngest son, Billy, is now in jail. He had been suspended from high school for fighting but with a great deal of hard work on Billy's part was allowed to continue and graduated last spring. Since then he began attending college in Maryland. He got into a fight with someone who insulted a friend of his and is now in custody awaiting trial. Lilly was furious with him, in part because she had high hopes for his education. "Now," she says, "I have it triple. My brother, my son, and my grandson." She remains a whirlwind of familial activity, baby-sitting, organizing family gatherings, and keeping the family in touch with the three men now behind bars. Her daughter, an entrepreneur, is struggling in the slowing economy but still helps out a great deal. As Lilly says, "I couldn't get by without her. She's really supporting me and a lot of people."

Londa recovered from her broken leg but was diagnosed with Grave's disease, an autoimmune hyperthyroid disorder that is triggered by stress. Complications and other conditions exacerbated the problem, and she's been out of work and in and out of the hospital for the last two years. She has a new boyfriend, although she's a bit shy about telling me much about him. She still thinks of Derek but harbors no illusions about them getting back together.

I spoke to David a week after his release from prison. He moved back in with his wife, Sandra, who found work in a fitness center closer to home. He is unemployed but has the determination of most men newly released from prison. His daughter, Davida, has two children and is living with the father of the second child. He is unemployed, but David is planning to have a serious talk with him to set him straight on what happens to those who work outside of the legal economy. David's son, Charles, maintains his flawless grade point average but has been in a juvenile facility since a month prior to his father's release for stealing a car.

Tina is doing well. She moved to Georgia to be closer to Dante, who was transferred to another private prison there, then moved back after growing frustrated with the job market there.

I've lost touch with Zelda and Clinton. As happened many times with families during my fieldwork, I called only to find that the phone was disconnected. Having moved out of the District and on to other projects, I don't have the resources I once did to track them down. I still think of them, though, and hope to see them again. (My old phone number still works.)

Appendix Methodology and Data Sources

Prior to beginning fieldwork, I traveled to five large cities and the prisons they fed. I selected the District of Columbia over Baltimore, Houston, Los Angeles, New Haven, New York City, and San Francisco for a number of reasons, though I suspect the results would not have been significantly different in any of those cities. The District is about average in ways that matter. For example, the District ranks in the middle of the largest fifty cities by population. It also has an incarceration rate that is neither particularly high nor low and (at least prior to federal takeover of the correctional system) faced the same difficulties that many states have with regard to prison overcrowding and corrections funding.

The District is atypical in ways that were useful to this study as well. Unlike most other mid-sized cities, a number of excellent ethnographies and histories have already been written about it.[1] Also unlike most cities large and small, the District has its own Department of Corrections, making analysis of incarceration rates, demographic data, and so on far easier than would have been the case elsewhere. And, not unimportantly, as our nation's capital city it is uniquely familiar to many of the nation's lawmakers and the millions of tourists who visit each year, lending it a ready familiarity.

The inmates in this study were housed in a mix of municipal facilities in and around the District, in privately run facilities both in the District and in several other states, and in federal facilities in other states. This mix helped me to understand which aspects of incarceration were specific to the District and which were not. Nearly all the families in this study lived in the District or its surrounding suburbs.

I began my research in a manner typical of ethnographic inquiries, asking if friends and contacts could introduce me to other people, then asking each new participant to introduce me to someone new. This is an easy way to get a study going, as it spreads through trusted relationships. However, it has the disadvantage of being self-selecting in ways that are impossible to predict for just this reason. To address this potential problem, once I felt I understood the major concerns of the twenty families in my "snowball sample," I selected another thirty families using a stratified random sample of the population of the Department of Corrections. Incarcerated family members were approached and asked if they would be interested in the study and whether they would provide contact information for family members. Only two of the thirty declined to participate.

All the inmates who participated listed the District as their place of residence; some family members, however, lived in the surrounding suburbs. District inmates who were interviewed were located in one of the following facilities: the D.C. Jail, located in Southeast Washington; the Correctional Treatment Facility, privately operated by the CCA adjacent to the D.C. Jail; the Lorton Correctional Facilities, located twenty minutes west of the District in Lorton, Virginia; the Sussex II facility, located two hours south of the District in Sussex, Virginia; the Red Onion facility, located six hours southwest of the District in Pound, Virginia; and the Youngstown Correctional Facility, operated by the CCA in Youngstown, Ohio.

The quotations are, for the most part, taken from the over two hundred recorded interviews I conducted with participants. Interviews were conducted over the course of three years starting in 1998. Most interviews were conducted either in the home of the person I interviewed or, for most inmates, in a private visiting room designed for legal consultations. Most interviews were audio recorded, but for various reasons some were not. The largest number of interviews not audio recorded were conducted in facilities managed by the Virginia Department of Corrections, which declined to authorize the use of a recording device for this study. In other rare instances, I found an unexpected opportunity for an interview and did not have a recording device handy or, the lament of interviewers everywhere, my batteries ran out. In these instances I recorded the interview by hand, with detailed notes. I have made every attempt to rely on audio-recorded conversation where possible but occasionally quote from my written notes.

Transcriptions differ from the actual spoken words of the interview in three ways. First, names and other identifying information have been altered. Second, a few interviewees had a linguistic tic (for example, saying "like" every few words) that distracted from the content of the quotation; where the removal of the tics did not alter the content in any significant way, I removed them. Third, unless the pronunciation was highly irregular, rather than emphasize vernacular pronunciation I used the dictionary spelling of the word the person used (e.g., "doing" rather than "doin'"). I decided not to indicate vernacular pronunciation at every instance for three reasons. First, after many attempts, I found that it was very difficult to do this accurately and consistently—attempting to indicate the difference between elisions, faint inclusions, and atypical phonemes came to seem arbitrary and my indications of them variable. Second, readers of early papers in which I tried to indicate alternative pronunciations found it distracting. Third, many participants expressed concerns about their ability to speak articulately to the issues that mattered greatly to them, and it thus seemed counter to both their intentions and the general project to mark their language in ways that placed undue emphasis on pronunciation.

Any other deviations from the original wording of a quotation are indicated in one of two ways. First, square brackets ([ ]) indicate that the wording is mine or, if surrounding the first letter of a sentence, that the beginning of the sentence was truncated. They are used in cases where the person clearly omitted a word, where alternate phrasing was much more succinct or clear, or where the beginning of a sentence did not add significant meaning to the quoted material (e.g., "Well, like I was saying"). Second, brief ellipses (. . .) indicate a recorded pause in conversation and extended ellipses (. . . .) are used to indicate that the sentences did not directly follow one another in the original interview (usually indicating that a repetition or aside was deleted).

Statistical analyses drew upon data from five sources:

- *Historical census data.* These data sets provided information on the demographic composition of the District.
- *D.C. Department of Corrections records.* These records provided inmates' last residence, crime for which convicted, time incarcerated, length of sentence, and so forth, for 1998 population and 1999 admissions.
- *Police Department crime data.* Geocoded records from the D.C. Police Department on 1999 crime reports and arrests provided information on the date, time, and location of crimes reported in the District.
- *Street map layers for geocoding data sets 1, 2, and 3.* Layers for all the streets and addresses in the District are publicly available. These data provide the physical layout of the city and the location of schools, churches, state agencies, banks, and stores, all of which helped develop a geographic portrait of the neighborhoods in and around the District.
- *National data on incarceration in urban areas.* Data on incarceration for individual cities were, unless otherwise noted, obtained from the relevant Department of Corrections.

Acknowledgments

Having spent five years working to finish this book, it seems much less a writing project than a series of extended and often intense discussions. Many of these were in backyards, kitchens, and living rooms; some were in prisons, halfway houses, and vans that served as temporary homes; others were in offices, over the phone, or by e-mail. All were important.

The not so simple act of getting to know people is at the heart of ethnography, and this project has led me into hundreds of relationships I would not otherwise have had. I now know why so many anthropologists love fieldwork. I was continually surprised by the generosity of participants in this study; I owe them an unpayable debt. They opened up their lives so that I could learn from them and helped me to discard many of my assumptions along the way. Their hospitality and friendship, often in the most trying of circumstances, were things I was trained not to expect but without which this work would have been impossible. Over dinner, in church, at work, or just when they had a few free moments, the families in this study shared not only their time but intimate and often painful details of their lives. Their names do not appear here because they were promised anonymity, but they know who they are and so do I. My objective throughout has been to do their accounts justice.

My friends and colleagues were expert where I was not, helping me to understand the many arguments that had already been made about families, communities, and the law and often pointing out lapses in logic or contradictions in my own. More importantly, they both prodded and reassured me at the necessary times and places. I will be forever grateful to Kathryn Dudley, who has become my model for academic mentorship. I would not have undertaken this study, let alone finished it, were it not for her sure guidance and unwavering encouragement. Hal Scheffler provided a solid and reassuring sounding board throughout this project and read more than most advisors should ever have to. Dan Kahan was generous beyond measure, opening my eyes to ways of viewing the law that were entirely new to me. Kai Erikson was and is precisely the kind of person and scholar I aspire to be: inspired but careful, worldly but never jaded. Linda-Anne Rebhun provided not only excellent comments but, by example, a model of thoughtful scholarship. Dana Goldblatt, Ryan Goodman, Kate Masur, Marc Mauer, Tracey Meares, Michelle Gates-Moresi, Karen Nakamura, Maya Nayak, Tom Pertersik, Galit Sarfaty, Tahlia Townsend, Jeremy Travis, and Paul Wood all read and gave very helpful comments on papers and drafts over the last two years. My family has been patient with my endless talk about this project. I thank them from the bottom of my heart. I give special thanks to Jenifer Wood, who was my closest friend and most careful reader throughout.

A number of people welcomed me to Washington and helped me to find my feet. Betsy Biben, Michael Bryant, Brenda Smith, Charlie and Pauline Sullivan, and the many people they introduced me to were especially kind to me, patiently listening to my endless questions, answering where they could, and directing me to others where they could not. They often made my fieldwork enjoyable where it could easily have been frustrating.

A number of people who work on behalf of the many inmates, families, and communities in the District shared their time and insight. In particular, I want to thank John Bess, Mary Bissel, Luis Cardono, Beth Carter, Audrey Epperson, Jenni Gainsborough, Dianna Guinyard, Pastor Greylan Ellis Hagler, Ronald Hampton, Stephanie Harrison, Gayle Hebron, the Reverend D. H. Beecher Hicks Jr., Jeffery Jay, Gail Johnson, Ambrose Lane Jr., Keith Langston, Jennifer Lanoff, Eric Lotke, Catherine Thomas Pinknee, Khalid Pitts, Patty Puritz, Bill Sabol, Michael Schaffer, Vincent Schiraldi, Giovanna Shay, Brenda Shepherd-Vernon, David A. Singleton, the Reverend A. Noris Smith, Michael Spevak, Fred Taylor, Shari L. Thomas, Edward J. Ungvarsky, Pastor Willy Wilson, and Bob Woodson.

Many of the greatest obstacles to a study of this kind are bureaucratic. I am deeply indebted to the many public servants who helped guide my queries and requests through the shoals of red tape that would otherwise have wrecked this project. This research could not have been conducted without the cooperation of the District of Columbia Department of Corrections, the Virginia Department of Correction, and the various federal agencies working with District inmates. In particular, I want to thank Farshad Amirkhizi, Clinton Boyd, Mary Buel, Jay Carver, John Clark, Sylvester Ezeani, Melinda Fallen, Dena Hanley, Stephanie Harrison, Gayle Hebron, Tom Hoey, Nancy Holt, Louis N. Jones, John P. May, Bill Meets, Margaret Moore, Polly Nelson, Jasper Ormand, Emanual Ross, John Thomas, Ed Walsh, Frances Washington, Odie Washington, Wendel Watkins, Andrea Weissman, Ed Wiley, Brett Williams, Earnest L. Williams, Joseph Willmore, Walter Woodward, and Elwood York.

This study was generously supported by the National Institute of Justice (Award Number 98-CE-VX-0012), the National Science Foundation (Award Number SBR-9727685), the Wenner-Gren Foundation for Anthropological Research, and the Yale Center for the Study of Race, Inequality, and Politics.

Notes

Introduction

1. Eric Lotke, *Hobbling a Generation: Young African American Men in D.C.'s Criminal Justice System Five Years Later*, National Center on Institutions and Alternatives (1997). The latter figure includes jail, prison, parole, probation, and warrants.

2. D.C. Department of Corrections (2000). *See infra* note 16 (chap. 4), and accompanying text for further data lifetime likelihood. *See* appendix for discussion of estimation methods. Nationally, about one in three black men can expect to spend time in jail or prison.

3. For example, the overall rate of incarceration in the District is 1.8 percent, while in Baltimore, Maryland, it is 2.1 percent and in New Haven, Connecticut, it is 1.7 percent. Estimates are based on census data and data provided by the D.C., Maryland, and Connecticut Departments of Corrections.

4. *See* Ed Marciniak, *Standing Room Only*, 2 COMMONWEAL 129, 10 (2002).

5. This is the thrust of David Cole's recent work. *See, e.g.,* DAVID COLE, NO EQUAL JUSTICE (1999); *see also* Angela J. Davis, *Incarceration and the Imbalance of Power, in* INVISIBLE PUNISHMENT (Marc Mauer and Meda Chesney-Lind eds., 2002).

6. *See, e.g.,* Angela J. Davis, *Incarceration and the Imbalance of Power,* in INVISIBLE PUNISHMENT: THE COLLATERAL CONSEQUENCES OF MASS IMPRISONMENT 63 (Marc Mauer and Meda Chesney-Lind eds., 2002) (stating that prosecutors have an "almost unlimited amount of discretion" in making charging decisions).

7. *See, e.g.,* John DiIulio, *Arresting Ideas: Tougher Law Enforcement Is Driving Down Urban Crime*, POL'Y REV. (fall 1995); JAMES Q. WILSON, THINKING ABOUT CRIME (1985). *See also* WILLIAM J. BENNETT ET AL., BODY COUNT: MORAL POVERTY AND HOW TO WIN AMERICA'S WAR AGAINST CRIME AND DRUGS (1996).

8. *See, e.g.,* John DiIulio, *Lock 'Em Up or Else*, LEDGER, March 23, 1996, at A11.

9. Few victims of crime, for example, would want a criminal found innocent because the evidence against him, though proving his guilt, was inadmissible on Fourth Amendment grounds. This, however, is part of the standard liberal line. David Cole, for example, argues that the charges against a man who consented to having his bags searched on a bus and was found to be carrying a pound of cocaine should be dismissed because the

police could provide no justification for their search. *See* COLE, *supra* note 5 (introduction). There are interesting exceptions to this hard-line approach to the rights of criminal defendants. Akhil Amar, for example, has argued convincingly against Fourth Amendment exclusions accompanied by civil police liability for rights violations. Akhil Amar, *Fourth Amendment First Principles,* 107 HARV. L. REV. 757 (1994). *See also* RANDALL KENNEDY, RACE, CRIME, AND THE LAW 375 (1997) (criticizing those who, in the interest of the criminal offender, ignore those "who must share space on the streets and in buildings" with those offenders); TRACEY MEARES AND DAN KAHAN, URGENT TIMES (1999) (noting that an insistence on strict limitations on police discretion, while a sensible response to police racism in the 1950s and 1960s, makes less sense in contemporary struggles against the far greater problem of inner-city crime).

10. *See* Donald Braman and Jenifer Wood, *From One Generation to the Next, in* PRISONERS ONCE REMOVED (Jeremy Travis and Michelle Waul eds., 2003).

11. Deterrence and desert are shorthand for the two main theoretical contenders in the criminal law: utilitarianism (usually described in terms of deterrence) and retributivism (usually described as moral desert). These warring factions are typically represented by early proponents Jeremy Bentham and Immanuel Kant. *See, e.g.,* JEREMY BENTHAM, THE PRINCIPLES OF MORALS AND LEGISLATION (1948) (1823); IMMANUEL KANT, GROUNDWORK OF THE METAPHYSICS OF MORALS (Mary Gregor trans. and ed., 1997) (1785). Following Bentham, theories of legal utility tend to be economistic–that is, developed with the goal of maximizing something like human health, wealth, and happiness. *See, e.g.,* Louis Kaplow and Steven Shavell, *Fairness Versus Welfare,* 114 HARV. L. REV. 961 (2001) (an insistent defense of the utilitarian ideal). Following Kant, legal retributivists are less concerned with human welfare than they are with distributing just deserts. *See, e.g.,* Jean Hampton, *An Expressive Theory of Retribution, in* RETRIBUTIVISM AND ITS CRITICS 1 (Wesley Cragg ed., 1992).The policy pendulum that once swung toward utility has now swung rather sharply back toward retribution. *See* Michele Cotton, *Back with a Vengeance: The Resilience of Retribution as an Articulated Purpose of Criminal Punishment,* 37 AM. CRIM. L. REV. 1313 (2000). *See also* Paul J. Hofer and Mark H. Allenbaugh, *The Reason Behind the Rules: Finding and Using the Philosophy of the Federal Sentencing Guidelines,* 40 AM. CRIM. L. REV. 19 (2003) (arguing that the Federal Sentencing Guidelines are, despite protestations to the contrary, retributivist).

12. For a recent review of the research in this area, see William Spelman, *What Recent Studies Do (and Don't) Tell Us about Imprisonment and Crime,* 27 CRIME & JUST. 419 (2000).

13. We do know a great deal about family, community, and criminal sanctions as distinct subjects. Treatises on family life range from economic inquiries and political treatises to sociological surveys and ethnographic studies. *See, e.g.,* CAROL STACK, ALL OUR KIN: STRATEGIES FOR SURVIVAL IN A BLACK COMMUNITY (1974) (describing the importance of extended family to

material and emotional well-being of housing project residents in Chicago); GARY S. BECKER, A TREATISE ON THE FAMILY (1981) (describing families in economic terms); REBUILDING THE NEST (David Blankenhorn et al. eds., 1990) (assessing the importance of varied family arrangements to child health and welfare); STEPHANIE COONTZ, THE WAY WE REALLY ARE (1997) (describing importance and diversity of family life in America); SYLVIA ANN HEWLETT AND CORNEL WEST, THE WAR AGAINST PARENTS (1998) (describing the impact of various public policies on family life in America).

A growing number of ethnographies are focusing on the positive aspects of community life in urban America and the strengths of community organizations. *See, e.g.,* STEVEN GREGORY, BLACK CORONA (1998) (describing political activism in an African-American neighborhood in New York City); KENNETH W. W. GOINGS AND RAYMOND A. MOHL, THE NEW AFRICAN AMERICAN URBAN HISTORY (1996) (describing a "New African American Urban History" emphasizing "a sense of active involvement, of people empowered, engaged in struggle, living their lives with dignity and shaping their own futures"); RHODA H. HALPERIN, PRACTICING COMMUNITY (1998) (describing the daily activities of ordinary people that create community in an urban setting). Generally, these accounts describe people working together to overcome adversity. Sadly, while there are national and even local organizations active on the issue of incarceration, the present study suggests that the type of community organizing described in these works has failed to counter the effects of incarceration.

The criminological literature on sanctions is vast, and, as incarceration rates have risen precipitously during the last thirty years, numerous and highly publicized analyses of criminal justice policy have told us how grossly disproportionate the rates of incarceration are among poor, urban, and minority populations. *See, e.g.,* MICHAEL TONRY, SENTENCING MATTERS (1996); GEORGE L. KELLING AND CATHERINE M. COLES, FIXING BROKEN WINDOWS (1998); NATIONAL CRIMINAL JUSTICE COMMISSION, THE REAL WAR ON CRIME (1996); KENNEDY, *supra* note 9 (introduction); ELLIOTT CURRIE, CRIME AND PUNISHMENT IN AMERICA (1998); DAVID COLE, NO EQUAL JUSTICE (1999), *supra* note 5; MARC MAUER, RACE TO INCARCERATE (1999); AND MICHAEL TONRY, MALIGN NEGLECT (1995).

14. *But see* Tracey L. Meares, *Place and Crime,* 73 CHI.-KENT. L. REV. 669 (1998) (arguing for a social understanding of crime prevention).

15. THOMAS J. SUGRUE, THE ORIGINS OF THE URBAN CRISIS: RACE AND INEQUALITY IN POSTWAR DETROIT (1996). Michael Taussig has written of the numbness that the permanency of "crisis" can bring, preventing any meaningful understanding of the severity of the problems people face in their daily lives. *See* Michael Taussig, *Terror as Usual: Walter Benjamin's Theory of History as State of Siege, in* THE NERVOUS SYSTEM (1992). One of the tasks of the contemporary ethnographer is to resurrect the public's connection with lived reality of those in crisis.

16. A return to the anthropological runs against a trend in anthropology itself. Paradoxically, while other disciplines have been plundering anthro-

pology's own rich theoretical trove—with political scientists discovering social exchange, economists discovering kinship, and legal scholars discovering the power of social norms and informal sanctions—anthropologists have been looking elsewhere. But as much as other disciplines have added to our understanding of these core anthropological concerns, they have also made them more abstract and hypothetical, less grounded in the careful fieldwork that originally imbued them with their depth of meaning. Part of my goal in lending an anthropological perspective to contemporary political and policy debates, then, is to reclaim these concepts in a way that is both insistently anthropological and empirically grounded.

17. The literatures on exchange, reciprocity, kinship, and social norms are often tightly integrated. For example, both Marcel Mauss and Claude Lévi-Strauss, perhaps two of the best known and earliest major analysts of exchange, note the fundamental role of kinship in modeling and regulating how the norm of reciprocity is articulated in exchange. *See* MARCEL MAUSS, THE GIFT passim (1990) (1925); CLAUDE LÉVI-STRAUSS, THE ELEMENTARY STRUCTURES OF KINSHIP passim (1949). These concerns have been developed by anthropologists in a number of works, only a few of which can be mentioned here. On exchange and reciprocity, see MARSHAL SAHLINS, STONE AGE ECONOMICS (1972). For a classic introduction to household economy, see Donald Bender, *A Refinement of the Concept of Household,* 69 AM. ANTHROPOLOGIST 493 (1983). On kinship, see ROBIN FOX, KINSHIP AND MARRIAGE (1967); IRA R. BUCHLER AND HENRY A. SELBY, KINSHIP AND SOCIAL ORGANIZATION (1968); BERNARD FARBER, COMPARATIVE KINSHIP SYSTEMS (1968); ROGER M. KEESING, KIN GROUPS AND SOCIAL STRUCTURE 131, 142 (1975); DAVID M. SCHNEIDER, AMERICAN KINSHIP (1980); COONTZ, *supra* note 13 (introduction). For a review of social networks literature, see ULF HANNERZ, EXPLORING THE CITY 163–201 (1980).

18. *See, e.g.,* Francis Fukuyama, *Social Capital, in* CULTURE MATTERS (Lawrence E. Harrison and Samuel P. Huntington eds., 2000); ADAM B. SELIGMAN, THE PROBLEM OF TRUST (1997); ROBERT PUTNAM, BOWLING ALONE (2000).

19. Putnam, *supra* note 18 (introduction).

20. I suspect that few scholars of social norms working outside the field of anthropology have read the early works in this area. *See, e.g.,* BRONISLAW MALINOWSKI, CRIME AND CUSTOM IN SAVAGE SOCIETY 30–50 (1926) (discussing the norm of reciprocity); FREDRIK BARTH, POLITICAL LEADERSHIP AMONG SWAT PATHANS (1959) (developing an "interactionist" theory of norm formation); F. G. BAILEY, STRATAGEMS, AND SPOILS (1969) (describing the pragmatic negotiation of social norms in India, England, and France). *See also* KEESING, *supra* note 17 (introduction) (describing the dynamic negotiation of norms in relation to structural understandings of kinship).

21. There has been an "explosion of interest" in social norms over the last five years. Robert C. Ellickson, *Law and Economics Discovers Social Norms,* 27 J. LEGAL STUD. 537, 542 (1998). Those associated with bringing discussions about social norms into the legal mainstream have been called the "new

Chicago school"–"new" because it has displaced much of the previous law-and-economics scholarship conducted by the "old" Chicago school. *See* Lawrence Lessig, *The New Chicago School,* 27 J. LEGAL STUD. 661 (1998) (suggesting the utility of viewing the social norms analysis of the new Chicago school as the successor of the law-and-economics analysis of the old Chicago school).

22. Putnam's work has brought the importance of social networks to individual and collective well-being to public attention, making three core arguments: (1) the last half century has been witness to several trends, including an extended period of peace, declining leisure time, more television watching, and suburban sprawl; (2) as a result, social networks are both weaker and less dense than they used to be; and (3) this has a host of negative consequences. *See, generally,* PUTNAM, *supra* note 18 (introduction). Unfortunately, because Putnam does not observe or describe the lives of real people in any detail, his causal arguments are (as he admits) speculative and his policy recommendations vague. The lack of grounded detail in Putnam's work obscures the ways that pursuit of social capital may force compliance with norms that, while normally beneficial, can be quite costly for those from whom assistance is expected but to whom little help is given. This concern is similar to that raised by Bourdieu when he argues that the norms that obtain in social exchange can be enforced in ways that are exploitative, abusive, and dominating. *See, e.g.,* PIERRE BOURDIEU, THE LOGIC OF PRACTICE 108–10 (1990).

23. Putnam, for example, focuses less on policies that erode social capital and more on what individuals and communities can do outside of the realm of law and policy. *See, generally,* ROBERT D. PUTNAM, LEWIS M. FELDSTEIN, AND DON COHEN, BETTER TOGETHER: RESTORING THE AMERICAN COMMUNITY (2003).

24. *See supra* note 21 (introduction).

25. Dan Kahan, a leading figure in the social norms movement, puts the matter succinctly when he writes that "[e]conomic analyses of criminal law that abstract from social meaning fail, on their own terms, because social meaning is something people value." Dan M. Kahan, *Social Meaning and the Economic Analysis of Crime,* 27 J. LEGAL. STUD. 609 (1998). Ann Oakley and John Ashton have also described the predicament that the "accountancy-driven" approach brings with it, noting that "while we have begun to understand the cost of everything, we are in danger of losing track of the value of anything." Ann Oakley and John Ashton, *Introduction to the New Edition, in* RICHARD TITMUSS, THE GIFT RELATIONSHIP: FROM HUMAN BLOOD TO SOCIAL POLICY 11 (Ann Oakley and John Ashton eds., 1997).

26. For two notable exceptions, see ROBERT ELLICKSON, ORDER WITHOUT LAW (1991) (describing how extra-legal norms shape fence-sharing practices among ranchers in Shasta County, California); and Ryan Goodman, *Beyond the Enforcement Principle,* 89 CALIF. L. REV. 643 (2001) (describing the effects of constitutionally endorsed social norms on gay life in South Africa).

27. This is acknowledged in the literature and is a matter of regular complaint. Mark Tushnet, for example, notes:

> The problem . . . is that norms are really complicated things. Indeed, they are hardly "things" at all. They are unstable, subject to constant renegotiation and redefinition through processes of interaction that lead the new Chicago School to develop models. But modeling requires abstraction, and abstracting from norms is quite likely to generate either models that have essentially nothing to do with the real world of norms, or entirely formal results. Moreover, to the extent that one is interested in real norms in the real world, one would have to do a fair amount of empirical investigation. Aficionados of law and society studies know that legal academics are not well-trained to do such research and, even more, that the legal academy's reward structure actively discourages it. This may account for the fact, as it seems to me, that articles [from the legal academy that focus on social norms] have a rather high ratio of programmatic statements and illustrative (and short) anecdotes to actual investigations of real norms in real social settings.

Mark V. Tushnet, *"Everything Old Is New Again": Early Reflections on the "New Chicago School,"* 1998 WIS. L. REV. 579, 586–87 (1998) (footnotes excluded). *See also* Goodman, *supra* note 26 (introduction), at 645 ("These scholarly efforts have developed analytic models to describe law's impact, but little empirical work has been conducted to examine law's actual effects in society.").

28. *See, e.g.,* Dan Kahan, *What Do Alternative Sanctions Mean?* 63 U. CHI. L. REV. 591, at 591 (1996) ("Social norms permit the construction of a rich array of shaming practices, all of which unambiguously convey moral condemnation. By using these practices, either alone or in combination with conventional sanctions such as fines and community service, American jurisdictions can fashion politically acceptable alternative sanctions."); Stephen P. Garvey, *Can Shaming Punishments Educate?* 65 U. CHI. L. REV. 733, 739 (1998) ("Under the right circumstances shaming may live up to its billing as a cost effective and politically viable alternative to imprisonment.").

29. Jeremy Travis, *Invisible Punishment: An Instrument of Social Exclusion, in* INVISIBLE PUNISHMENT: THE COLLATERAL CONSEQUENCES OF MASS IMPRISONMENT (Marc Mauer and Meda Chesney-Lind eds., 2002).

Chapter 1

1. There were five subsequent Zoning Commission hearings. *See* Zoning Commission Hearings In the Matter of: Consolidated PUD and Related Map Amendment at Oxon Cove–D.C. Correctional Facility, Case No. 98–16C, November 16, 1998; November 19, 1998; May 17, 1999; May 24, 1999; and May 27, 1999 (hereinafter "November 16 Hearing," "November 19 Hearing," "May 17 Hearing," "May 24 Hearing," and "May 27 Hearing").

2. *Job Training Program Comes to Ward Eight–But You'll Have to Go to Prison to Get It*, COMMON DENOMINATOR, Nov. 19, 1998, at A2.

3. Testimony of Marion Barry, May 24 Hearing, *supra* note 1 (chap. 1). It should be noted that inmates are excluded from unemployment rates.

4. Testimony of Naomie K. Martin, May 24 Hearing, *supra* note 1 (chap. 1).

5. Testimony of Eugene Kinlow, May 24 Hearing, *supra* note 1 (chap. 1) ("The second document lists those groups and organizations that are opposed to a prison at the Oxon Cove location and it starts off, it's broken out in sections. The first section are letters from the economic development organizations that operate in Ward Eight including the Anacostia Economic Development Corporation, the East of the River Development Corporation and the Far Southwest Southeast Community Development Corporation. The second part indicates those officials, elected officials in Washington, D.C. who are opposed to a prison, including Mayor Anthony Williams; our Council Member on Ward Eight, Sandy Allen; Council Member David Cattania, Howard Brazil, Phil Mendelssohn, Kevin Chavez, etcetera. So it lists all the groups, coalitions, Maryland government officials, coalitions of associations and federations, political parties and entities and others, including churches and so on.")

6. Testimony of the Reverend Dennis Wiley, May 27 Hearing, *supra* note 1 (chap. 1).

7. Covenant House of Washington Youth Congress. As Mr. Pair described it, "Youth Congress is a youth advocacy program located in Southeast Washington. We strive to work together to make positive and sustaining changes in our community."

8. Testimony of David Pair, May 27 Hearing, *supra* note 1 (chap. 1).

9. Testimony of Damion Cain, May 27 Hearing, *supra* note 1 (chap. 1).

10. In the District of Columbia property insurers are not allowed to practice geographic discrimination and insurance redlining. *See Fireman's Insurance Co. of Washington, D.C. v. Washington*, 483 F.2d 1323 (D.C. Cir. 1973) (affirming judgment holding invalid regulations prohibiting geographic discrimination as to basic property insurance).

11. *See* United States Conference of Mayors, *America's Homeownership Gap: How Urban Redlining and Mortgage Lending Discrimination Penalize City Residents* 1 (1998) (finding that "urban redlining has ruined and continues to ruin thousands of minority communities") <http://www.usmayors.org/uscm/news/press_releases/press_archive.asp?doc_ id=98>.

12. Testimony of Robin Ijames, May 24 Hearing, *supra* note 1 (chap. 1).

13. *See* LOTKE, *supra* note 1 (introduction).

14. *See infra* figure 6 (chap. 4) and accompanying text.

Chapter 2

1. Elijah Anderson gives the most extensive description of what it means to be "decent." *See* ELIJAH ANDERSON, THE CODE OF THE STREET 37–45 (2000).

2. There are plenty of projects in the District that have been near disasters: Ellen Wilson, Valley Green, Stanton Dwellings, Frederick Douglass, Montana Terrace, Frontiers, Capital View Townhouses, Judiciary House, Carroll Apartments, East Capitol Dwellings, and Sheridan Terrace. Many are currently being demolished or rebuilt using Hope VI monies.

3. D.C. Police Department data, on file with author. *See* appendix for data description.

4. Usually fugitive, larceny, burglary, or robbery charges. DC Department of Corrections data, on file with author.

Chapter 3

1. Frederick Douglass, "Government of the District." THE NEW ERA, January 27, 1870, at 2. *See also* Kate Masur, *Reconstructing the Nation's Capital* (Ph.D. diss., University of Michigan, 2001).

2. Masur, *supra* note 1 (chap. 3).

3. *Plessy v. Ferguson*, 163 U.S. 537 (1896).

4. *Civil Rights Cases*, 109 U.S. 3 (1883).

5. *Shelley v. Kraemer*, 334 U.S. 1 (1948).

6. *See, e.g.*, Federal Housing Administration, Underwriting Manual: Underwriting and Valuation Procedure Under Title II of the National Housing Act With Revisions to April 1, 1936 (Washington, D.C.), Part II, Section 2, Rating of Location (recommending underwriting in cases where deed restrictions include "racial occupancy" restrictions and against underwriting in neighborhoods that allow for "inharmonious racial groups").

> The Valuator should realize that the need for protection from adverse influences is greater in an undeveloped or partially developed area than in any other type of neighborhood. Generally, a high rating should be given only where adequate and enforced zoning regulations exist or where effective restrictive covenants are recorded against the entire tract, since these provide the surest protection against undesirable encroachment and inharmonious use. To be most effective, deed restrictions should be imposed upon all land in the immediate environment of the subject location. . . . Recommended restrictions should include provisions for the following . . . Prohibition of the occupancy of properties except by the race for which they are intended.

7. "Black communities" is, admittedly, a gloss. *See* GODFREY FRANKEL AND LAURA GOLDSTEIN, IN THE ALLEYS: KIDS IN THE SHADOW OF THE CAPITOL 47 (1995) ("It was still a segregated city, but believe it or not, there was mixed housing you could have half a block that was white from one section up to the end, and the next section would be black from one end to the other."). While some neighborhoods were mixed, the vast majority were two-thirds majority black or white. JAMES BORCHERT, ALLEY LIFE IN WASHINGTON: FAMILY, COMMUNITY, RELIGION, AND FOLKLIFE IN THE CITY, 1850–1970 44 (1982).

8. Elanine B. Todd, *Urban Renewal in the Nation's Capital: A History of*

the RLA in Washington, D.C. 1946–1973, at 41–47 (Ph.D. diss., Howard University, 1986).

9. BORCHERT, *supra* note 7 (chap. 3), at 219–20. *See also, generally,* EUGENE D. GENOVESE, ROLL JORDAN ROLL (1974); and HERBERT G. GUTMAN, THE BLACK FAMILY IN SLAVERY AND FREEDOM, 1750–1925 (1976).

10. Medell E. Ford, *quoted in* FRANKEL AND GOLDSTEIN, *supra* note 7 (chap. 3), at 51, 58.

11. Hilton O. Overton Jr., *quoted in* FRANKEL AND GOLDSTEIN, *supra* note 7 (chap. 3), at 49.

12. DOLORES HAYDEN, THE GRAND DOMESTIC REVOLUTION 7 (1981). *See also* DOLORES HAYDEN, REDESIGNING THE AMERICAN DREAM (1984); KENNETH JACKSON, CRABGRASS FRONTIER: THE SUBURBANIZATION OF THE UNITED STATES (1985); MARK BALDASSARE, TROUBLE IN PARADISE: THE SUBURBAN TRANSFORMATION IN AMERICA (1986); David W. Bartlet, *Housing the Underclass, in* THE "UNDERCLASS" DEBATE: VIEWS FROM HISTORY (Michael B. Katz ed., 1993); Thomas J. Sugrue, *The Structure of Inequality, in* THE "UNDERCLASS" DEBATE: VIEWS FROM HISTORY (Michael B. Katz ed., 1993); and Michael B. Katz, *Reframing the Underclass Debate, in* THE "UNDERCLASS" DEBATE: VIEWS FROM HISTORY (Michael B. Katz ed., 1993).

13. Tim Wise, *The Mother of All Racial Preferences,* March 20, 2003, at <http://.zmag.org///-03/.cfm>.

14. Hayden, *supra* note 12 (chap. 3), REDESIGNING THE AMERICAN DREAM. This occurred not only in Washington but across the nation. *See* WILLIAM JULIUS WILSON, WHEN WORK DISAPPEARS 46 (1996) ("By manipulating market incentives, the federal government drew middle-class whites to the suburbs and, in effect, trapped blacks in the inner cities. Beginning in the 1950s, the suburbanization of the middle class was also facilitated by a federal transportation and highway policy, including building freeway networks through the hearts of many cities, mortgages for veterans, mortgage-interest tax exemptions, and the quick, cheap production of massive amounts of tract housing.")

15. Early plans to run freeways through white neighborhoods were quickly quashed in Congress. *See* HOWARD GILLETTE JR., BETWEEN JUSTICE AND BEAUTY 165 (1995) ("Formidable opposition, much of it from members of Congress whose own homes were threatened, managed to kill the proposed Wisconsin Avenue Interstate in affluent Northwest Washington.")

16. *Id.* at 169.

17. *Id.*

18. *Brown v. Board,* 347 U.S. 483 (1954).

19. Martin Luther King, Jr. I Have a Dream, Address to the March on Washington (Aug. 28, 1963).

20. This was one of the main concerns that conservatives had with Brown at the time. *See, e.g.,* Albert A. Mavrinac, *From Lochner to Brown v. Topeka: The Court and Conflicting Concepts of the Political Process,* 52 AM. POL. SCI. REV. 3, 641 (1958) (complaining that the Court had abandoned the individualist conception of justice embodied in *Lochner* for a group-based

conception in *Brown*). *See also,* Alan F. Westin, *The Supreme Court and Group Conflict,* 52 AM. POL. SCI. REV. 3. 665 (1958) (arguing that this was an appropriate response to a new and "contemporary" understanding of equal protection under the law).

21. The problems that the concentration of poverty created in the inner cities are now well documented, and there are excellent suggestions about what should be done. *See, especially,* OWEN FISS, A WAY OUT (2003).

22. *See* WILSON, *supra* note 14 (chap. 3).

23. This happened for many reasons. Land was much cheaper in the suburbs; suburbs were offering massive incentives; and transportation allowed many firms to relocate. Crime rates in 1970 were also at all-time highs in the inner cities, and many employers simply saw the costs of crime as too great. Some of the move may also have been related to racial bias as well; many employers viewed white suburban workers as simply more qualified than urban black workers.

24. While the overall number of jobs grew with the aggressive development of the downtown area, the job base for those living in local neighborhoods actually shrank, as positions were filled by those living outside of the District. GILLETTE, *supra* note 15 (chap. 3), at 198. The jobs that were available to District residents were nearly inaccessible to the population living in areas that had been cut off by the freeways and that mass transit did not reach–again, mostly poor, mostly black neighborhoods. The District's subway did not reach Shaw or Southeast Washington until 1991. WASHINGTON METROPOLITAN AREA METRO AUTHORITY, CAPSULE HISTORY OF WMATA 5–6 (2002).

25. *See* HEWLETT AND WEST, *supra* note 13 (introduction), at 98–99 (describing "a uniform $600 exception per dependent person" in the late 1940s, "which would be worth $6500 in 1996 dollars"). Both Presidents Kennedy and Nixon failed to include increases in the deduction to account for inflation (*id.* at 103).

26. *See id.* at 103 ("Richard Nixon's tax reform package of 1969 [limited] the gains from income splitting to 20 percent of total income.").

27. *Id.* at 104. While Republicans were the most vocal proponents of tax cuts, Democrats from Kennedy to Clinton followed suit, though to a lesser extent. *See id.* at 103 and 109 ("Direct dismantling [of the pro-family tax code] began mildly enough with Kennedy's 1963 tax cut. Kennedy's tax bill instituted a new minimum standard deduction that paid no attention to the presence or absence of children." "In the summer of 1996, President Clinton, in a preelection bid for the support of affluent voters, all but eliminated capital gains taxes on the sale of expensive homes.").

28. Liberals generally accept the conservative claims that welfare benefits encourage single-parent households; they simply disagreed that this is undesirable. June Axinn and Amy Hirsch, for example, argue the point this way:

The current furor over "family disintegration" is a protest against the increased choices women have made in the past several decades. For women in abusive relationships, AFDC has offered hope and choice by supporting women and children outside of marriage. Welfare reform that attacks women for having children outside marriage represents a backlash against women's life options outside the traditional family system.

June Axinn and Amy Hirsch, *Welfare and the "Reform" of Women*, 74 FAMILIES IN SOCIETY 571 (1993). *See also* JOHNETTA COLE, CONVERSATIONS 140 (1994) (advocating an array of options from a "fairly permanent state of singleness to lesbianism to significant-othering" as solutions to the burdens that welfare laws place on marriage); Bonnie Angleo, *The Pain of Being Black*, TIME, May 22, 1989, at 122 (quoting Toni Morrison: "Why we are hanging on to [the nuclear family], I don't know. I don't think a female running a household is a problem.").

29. There is considerable debate over whether men's wages have been falling overall, after adjusting for inflation. *See* John M. Berry, *BLS to Test Experimental CPI*, WASH. POST, April 11, 1997, at G03. There is no debate, however, over the fact that during the 1970s, 1980s, and 1990s, while the top quarter of wage earners saw their pay increase, the bottom quarter of wage earners saw their pay drop off considerably.

Chapter 4

1. Some still see the District this way. *See* FRED SEIGEL, THE FUTURE ONCE HAPPENED HERE (1997).

2. *See, e.g.,* OWEN FISS, A WAY OUT (2003). Thomas J. Sugrue provides a more detailed account of this process in postwar Detroit. *See, generally,* SUGRUE, *supra* note 15 (introduction).

3. *See* U.S. DEPARTMENT OF JUSTICE, CORRECTIONS PROGRAMS OFFICE, CRIME AND JUSTICE ATLAS 40–41 (2000) (describing and depicting the historical incidence of various drug offenses).

4. *See* Alfred Blumstein and Allen J. Beck, *Population Growth in U.S. Prisons, 1980–1996*, 26 CRIME & JUST. 17, 28 (1999). *See also* Sandra Evans Skovron, *Prison Crowding: The Dimensions of the Problem and Strategies of Population Control, in* CONTROVERSIAL ISSUES IN CRIME AND JUSTICE 183 (Joseph E. Scott and Travis Hirschi eds., 1988) (arguing that, due to demographic shifts, the "baby-boom" generation reached an age bracket more likely to commit crimes at that time).

5. Richard Nixon effectively capitalized on the unexpected rise of crime, attributing it to Democratic failings and "conjur[ing] up the image of Washington as the 'crime capital of the world.'" *See* GILLETTE, *supra* note 15 (chap. 3), at 182.

6. An influential review of hundreds of rehabilitation programs published in 1975 convinced many that "nothing works." *See* DOUGLAS LIPTON ET AL., THE EFFECTIVENESS OF CORRECTIONAL TREATMENT: A SURVEY OF EVALUA-

TION STUDIES (1975). *See also* Robert Martinson, *What Works?–Questions and Answers about Prison Reform*, 35 PUB. INTEREST 22, 25 (1974) (concluding that "with few and isolated exceptions, and rehabilitative efforts that have been reported so far have had no appreciable effect on recidivism").

7. For a review of the literature, see Lawrence W. Sherman et al., *Preventing Crime: What Works, What Doesn't, What's Promising*, NATIONAL INSTITUTE OF JUSTICE–RESEARCH IN BRIEF (July 1998).

8. *See* John J. Diiulio Jr. *Prisons Are a Bargain, by Any Measure*, NEW YORK TIMES, January 16, 1996, at A17 ("All 30 Republican governors elected or re-elected in 1994 promised to get tough on crime.").

9. Until the mid-twentieth century, the view that prisoners were "slave[s] of the state" (*Ruffin v. Commonwealth* [1871]) held sway. But starting with the Supreme Court's decision in *Ex Parte Hull* (1941), the federal judiciary and legislative branches have intervened on behalf of prisoners in a number of ways. Under the federal Civil Rights Act of 1964, for example, inmates may challenge the conditions of their imprisonment based on the Equal Protection Clause of the Fifth and Fourteenth Amendments.

10. Comprehensive Crime Control Act of 1984, Pub. L. No. 98–473, 98 Stat. 1837 (1987) (codified as amended in scattered sections of 18 and 28 U.S.C.). Federal guidelines restricted the ability of judges to reduce sentences and provided model sentencing code for state and local jurisdictions.

11. Anti-Drug Abuse Act of 1986, Pub. L. No. 99–570, 100 Stat. 3207 (1989) (codified as amended in scattered sections of 16, 19, 20, 21 and 48 U.S.C.).

12. Omnibus Anti-Drug Abuse Act of 1988, Pub. L. No. 100–690, 102 Stat. 4181 (codified as amended at 28 U.S.C. ch. 13 [1988]). The mandatory minimum for possession of crack cocaine is viewed by many as having targeted black populations. *See* KENNEDY, *supra* note 9 (introduction), at 364–86 (describing the debate).

13. Violent Crime Control and Law Enforcement Act of 1994, Pub. L. No. 103–322, 320935(a), 108 Stat. 1796, 2136–37.

14. Violent Offender Incarceration/Truth in Sentencing Act 42 U.S.C. §§ 13701–712 (2000) (providing appropriations of over $997 million in authorized appropriations to eligible states for the 1996 fiscal year and providing for these amounts to increase yearly until 2000. For the 1997 fiscal year, over $1.3 billion was made available to states. In 1998 that amount increased to over $2.5 billion. In the 1999 fiscal year over $2.6 billion was available. In year 2000 over $2.75 billion was made available to states to subsidize the incarceration of violent offenders to facilitate a greater amount of prison time actually served.).

15. *See* Laura A. Kiernan and Al Kamen, *Crimes Involving Guns, Drug Sales; Mandatory Sentence Proposal Strongly Backed in D.C. Vote*, WASH. POST, September 15, 1982, at A15 ("District voters yesterday gave overwhelming approval to a proposal requiring mandatory minimum prison terms for most crimes involving guns and for certain drug offenses.").

16. *See* Neely Tucker, *New Sentencing Rules Take Effect in District; Set Terms Mandated; Parole Eliminated*, WASH. POST, August 6, 2000, at C01.

17. Estimates based on D.C. Department of Corrections statistics and U.S. Census data for the year 2000. Estimate assumes stable incarceration rates by age cohort and no in- or out-migration.

Part II

1. *See, generally,* HAROLD SCHEFFLER, FILIATION AND AFFILIATION (2000).

2. Of course, families can also be draining and oppressive, modeling selfish calculation and exploitation of others rather than reciprocal concern and support. This, essentially, is the point that Bourdieu makes in discussing kinship. *See* Bourdieu *supra* note 22 (introduction). *But cf.* MARGARET TRAWICK, NOTES ON LOVE IN A TAMIL FAMILY 135–39 (1990) (criticizing Bourdieu's reliance on selfish calculation as a universal explanation, seeing only the "hypocritical, oppressive side" of family relationships [at 139]); *cf. also* Hans Medick and David Warren Sabean, *Introduction, in* INTEREST AND EMOTION: ESSAYS IN THE STUDY OF FAMILY AND KINSHIP (Hans Medick and David Warren Sabean eds., 1984).

3. Erik Erikson and J. M. Erikson, *On Generativity and Identity,* 51 HARV. ED. REV. 2, 249, 288 (1981) (describing generativity as "the link between the life cycle and the generational cycle"). *See also, generally,* JOHN SNAREY, HOW FATHERS CARE FOR THE NEXT GENERATION (1993). Of course, generativity is not limited to those with children, and, as Erik Erickson describes, it infuses life with what is perhaps its greatest meaning.

4. The effects of impoverishment and reduced options on family life are, of course, not simply an American phenomenon. Parker Shipton has described how, in many African nations, "when reserves run low . . . family may change radically in meaning, or lose meaning." Parker Shipton, *African Famines and Food Security,* 19 ANN. REV. ANTHROPOLOGY 353, 357 (1990).

Chapter 5

1. For a history of this neighborhood, see Jenell Williams Paris, *"We've Seen This Coming": Resident Activists Shaping Neighborhood Redevelopment in Washington, D.C.,* unpublished manuscript, on file with author.

2. The phrase "sick and tired of being sick and tired" runs through the literature on recovery, particularly twelve-step programs. *See* ALCOHOLICS ANONYMOUS WORLD SERVICES, INC., ALCOHOLICS ANONYMOUS (3D ED. 2001).

3. ANDERSON, *supra* note 1 (chap. 2).

4. *See infra* note 8 (chap. 7) and accompanying text.

5. The National Center on Addiction and Substance Abuse, Columbia University, *"Behind Bars: Substance Abuse and America's Prison Population,"* January 1998.

6. Peter Slevin, *In D.C., Many Addicts and Few Services; Lack of Treatment Programs Keeps Substance Abusers in Jail or in Trouble,* WASH. POST, August 25, 1998, at A01.

7. DRUG STRATEGIES, FACING FACTS 1 (1999).

8. *Id.*

9. *See* Slevin, *supra* note 6 (chap. 5) ("Because drug treatment is so scarce in the District, prisoners who need help routinely spend extra time behind bars, just waiting.").

10. There are numerous descriptions of the behavioral and academic consequences of imprisonment on children in the social science literature. *See, e.g.,* T. A. Fritsch and I. D. Burkhead, *Behavioral Reactions of Children to Parental Absence Due to Imprisonment,* 83 FAMILY RELATIONS 88, at 30 (1981); L. ALES SWAN, FAMILIES OF BLACK PRISONERS: SURVIVAL AND PROGRESS (1981); A. Lowenstein, *Temporary Single Parenthood: The Case of Prisoners' Families,* 35 FAMILY RELATIONS 79 passim (1986).

Chapter 6

1. Murder and felony weapons counts are high-prestige arrests for police officers, so those hoping to move up in the ranks are more interested in homicide and weapons charges than drug charges.

2. Many families describe in strong terms the negative effect of incarceration on the attitude and schoolwork of children. *See, e.g., supra* chap. 5 (discussing Derek and Londa's daughter), chap. 8 (discussing Kenny's boys), and chap. 13 (discussing the Smiths' son). There are also descriptions of the behavioral and academic consequences of imprisonment on children in the social science literature. *See supra* note 10 (chap. 5).

3. Several studies have found the absence of a biological father to be a strong predictor of abuse. *See, e.g.,* Leslie Margolin, *Child Abuse by Mothers' Boyfriends,* 16 CHILD ABUSE AND NEGLECT 541–51 (1992); Margo I. Wilson and Martin Daly, *Risk of Maltreatment of Children Living with Stepparents, in* CHILD ABUSE AND NEGLECT: BIOSOCIAL DIMENSIONS (Richard J. Gelles and Jane B. Lancaster eds., 1987).

4. Figures are for men and women over the age of eighteen and are based on D.C. Department of Corrections and U.S. Census data. Figures were obtained by examining incarceration rates and adult male and female populations by census tract. Incarceration is one of many contributing factors that lead to such a high ratio of women to men, including higher male mortality rates. Unfortunately, at the time of this writing, separate population data for men and women in the specific age groups most affected by incarceration (ages eighteen to thirty-five) were not available.

5. *Cf.* ARLIE HOCHSCHILD, THE SECOND SHIFT 51 (1989) (describing the way that men and women perceive a "going rate" for gendered behavior–that is, men need not behave as their wives do, just as well or better than their partner's perceptions of other men); and Willard Waller, *The Rating and Dating Complex,* 2 AM. SOC. REV. 5, 727–34 (1934) (arguing that the person who has the least interest in continuing a romantic relationship can demand more from the relationship).

6. *See* Bruce Western, *Incarceration and Employment Inequality among*

Young, Unskilled Men 16 (visited Feb. 20, 2002) <http://opr.princeton.edu/pub/western/papers/employ.pdf> (finding a "pervasive influence of the penal system on the life chances of disadvantaged minorities").

7. WILSON, *supra* note 14 (chap. 3), at 63–92 (discussing the impact of poverty on family structure).

8. The psychiatric unit in Los Angeles County Jail, for example, is the largest mental health facility in the United States.

9. *See, e.g.,* CANADIAN PSYCHIATRIC ASSOCIATION, HIV & PSYCHIATRY, <http://www.cpa-apc.org/Publications/HIV/HIV.asp> (describing the loss of trust that clinicians encounter in counseling HIV-positive patients). HIV status also affects other relationships in other ways. David, Sandra, and Carla, for example, were all concealing their HIV status from their parents, siblings, and children.

Chapter 7

1. ORLANDO PATTERSON, RITUALS OF BLOOD 167 (1998).

2. *See* Bruce Western and Sara McLanahan, *Fathers Behind Bars: The Impact of Incarceration on Family Formation, in* FAMILIES, CRIME, AND CRIMINAL JUSTICE 309, 322 (Greer Litton Fox and Michael L. Benson eds., 2000) (citing evidence that incarceration has a "large destabilizing effect" on low-income families). *See also* Mark Testa and Marilyn Krogh, *The Effect of Employment on Marriage among Black Males in Inner-City Chicago, in* THE DECLINE IN MARRIAGE AMONG AFRICAN AMERICANS (M. Belinda Tucker and Claudia Mitchell-Kernan eds., 1995); Robert J. Sampson, *Unemployment and Imbalanced Sex Ratios, in* THE DECLINE IN MARRIAGE AMONG AFRICAN AMERICANS (M. Belinda Tucker and Claudia Mitchell-Kernan eds., 1995) (describing the influence of incarceration on joblessness and sex ratios). These findings logically reverse the causal relationship implicit in many other studies that describe familial environment as influencing rather than being influenced by involvement in the criminal justice system. *See, e.g.,* Robert Joseph Taylor et al., *Recent Demographic Trends in African American Family Structure, in* FAMILY LIFE IN BLACK AMERICA 46 (Robert Joseph Taylor et al. eds., 1997) (reviewing the literature on female-headed households and crime).

3. *See infra* note 8 (chap. 7).

4. *See* CAROL STACK, CALL TO HOME (1996) (describing reversal of the "great migration" from rural to urban America); Isaac Robinson, *Blacks Move Back to the South,* 8 AMERICAN DEMOGRAPHICS 40 (1986); Issac Robinson, *The Relative Impact of Migration Type on the Reversal of Black Out-Migration from the South,* 10 SOCIOLOGICAL SPECTRUM 373 (1990).

5. According to a recent Senate Report, "children of prisoners are six times more likely than other children to be incarcerated at some point in their lives." S. Rep. No. 106–404, at 56 (2000). *See also* Denise Johnston, *Effects of Parental Incarceration, in* CHILDREN OF INCARCERATED PARENTS 80 (Katherine Gabel and Denise Johnston eds., 1995) ("children of offenders

are far more likely than other children to enter the criminal justice system"). Recent studies have also shown that generative parenting also improves the quality of life of fathers, increasing not only fathers' occupational mobility but also their marital success and contributions to society at large. *See* SNAREY *supra* note 3 (part II), at 105–19.

6. *See* MAUSS, *supra* note 17 (introduction). *See also infra* notes 14–18 (chap. 11) and accompanying text.

7. Jacques Godbout has nicely deflated the utilitarian model of marriage. *See* JACQUES T. GODBOUT, ALAIN CAILLÉ, AND DONALD WINKLER, THE WORLD OF THE GIFT 30–33 (1998). *See also* Arlie R. Hochschild, *The Economy of Gratitude, in* THE SOCIOLOGY OF EMOTIONS (David D. Franks and E. Doyle McCarthy eds., 1989).

8. This finding is consistent with findings from a number of empirical studies of low-income and minority populations. *See, e.g.,* M. Belinda Tucker, *Marital Values and Expectations in Context: Results from a 21-City Survey, in* THE TIES THAT BIND 166, 182–83 (Linda J. Waite ed., 2000). *See also, generally,* Wendy D. Manning and Pamela J. Smock, *Why Marry? Race Relations and Transition to Marriage among Cohabitors,* 95 DEMOGRAPHY 509 (1995); Michael J. Brien and Lee A. Lillard, *Interrelated Family-Building Behaviors: Cohabitation, Marriage and Non-Marital Conception,* 36 DEMOGRAPHY 535 (1999).

9. This is consistent with the findings of the only longitudinal statistical study to date of incarceration's effect on family formation using individual-level data. The study found that incarceration had a much smaller effect on separation rates among married couples than it did among unmarried couples. *See* Western and McLanahan *supra* note 2 (chap. 7).

10. *See, e.g.,* DINESH D'SOUZA, THE END OF RACISM 24 (1995) (arguing that the black underclass suffers not from lack of opportunity or racism but from "excessive reliance on government, conspiratorial paranoia about racism, a resistance to academic achievement as 'acting white,' a celebration of the criminal outlaw as authentically black, and the normalization of illegitimacy and dependency"); CHARLES MURRAY, THE UNDERCLASS REVISITED 33 (1999) ("[D]uring the last three decades [urban black culture] has increasingly been infiltrated by an underclass subculture that celebrates a bastardized code duello, predatory sex, and 'getting paid'—a euphemism for forcibly extracting money from someone else. The violence and misogyny that pervade certain forms of popular music are coordinate with these values. So is the hooker look in fashion and the flaunting of obscenity and vulgarity in comedy. Perhaps most disturbing is the widening expression, often approving, of underclass ethics: take what you want; respond violently to anyone who antagonizes you; despise courtesy as weakness; take pride in cheating (stealing, lying, exploiting) successfully."). *See also* MARTIN ANDERSON, WELFARE (1978); MARVIN OLASKY, THE TRAGEDY OF AMERICAN COMPASSION (1992); MYRON MAGNET, THE DREAM AND THE NIGHTMARE (1993); CHARLES MURRAY, THE UNDERCLASS REVISITED (1999).

11. This is, in many ways, a lopsided criminal application of a "normative failure" theory of law. *See* Robert Cooter, *Normative Failure Theory of Law*, 82 CORNELL L. REV. 947, 948 (1997) ("Just as regulations ideally correct failures in markets, laws ideally correct failures in social norms. No law is required when the 'market' for social norms works, but when it fails, law may improve the situation by enforcing a beneficial social norm, suppressing a harmful social norm, or supplying a missing obligation. The theory of normative failures is a diagnostic tool for explaining if, when, and how the state should intervene by imposing law."). *See also* ERIC A. POSNER, LAW AND SOCIAL NORMS 221 (2000) ("The rule of law . . . can be understood as the appropriate legal response to dysfunctions of nonlegal enforcement mechanisms. Social norms keep a rudimentary sort of order, and are surely superior to chaos, but they provoke a longing for predictability, a longing that can be satisfied only by a wealthy and powerful government. So if a side effect of the rule of law is the loss of certain collective benefits that can be obtained only through nonlegal enforcement, that might seem a straightforward improvement.").

12. *See* FRANCIS FUKUYAMA, THE GREAT DISRUPTION 82 (1999) ("Family breakdown often proves to be an important mediating variable that explains how poverty is related to crime: poor families are not simply ones whose job opportunities are blocked by lack of education or transportation; they are often ones without fathers present in the home who can encourage, discipline, serve as role models, and otherwise socialize sons."); James H. Andrews, *Cities Identify "Risk Factors" That Lead to Juvenile Crime*, CHRISTIAN SCIENCE MONITOR, Nov. 18, 1986, at 25; WILLIAM A. GALSTON AND ELAINE CIULLA KAMARK, PUTTING CHILDREN FIRST: A PROGRESSIVE FAMILY POLICY FOR THE 1990S 14–15 (1990) (noting that "controlling for family configuration erases the relationship between race and crime and between low income and crime").

Chapter 8

1. Kenny's daughter was by a previous relationship, but also lived with Kenny and Edwina.

2. *See* STACK, *supra* note 4 (chap. 7).

3. *See, e.g.,* GEORGE SHER, DESERT (1987).

4. Sixty-seven percent of urban blacks feel that courts are "not harsh enough" in dealing with criminals, 17 percent feel courts are "too harsh," and 16 percent feel courts get it "about right." General Social Survey (2000).

5. *See infra* fig. 3 (chap. 4) and accompanying text.

6. *See* KENNEDY *supra* note 9 (introduction), at 29 (arguing that lack of protection against criminality "is one of the most destructive forms of oppression that has been visited upon African-Americans"); Dan M. Kahan, *Social Influence, Social Meaning, and Deterrence*, 83 VA. L. REV. 349 (1997) ("[A]ggressive panhandling, prostitution, open gang activity and other visible signs of disorder . . . are cues about the community's attitude toward more serious forms of criminal wrongdoing.").

7. ANDERSON, *supra* note 1 (chap. 2), at 109.

8. *See infra* pages 55–56 (chap. 5) and accompanying notes for more discussion.

9. Christopher J. Mumola, Bureau of Justice Statistics, Special Report, Incarcerated Parents and Their Children 5 (2000). Estimates from the 1999 prison survey indicate that 1,372,700 children have a father who is incarcerated; a majority (667,900) of prisoners are fathers; and over 60 percent of incarcerated fathers have at least monthly contact with their children.

10. Bureau of Justice Statistics, Survey of State Prison Inmates, 1991 (1993).

11. While not all inmates in this study were as gainfully employed as Kenny, most families felt they contributed more than they took.

Chapter 9

1. *See infra* page 116 for these "prison worries."

2. This is precisely the kind of relationship that Marcel Mauss describes in his classic study of reciprocity and exchange. MAUSS *supra* note 17 (introduction). As David Graeber has noted, the type of "total prestations" described by Mauss

> create permanent relationships between individuals and groups, relations that were permanent precisely because there is no way to cancel them out by a repayment. The demands one side could make on the other were open ended because they were permanent. . . . Most of us treat our closest friends this way. No accounts need be kept because the relation is not treated as if it will ever end.

DAVID GRAEBER, TOWARD AN ANTHROPOLOGICAL THEORY OF VALUE 218 (2001).

3. She does this either when they are at her home or by calling them using three-way dialing when they are not. The use of three-way dialing is prohibited but widely used by families. For further discussion, see *infra* note 16 (chap. 9) and accompanying text.

4. This is a central argument of Jonetta Rose Barras's recent memoir. *See* JONETTA ROSE BARRAS, WHATEVER HAPPENED TO DADDY'S LITTLE GIRL (2000).

5. Ann Quigley, *Father's Absence Increases Daughter's Risk of Teen Pregnancy,* HEALTH BEHAVIOR NEWS SERVICE, May 14, 2003.

6. *Id.*

7. *See, e.g.,* Marianne E. Page and Ann Huff Stevens, *The Economic Consequences of Absent Parents,* unpublished manuscript, on file with author.

8. Megan Lee Comfort, *32 In the Tube at San Quentin: The "Secondary Prisonization" of Women Visiting Inmates* 1, 77 (2003).

9. *Id.* at 23.

10. See part III for further discussion of stigma and stereotype threat.

11. *See supra* note on page 90 (chap. 7).

12. *See supra* pages 80–84 in chap. 6 (discussion of David's son, Charles).

13. In his trilogy on attachment, separation, and loss, John Bowlby

describes anger as one of the most common responses to separation, particularly childhood separation. *See, generally,* JOHN BOWLBY, SEPARATION: ANXIETY AND ANGER (2000): 245–57. Bowlby describes separation as often leading to "aggressive and/or destructive behavior during a period of separation," behavior that is sometimes directed "towards all and sundry." *Id* at 248. He also notes that children "who have experienced long and/or repeated separations" are far more likely to have "angry and fault-finding responses" than are children raised in stable families. *Id.* at 253. This is, of course, significant given that many poor inner-city children do not grow up in stable families and are far more likely than average to be moved from one caretaker to another. It also bears on the responses that young men may have to criminal convictions. For further discussion, see *infra* notes 7–16 (chap. 12) and accompanying text.

14. *See, e.g.,* Ronald Glaser et al., *Stress-Induced Immunomodulation: Implications for Infectious Diseases* 281 JAMA 2268 (1999) (describing the effects of stress on susceptibility to and recovery from infectious diseases). *See also* Michael L. Blakey, *Psychophysiological Stress and Disorders of Industrial Society, in* DIAGNOSING AMERICA (Sheperd Foreman ed., 1995); HANDBOOK OF HUMAN STRESS AND IMMUNITY (Ronald R. Glaser and Janice Kiecolt-Glaser eds., 1994). For an illuminating example of the influence of emotion on the body, see Linda-Anne Rebhun's description of "nerves" in Northeast Brazil. LINDA-ANNE REBHUN, THE HEART IS UNKNOWN COUNTRY 19–35 (2001) (describing the sometimes unexpected physical effects of emotional responses).

15. I discuss this coping strategy in more detail in chapter 5.

16. Paul Duggan, *Captive Audience Rates High; Families Must Pay Dearly When Inmates Call Collect,* WASH. POST, January 23, 2000, at A03. As a result, collect calls from prisons can be as much as twenty times as expensive as standard collect calls.

Chapter 10

1. During our interview, Clinton recalled being about six years old, but subsequent discussions with him and other family members indicated that he was closer to eight at the time.

2. For discussion of the problems with part-time work, see Jeffery Wenger, *The Continuing Problems with Part-Time Work,* Economic Policy Institute Issue Brief #155, April 24, 2001.

3. The criticism of prison labor as a modern-day form of slavery, while not prominent, has been a regular criticism of both over-incarceration in general and prison labor in particular. *See, e.g.,* Graham Boyd, *The Drug War Is the New Jim Crow,* 35 NACLA REPORT ON THE AMERICAS 18 ("Slaves were forced to work in inhuman conditions with no control over their situation and no remuneration. Public authorities today, intimidated by the rising costs of building and maintaining prisons, have introduced an innovative program as the panacea of incarceration: prison labor."); Kim Gilmore,

Slavery and Prison–Understanding the Connections, 3 SOCIAL JUSTICE 27, 195 (2000) ("Built into the 13th Amendment was state authorization to use prison labor as a bridge between slavery and paid work.").

4. One of the major factors leading to a near-riot in a prison contracted by the District was the mixing of populations that were supposed to be separated for security reasons. Two inmates were killed in the incident. *See* John L. Clark, Corrections Trustee of the District of Columbia, Report to the Attorney General Inspection and Review of the Northeast Ohio Correctional Center, November 25, 1998.

5. *See* Nurith C. Aizenman, *Laborers Ousted from Gathering Spot,* WASH. POST, June 1, 2001, at B01; Nurith C. Aizenman, *Day Laborers Seeking Gathering Place; Owner of Current Site Vows to Bar Them,* WASH. POST, Prince George's Extra, June 7, 2001, at T03. Nurith C. Aizenman, *Day Laborers in Search of New Place to Seek Work; Mall Owner Moves to Make One Gathering Spot Off Limits,* WASH. POST, Montgomery Extra, June 14, 2001, at T07.

6. Incarcerated fathers face a more extreme and stigmatized version of the fears about providing enough for and spending enough time with their children than many middle-class fathers. *See, generally,* NICHOLAS TOWNSEND, THE PACKAGE DEAL (2002) (describing the pressures that middle-class fathers feel about family life).

7. *See* PHILIPPE BOURGOIS, IN SEARCH OF RESPECT: SELLING CRACK IN EL BARRIO (1995) (finding similarly meager income and lifestyles among low-level crack dealers in New York City).

8. General Social Survey 1988–2002.

9. *See, e.g.,* KATHRYN EDIN AND LAURA LEIN, MAKING ENDS MEET: HOW SINGLE MOTHERS SURVIVE WELFARE AND LOW-WAGE WORK 158 (1997) ("Mothers who relied on boyfriends for income sometimes had to choose between danger and destitution. . . . [M]any mothers reported that they or their children had been physically or sexually abused by their domestic partners at some point in the past. . . . [Some] ignored the abuse because they were so desperate for their boyfriends money."); Eleanor Lyon, *Welfare, Poverty, and Abused Women: New Research and Its Implications,* National Resource Center on Domestic Violence (2000); Randy Albelda, *What Has Happened to Those Who Left the Massachusetts Welfare Rolls?* BOSTON GLOBE, Oct. 30, 1997, at A23.

10. *See supra* note 16 (chap. 9) and accompanying text (discussing phone rates).

Chapter 11

1. *See* WILSON, *supra* note 14 (chap. 3), at 21. This, in turn, has a host of other deleterious effects on neighborhood norms regarding conduct and lawful behavior.

2. *See supra* notes 5–7 (chap. 10) and accompanying text.

3. *See* Mumola, *supra* note 9 (chap. 8).

4. *See, e.g.,* Bruce Western, Becky Pettit, and Josh Guetzkow, *Black Eco-*

nomic Progress in the Era of Mass Imprisonment, in INVISIBLE PUNISHMENT: THE COLLATERAL CONSEQUENCES OF MASS IMPRISONMENT (Marc Mauer and Meda Chesney-Lind eds., 2002) (arguing that offenders have greater difficulty finding work after release due to both their criminal record and their lack of employment history for the period of incarceration).

5. *See* Daniel Nagin and Joel Waldfogel, *The Effect of Conviction on Income through the Life Cycle,* 18 INT. REV. L. & ECON. 25 (1998).

6. Economists have recently become more aware of the importance of the care that family members provide for one another. Paula England and Nancy Folbre, for example, describe the significance of it this way:

> For one thing, had someone not developed these capabilities enough to nurture each of us when we were children, we would all be dead, or at least so anti-social as to be locked up. The broader point is that one's need to receive care from someone other than oneself flows from the fact that we are all sometimes unable to provide needed care for ourselves. Despite the glorification of autonomy in classical liberal theory, there are inevitable dependencies in human life.

Paula England and Nancy Folbre, *Reconceptualizing Human Capital,* paper presented at the annual meeting of the American Sociological Association, Toronto, Canada, August 1997.

7. There are other causes as well. For example, blacks don't live as long, on average, as whites and thus fail to reap the same benefits from Social Security and retirement benefits. *See, generally,* Marjorie Honig, *Minorities Face Retirement: Worklife Disparities Repeated? in* FORECASTING RETIREMENT NEEDS AND RETIREMENT WEALTH (Olivia S. Mitchell et al. eds., 1999).

8. Mark Jospeh, *The Economic Consequences of a Criminal Background* (Ph.D. diss., University of Chicago).

9. *See supra* note 13 (introduction) (listing major reviews of the literature on disparate impact).

10. Michael Lynch, *Piece of the Pie,* REASON MAGAZINE, July (1998). *See also* Francine D. Blau and John W. Graham, *Black-White Differences in Wealth and Asset Composition,* 105 QUART. J. ECON. 2, 321–39 (1990); MELVIN OLIVER AND T. SHAPIRO, BLACK WEALTH/WHITE WEALTH (1995).

11. *See, e.g.,* James P. Smith, *Racial and Ethnic Differences in Wealth in the Health and Retirement Study,* 30 J. HUM. RESOURCES, S158–83 (1995); Robert B. Avery and Michael S. Rendall, *The Contribution of Inheritances to Black-White Wealth Disparities in the United States,* BLCC Working Paper 97–08, June (1997); Paul L. Menchik and Nancy Jianakoplos, *Black-White Wealth Inequality: Is Inheritance the Reason?* 35 ECON. INQUIRY 428–42 (1997).

12. *See* STACK, *supra* note 13 (introduction), at 127 ("Welfare policy effectively prevents the poor from inheriting even a pitifully small amount of cash, or from acquiring capital investment typical for the middle class, such as home ownership.").

13. The phrase "human capital" is most strongly associated with Gary Becker's work. *See, e.g.,* BECKER *supra* note 13 (introduction). But, as a num-

ber of commentators have noted, Becker's neoclassical formulation of family life fails to capture the full breadth of human investment. *See, e.g.,* England and Folbre *supra* note 6 (chap. 11).

14. STACK, *supra* note 13 (introduction).

15. Johnnetta B. Cole, *All American Women: Lines That Divide, Ties That Bind, in* WOMEN AND POVERTY (Gelpi et al. eds., 1986); Rayna Rapp, *Urban Kinship in Contemporary America: Families, Classes, and Ideology, in* CITIES OF THE UNITED STATES: CASE STUDIES IN URBAN ANTHROPOLOGY (Leith Mullings ed., 1987).

16. The classic text on reciprocity in varied cultures is, of course, Marcel Mauss's *The Gift.* MAUSS, *supra* note 17 (introduction). For a review of the anthropological literature on exchange since then, see GRAEBER, *supra* note 2 (chap. 9), at 151–228.

17. Alvin W. Gouldner, *The Norm of Reciprocity: A Preliminary Statement,* 25 AM. SOC. REV. 161 (1960). Gouldner is, one can assume, referring to Lévi-Strauss's suggestion that the incest taboo itself is an effect of the norm of reciprocity. *See* LÉVI-STRAUSS, *supra* note 17 (introduction), at 144 (describing both dual organization and the prohibition against incest as "two extreme types of reciprocity").

18. JAMES C. SCOTT, THE MORAL ECONOMY OF THE PEASANT 167 (1976).

19. This can be thought of as "pooling risk," much the way that people who buy insurance pool risk. *See, generally,* Elizabeth A. Cashdan, *Coping with Risk: Reciprocity among the Basarwa of Northern Botswana,* 20 MAN 3 (1985).

20. *See* KATRINA HAZZARD-GORDON, JOOKIN': THE RISE OF SOCIAL DANCE FORMATIONS IN AFRICAN-AMERICAN CULTURE (2002).

21. This is a friendlier reading of the same logic behind Smith and Parker's conception of "tolerated theft." *See* J. Maynard Smith and G. Parker, *The Logic of Asymmetric Contests,* 24 ANIMAL BEHAVIOR 159 (1976). *See also* T. INGOLD, D. RICHES, AND J. WOODBURN, HUNTER GATHERERS: PROPERTY, POWER, AND IDEOLOGY (1998) (describing the same type of behavior as "demand" sharing that occurs based on perceptions of inequality and need).

22. Classically, transaction costs are defined as the costs of using the price mechanism, which includes the costs of discovering relevant prices, and negotiating and concluding contracts. *See, e.g.,* Ronald H. Coase, *The Nature of the Firm,* 4 ECONOMICA 16, 386 (1937).

23. Alejandro Portes and Particia Landolt, *The Downside of Social Capital,* THE AMERICAN PROSPECT 26 (May–June 1996).

24. In the anthropological literature, the influence is generally exerted through the norms surrounding kinship, a topic that I discuss in more detail in the next chapter. *See supra* notes 1–4 (part II) and accompanying texts.

25. *See* ANNE R. ROSCHELLE, NO MORE KIN xi (1997) (describing empirical findings that "informal social support networks typically found in minority communities are not as pervasive as they were in the past"); Mary Benin and Verna M. Keith, *The Social Support of Employed African American and Anglo Mothers,* 16 JOURNAL OF FAMILY ISSUES 275–97 (1995); R. Kelly Raley,

Black-White Differences in Kin Contact and Exchange among Never Married Adults, 16 JOURNAL OF FAMILY ISSUES 77–103 (1995).

26. ROSCHELLE, *supra* note 25 (chap. 12). One commentator has even suggested that the "contemporary black underclass in America today represents what is perhaps one of the most thoroughly atomized societies that has existed in human history." FRANCIS FUKUYAMA, TRUST 303 (1995). In contrast, Putnam, *supra* note 18 (introduction), argues that the recent decline in social capital has occurred across racial and class divides. However, he also acknowledges that social capital (both the extent of social networks and the material resources available through them) has been and continues to be much lower among poor and minority families and communities. He fails to note that, because these families and communities already had far less to spare, the loss of social capital is experienced in different ways. While a decline in social capital may be correlated with more television watching or longer commutes for middle- and upper-class families, for poor families it can mean lack of clothing, food, or shelter. The precipitous decline in social capital in inner-city populations is exacerbated because the resulting increase in physical stress, emotional frustration, and potential for violence is also less mitigated by the ties that hold extended family and communities together. Social capital, as Putnam measures it, may be declining across the board, but that decline also means something very different depending on who one is and where one lives.

27. For discussion of the concept see *supra* notes 18–22 (introduction), 26 (chap. 11), and accompanying text.

Part IV

1. While the hearing over the private prison described in chapter 1 provided a forum for discussion about prisons and prisoners, very few family members (none in this study's sample) actually testified.

2. Unexpected to me, anyway. For several months I was puzzled and frustrated because my interviews were not confirming one of the central hypotheses I had originally formulated for this study–that high incarceration rates would generate significant political resistance and community sympathy for offenders.

3. *See supra* note 21 (introduction) and accompanying text.

4. It has been argued that the last decade will be remembered as that "in which criminal law . . . rediscovered . . . the power of social norms as a regulatory device." Kahan, *supra* note 28 (introduction), at 591.

5. *See, e.g.,* JOHN BRAITHWAITE, CRIME, SHAME AND REINTEGRATION (1989); Kahan *supra* note 28 (introduction).

6. *See, e.g.,* Lawrence Lessig, *The Regulation of Social Meaning*, 62 U. CHI. L. REV. 943, 957 (1995) (describing how governments shape "social meanings to advance state ends"); Cass R. Sunstein, *On the Expressive Function of Law*, 144 U. PA. L. REV. 2021, 2036–43 (1996) (discussing the ways in which the "statement made by law" can be compared with the "conse-

quences produced by law"); Cass R. Sunstein, *Incommensurability and Valuation in Law*, *92* Mich. L. Rev. *779*, 820–24 (1994) (discussing how social norms are affected by the "expressive power" of law); Cass R. Sunstein, *Problems with Rules*, 83 CALIF. L. REV. 953, 970 (1995) ("We might say that the expressive function of law includes the effects of law on social attitudes about relationships, events, and prospects, and also the 'statement' that law makes independently of such effects.").

Chapter 12

1. This distinction is at the heart of many other debates about identity and action. For example, many people would understand someone who stated that a married man, while never having engaged in sex with another man, is *really* a closeted gay man—or, conversely, that a man who had sex with another man, but subsequently dated women, is not gay. Or, as the debate over Clarence Thomas's nomination to the Supreme Court made apparent, a single person can be described as not only black, ashamed of being black, or harming blacks, but as someone whose actions render his identity *as a black person* suspect. The relative durability and contingencies of sexual orientation, race, and criminality illuminate how complex identity and stigma can be.

2. *Cf.* Claude Steele and David A. Sherman, *The Psychological Predicaments of Women on Welfare*, *in* CULTURAL DIVIDES 422 (Deborah Prentice and Dale Miller eds., 1999) (describing the emphasis that women in a shelter in the South Bronx place on self-reliance).

3. Carol Stack's description of the inner-city environment still fits: "the social-economic conditions of poverty, the inexorable unemployment of black women and men, and the access to scarce resources of a mother and her children" (*supra* note 13, introduction). The decline of extended networks of exchange in inner cities makes the social supports that families do have all the more important.

4. Or, as Stack writes, the "black urban family, embedded in cooperative domestic exchange, proves to be an organized tenacious, active, lifelong network." *Id.* at 124. Opal Palmer Adisa also puts a fine point on it, writing in her poetic essay *Rocking in the Sunlight:*

> Truth be told, black women would cease to exist if we didn't have each other. . . . For who but a sister can you call up at 2:00 a.m. in the middle of the week and ask, "Do you have time to talk?" Who but a sister can you go to on payday to borrow twenty dollars to tide you over? . . . We use each other's strength and tenacity to fight the stress that would put us in our graves before our time.

Opal Palmer Addisa, *Rocking in the Sunlight, in* THE BLACK WOMEN'S HEALTH BOOK 12 (Evelyn C. White ed., 1990).

5. Indeed, there has probably been no greater institutional change

among families like those that Stack studied than the dramatic rise of incarceration rates in poor urban neighborhoods over the last quarter century. The incarceration rate in major metropolitan areas is nearly five times what it was in 1970.

6. Robert was located at a Virginia facility under contract to the District. While I met with Robert and interviewed him there, the Virginia Department of Corrections prohibited me from recording the interview. Although I did take notes while interviewing inmates there, Robert's quick speaking ran well ahead of my ability. For that reason, I quote sparingly from my notes. Thankfully, he is a good writer and correspondent.

7. While there is some debate about the social and psychological models that explain shame, there is a broad agreement in the literature on shame's most basic characteristics and effects. *See, generally,* MICHAEL LEWIS, SHAME: THE EXPOSED SELF (1995); HELEN MERREL LYND, ON SHAME AND THE SEARCH FOR IDENTITY (1958); HEBERT E. THOMAS, THE SHAME RESPONSE TO REJECTION 16–17 (1997); ERVING GOFFMAN, STIGMA 4 (1963); THE ROLE OF SHAME IN SYMPTOM FORMATION (Helen Block Lewis ed., 1987); ANDREW P. MORRISON, SHAME (1989); THE MANY FACES OF SHAME (Donald L. Nathanson ed., 1987).

8. *See* LEWIS, *supra* note 7 (chap. 12), at 200 ("The impact of stigma is wide: it not only affects those who are stigmatized, but those who are associated with the person so marked. . . . Stigmas are contagious: they impact on members of the family and even the friends of the stigmatized person. Like an infectious disease, the stigma not only affects the victim of the stigma but all those who are associated with him or her.").

9. GOFFMAN, *supra* note 7 (chap. 12), at 48. Goffman writes of this contamination through association:

> [I]n certain circumstances the social identity of those an individual is with can be used as a source of information concerning his own social identity, the assumption being that he is what the others are. . . . In any case, an analysis of how people manage the information they convey about themselves will have to consider how they deal with the contingencies of being seen "with" particular others.

Id. at 47–48.

10. As Goffman puts it, stigma is related to one's "social identity." GOFFMAN, *supra* note 7 (chap. 12), at 2.

11. *See, e.g.,* KATHERINE NEWMAN, FALLING FROM GRACE (1988); Deborah E. S. Frable, Linda Platt, and Steve Hoey, *Concealable Stigmas and Positive Self-Perceptions: Feeling Better around Similar Others,* 74 J. PERSONALITY & SOC. PSYCH. 4, 909 (1998) (finding that "[o]nly the presence of similar others lifted the self-esteem and mood of [those] with concealable stigmas").

12. Of course, men and women can experience shame in many ways, and gender differences do not hold true in every case. It is also quite true that, when discussing broad social effects like shaming, "gender difference neither explains how the difference got there nor what maintains it."

Stephanie A. Shields, *Thinking about Gender, Thinking about Theory, in* GENDER AND EMOTION 18 (Agneta H. Fischer ed., 2000). What gender differences do help us appreciate (at least in this case) is the specific and differential influence of incarceration on the social and psychological lives of many men and women.

13. *See* LEWIS, *supra* note 7 (chap. 12), at 69. *See also* discussion at 103.

14. *Id.* at 72. Men, on the other hand, are less likely to blame themselves for failure, and when they do, they are more likely to experience guilt than shame, given the same circumstances. *See id.* at 103 (discussing studies supporting this finding).

15. *See id.* at 143–49.

16. *See* THOMAS, *supra* note 7 (chap. 12), at 29–34 (describing general effects of shame) and 156–61 (describing the link between prolonged shame and violent or criminal activity). *See also* JAMES GILLIGAN, VIOLENCE 110 (1997) (arguing that, in his work with male offenders, "shame is the primary or ultimate cause of all violence").

Chapter 13

1. *See, generally,* HOCHSCHILD *supra* note 5 (chap. 6).

2. There are, to be sure, diverse attitudes in any city. What is striking in the ethnographies of inner-city families during the last decade is the diversity of findings on behaviors and attitudes. Jonathan and Constance's values clearly fall closer to those held by the men in Mitchell Duneier's work on male respectability than those described by Lewis, Moynihan, or Wilson. *Id.*

3. Many scholars have documented the ways in which race consciousness is submerged in people's daily lives. *See, e.g.,* RUTH FRANKENBERG, WHITE WOMEN, RACE MATTERS 23 (1993) (describing how the subject of race prompted "memory lapse, silence, shame, and evasion" among her informants). Paul Sniderman and his colleagues have gone to great lengths to discern perceptions of race that are normally hidden from public discourse. *See, e.g.,* Paul M. Sniderman et al., *The New Racism,* 35 AM. J. POL. SCI. 2, 423–47 (1991).

4. The most comprehensive summary of these data is presented in RANDALL KENNEDY, RACE, CRIME, AND THE LAW (1997). The perceived divide between the "good" and "bad" black in America has been discussed extensively. David Shipler has discussed this aspect of stereotyping. DAVID K. SHIPLER, A COUNTRY OF STRANGERS (1997). This good/bad division is paralleled in public policy discussions of "deserving" and "undeserving" poor, described by Herbert Gans. HERBERT J. GANS, THE WAR ON THE POOR (1995).

5. *See, e.g.,* Richard Veilleux, Criminal Justice Poll Shows Distrust of America's Legal System (May 4, 2000) (reporting results of a Connecticut survey on attitudes toward the criminal justice system).

6. General Social Survey, 1987–2000.

7. *See* Amy C. Lewis & Steven J. Sherman, *Hiring you makes me look bad: Social-identity based reversals of the ingroup favoritism effect,* 90 ORGANIZATIONAL BEHAVIOR & HUMAN DECSION PROCESSES 2, 262 (2003).

Chapter 14

1. While one of Tina's main goals is to buy a house so that she and the kids can move out of the projects, she knows that it will mean moving to a community and school district with fewer resources.

2. Arlie Hochschild has noted that Americans are spending an increasing amount of time at work and are increasing the level of social and emotional involvement there. ARLIE HOCHSCHILD, THE TIME BIND (1997). As work relationships become more important in people's lives, however, privacy becomes harder to maintain.

3. *See* PUTNAM, *supra* note 18 (introduction), at 275.

4. CHRISTINA NIPPERT-ENG, HOME AND WORK: NEGOTIATING THE BOUNDARIES OF EVERYDAY LIFE 155 (1997). Nippert-Eng describes the "greedy workplace" as one that demands as much time as possible from employees and thus requires either the displacement of personal life entirely or an intense integration of personal and work life:

> For the greedy workplace employee, work is liable to be everywhere, all the time. It infiltrates so much of life that it may be consciously activated when the employee least expects it and when it would be unthinkable for the vast majority of us. Nearly everything one does and everyone one does it with reverberates from and through the workplace.

5. The growing significance of work in people's lives bucks what Putnam and others have described as a general trend of a declining sense of belonging and community in other areas of life. In three recent national surveys, for example, adults born after 1964 were more likely than previous generations to report that they found a "real sense of belonging" among co-workers, but they were less likely to report getting that sense of belonging from family, friends, neighbors, at church, in the local newspaper, in the local community, or through groups or organizations. *See* PUTNAM, *supra* note 18 (introduction), at 275.

6. This is particularly true in the United States, where the average time spent on the job is higher than in any other country and where, every year, the average amount of time spent at work increases. A number of studies have made this point. *See, e.g.,* JOANNE B. CIULLA, THE WORKING LIFE: THE PROMISE AND BETRAYAL OF MODERN WORK (2000); JILL ANDRESKY FRASER, WHITE COLLAR SWEATSHOP (2001); JULIET B. SCHOR, THE OVERWORKED AMERICAN (1991).

7. *See, generally,* HOCHSCHILD, *supra* note 2 (chap. 14) (describing both the increasing amount of time Americans are spending at work and the increasing role of personal relationships at work).

8. NIPPERT-ENG, *supra* note 4 (chap. 14), at 184 (noting that members of the more successful and productive workplaces she studied "actively seek occasional social activities with colleagues. These range from dinners together [and] attending out-of-town conferences together, to departmental parties and small, same-age gatherings at each others' houses. These [workers] are also more likely to eat lunch together, [etc.]").

9. *See, e.g.,* HOCHSCHILD *supra* note 2 (chap. 14), at 19 (describing a human resource workshop encouraging employees to "piggyback" work on friendships). *See also* NIPPERT-ENG, *supra* note 4 (chap. 14), at 186 (noting that families "form a regular, important part of . . . conversations and plans [at work]").

10. As Kathryn Dudley has noted, these discussions and personal disclosures also help to build a sense of solidarity and teamwork that workers value. KATHRYN DUDLEY, END OF THE LINE (1994).

Chapter 15

1. While depression itself is a serious negative outcome, it has broader social consequences as well. Suzanne Retzinger has noted that "[i]solation and shame are inseparable. . . . In itself, unacknowledged shame creates a form of self-perpetuating entrapment in one's own isolation. If one hides this sense from the other due to shame, it creates further shame, which creates a further sense of isolation." Suzanne Retzinger, *quoted in* LEWIS *supra* note 7 (chap. 12), at 188–89. Depression is also reciprocally related to the isolation that shame brings, and soon after the incarceration of a loved one the three are often combined in a cascading effect.

Not all of them have described themselves as "depressed," though all did describe feelings and patterns of behavior consistent with the symptoms of clinical depression. These include a persistent sad, anxious, or "empty" mood; sleeping too much or too little or middle-of-the-night or early morning waking; reduced appetite and weight loss or increased appetite and weight gain; loss of interest or pleasure in activities, including sex; irritability and restlessness; persistent physical symptoms that don't respond to treatment (such as chronic pain or digestive disorders); difficulty concentrating, remembering, or making decisions; fatigue or loss of energy; feeling guilty, hopeless, or worthless; and thoughts of death or suicide. From THE NATIONAL MENTAL HEALTH ASSOCIATION, DEPRESSION: WHAT YOU NEED TO KNOW (1999).

One of the difficulties in discussing depression with African-American women is that many are reluctant to use clinical language or to admit that they were defeated by a psychiatric illness. This point is further supported by the recent Surgeon General's Report on Mental Health:

> Mental illness is at least as prevalent among racial and ethnic minorities as in the majority white population. Yet many racial and ethnic minority group members find the organized mental health system to

be uninformed about cultural context and, thus, unresponsive and/or irrelevant. It is partly for this reason that minority group members overall are less inclined than whites to seek treatment, and to use out-patient treatment services to a much lesser extent than do non-His-panic whites.

David Satcher, Mental Health: A Report of the Surgeon General (2000) (cita-tions omitted).

2. A recent study of income and depression shows evidence of a strong relationship between income and depression.

Family Income	Parental Depression
<$20,000	22.40%
$20,000–29,000	16.80%
$30,000–39,999	13.20%
$40,000–49,999	10.70%
$50,000–59,999	13.40%
$60,000–79,999	9.80%
$80,000+	6.20%

DAVID P. ROSS AND PAUL ROBERTS, INCOME AND CHILD WELL-BEING (1999) <http://www.ccsd.ca/pubs/inckids/>. The relationship is probably so strong because it is bi-direction: depression makes lowered income more likely and lowered income makes depression more likely.

Chapter 16

1. *Cf.* NEWMAN, *supra* note 11 (chap. 12), at 143–72 (describing the solidar-ity that can be found in a "brotherhood of downward mobility" when mate-rially dispossessed individuals are politically organized).

2. The issue of allowing a child to visit a parent in prison is difficult for many women and, in some cases, for the judges. *See* Rachel Sims, *Can My Daddy Hug Me? Deciding Whether Visiting Dad in a Prison Facility Is in the Best Interest of the Child,* 66 BROOKLYN L. REV. 933 (2001).

3. SHAWSHANK REDEMPTION (Castle Rock, 1994).

4. I have reordered the three pieces of this transcript, set off by extended ellipses, to facilitate narrative flow.

Chapter 17

1. *See* Peter Benson and Bernard Spilka, *God Image as a Function of Self-Esteem and Locus of Control,* 12 J. SCI. STUD. RELIG. 297–310 (1970); Bernard Spilka and M. Lillynshohn, *Parents, Self, and God: A Factor-Analytic Approach,* 6 REVIEW OF RELIGIOUS RESEARCH 28–36 (1975); Bernard Spilka, Phillip Shaver, and Lee Kirkpatrick, *A General Attribution Theory for the Psychology of Religion,* 24 J. SCI. STUD. RELIG. 1–20 (1985).

2. *See* Jennifer Crocker and Jason S. Lawrence, *Social Stigma and Self-*

Esteem, in CULTURAL DIVIDES 382–84 (1999) (showing the results of factor analysis). *See also* Bruce Blaine and Jennifer Crocker, *Religiousness, Race, and Psychological Well-being,* 21 PERSONALITY & SOC. PSYCHOL. BULL. 1031–41 (1995).

3. CATHY COHEN, THE BOUNDARIES OF BLACKNESS 287 (1999). The reaction of churches in African-American communities to gay members and HIV/AIDS provides several striking parallels, not the least of which is a guarded familial silence on the subject of the incarceration or sexual orientation of family members in relation to the moral judgment they perceive may be visited on them.

4. Gail Walker, *Oh Freedom: Liberation and the African-American Church,* GUARDIAN, February 1992, at 10.

Chapter 18

1. As one commentator writes:

The social controls that deter most people from stealing–shame from peers and family members, being fired by an employer, the fear of incarceration–don't exist for state-raised convicts who have a low investment in conventional society. Breaking the law and going to jail become what sociologists describe as "normalized" experiences. Criminal behavior loses its stigma; sanctions lose their sting.

JENIFER WYNN, INSIDE RIKERS 13 (2001).

2. This perception may, in part, be related to the fact that many relatives of prisoners are unaware of the full extent of incarceration and of the similar experiences of their neighbors, friends, and fellow church members. For example, when I asked participants if they knew of other people in the neighborhood, many did know of one or two out of the dozens of households on the block that had members incarcerated but did not feel comfortable talking with others. This type of phenomenon is often described as pluralistic ignorance, in which people misjudge the norm. Perhaps the most well-publicized example is found in studies of college freshmen who share a pluralistic ignorance of drinking norms, commonly overestimating the extent of drinking among other freshmen. *See* D. A. Prentice and D. T. Miller, *Pluralistic Ignorance and Alcohol Use on Campus: Some Consequences of Misperceiving the Social Norm,* 64 JOURNAL OF PERSONALITY AND SOCIAL PSYCHOLOGY 2, 243–56 (1993). In the case of families of prisoners, however, their underestimation of the extent of incarceration exacerbates their sense of stigma by making the incarceration of their family member seem more abnormal than it is.

3. The historical anthropologist Gerald Sider once wrote, "We can have no significant understanding of any culture unless we also know the silences that were institutionally created and guaranteed along with it." Gerald Sider, *Against Experience, in* BETWEEN HISTORY AND HISTORIES 74–75 (Gerald Sider and Gavin Smith eds., 1997).

Similarly, the focus of most critical and popular literature on social institutions is on the development and regulation of interaction through them rather than the silences they produce. As Robin Sheriff, an anthropologist who has begun the difficult task of developing this area of work, recently noted, silence "is, in a Durkheimian sense, a type of 'social fact' long overdue for scholarly interrogation." Robin E. Sheriff, *Exposing Silence as Cultural Censorship*, 102 AMERICAN ANTHROPOLOGIST 1, 114 (2000). *See also* Robin Tolmach Lakoff, *Cries and Whispers, in* GENDER ARTICULATED 25 (Kira Hall and Mary Bucholtz eds., 1995) ("Feminists have devoted a great deal of attention over the past quarter century to speech and its effect on gender and power relations. Less consideration has been given to its compliment, the absence of speech, or silence, and that much more recently").

Appendix

1. *See e.g.,* ELIOT LIEBOW, TALLY'S CORNER: A STUDY OF NEGRO STREET-CORNER MEN (1967); CONSTANCE MCLAUGHLIN GREEN, THE SECRET CITY: A HISTORY OF RACE RELATIONS IN THE NATION'S CAPITAL (1967); HOWARD GILLETTE, JR, BETWEEN JUSTICE AND BEAUTY: RACE, PLANNING, AND THE FAILURE OF URBAN POLICY IN WASHINGTON, D.C. (1995) HN80.W3G55; JAMES ALAN BORCHERT, ALLEY LIFE IN WASHINGTON (1980); GODFREY FRANKEL, IN THE ALLEYS: KIDS IN THE SHADOW OF THE CAPITOL (1995).

Index